Myths in Disguise

Cross-Roads.

Polish Studies in Culture, Literary Theory, and History

Edited by Ryszard Nycz

Volume 10

PETER LANG

Michał Głowiński

Myths in Disguise

Translated by Grzegorz Czemiel and Stanley Bill

Edited by Jan Burzyński

PETER LANG

Bibliographic Information published by the Deutsche Nationalbibliothek
The Deutsche Nationalbibliothek lists this publication in the Deutsche
Nationalbibliografie; detailed bibliographic data is available in the
internet at http://dnb.d-nb.de.

Library of Congress Cataloging-in-Publication Data
A CIP catalog record for this book has been applied for at the Library of Congress.

The Publication is funded by Ministry of Science and Higher Education of the Republic
of Poland as a part of the National Programme for the Development of the Humanities.
This publication reflects the views only of the authors, and the Ministry cannot be held
responsible for any use which may be made of the information contained therein.

NATIONAL PROGRAMME
FOR THE DEVELOPMENT OF HUMANITIES

Cover Design: © Olaf Gloeckler, Atelier Platen, Friedberg
Cover Image: Courtesy of Benjamin Ben Chaim

Printed by CPI books GmbH, Leck

ISSN 2191-6179
ISBN 978-3-631-67430-7 (Print)
E-ISBN 978-3-653-06871-9 (E-PDF)
E-ISBN 978-3-631-70911-5 (EPUB)
E-ISBN 978-3-631-70912-2 (MOBI)
DOI 10.3726/978-3-653-06871-9

Contents

1 The mask of Dionysus

And Semele, daughter of Cadmus was joined with him in love
and bore him a splendid son, joyous Dionysus,
—a mortal woman an immortal son.

Hesiod, *Theogony* (transl. Hugh G. Evelyn-White)

Greetings, Denis, God bless you.
Jarosław Iwaszkiewicz, "Autumn Nuptials" ["Gody jesienne"]

1.1 Myth and cultural equations

He has largely fallen into oblivion. Swept from the face of the earth, Dionysus is locked in a long-gone past that nobody can recollect anymore. The forgotten deity made himself a nest at the bottoms of cups, celebrated solely by those lifting them on certain occasions to praise their contents in song. Once omnipotent, he later came to exist merely "between the cup and the lip." However, he has made a glorious return; after all,

[e]verything goes, everything comes back; the wheel of being rolls eternally. Everything dies, everything blossoms again, the year of being runs eternally. Everything breaks, everything is joined anew; the same house of being builds itself eternally. Everything parts, everything greets itself again; the ring of being remains loyal to itself eternally.[1]

He has returned to reign over minds. He has returned with his entire train: satyrs and Bacchii, Pan and the maenads. He has returned wielding his inevitable thyrsus. He has returned invoked in apostrophes of philosophers and historians of the ancient era, as well as theoreticians of myth and poetry, whose words assumed the shape of incantations performed in praise of this godhead:

I enchanted, I made magic,
I called for Bacchus the god to come.
I have watched at empty crossroads,
In the heat of noon, in the night of Hecate,
Keeping my secret watch,
Yet the close god remained hidden.
[…]

---

1   Friedrich Nietzsche, *Thus Spoke Zarathustra*, transl. A. Del Caro, (Cambridge: Cambridge University Press, 2006), p. 175.

Have mercy on my harsh fate,
Come forth as stream or fire.
Spare me the torture.
Or, like a backward peasant,
Turn your charming, weary eyes
In my direction at night.[2]

Dionysus ultimately heeded these calls and came, abandoning the dark corners of antiquity and giving up the poetic convention of carefree Anacreontics. He has arrived to spread the kind of news that can be good or bad but always originates in what is most important: the appreciation of life in its earthly, material dimension, even in the face of inevitable destruction. The curtain rose, and Dionysus triumphantly entered the stage of this world and began his reign, becoming one of the fundamental symbols in literature: capable of expressing the spirit of an entire epoch, embracing all intricacies of world view and artistic matters.

He has thus freed himself from the shackles of a centuries-old topos[3] and ceased to be the conventional designator of life's joy and drunken passions (though he materialized in this role mainly as Bacchus, making playful appearances in learned or sometimes just frolicsome jokes). He ceased to be an insignificant literary ornament, or a fully conventionalized poetic embellishment. After becoming saturated with new symbolic content, he emerged as a figure expressing new attitudes and tendencies. Topoi not only comprise a reservoir of traditional, centuries-old images but are also updated, if conditions allow, as a result of which they can enter literary circulation without being mere museum pieces, i.e., respectable yet ossified testimonies to the past. A writer, a literary formation or even an entire epoch may reactivate a certain theme, lending it a new meaning and thus employing it to express that which is, in one way or another, most vital for the period. In this way, a traditional topos ceases to be a conventional device and becomes once again a vehicle for thoughts. It is in this spirit that Romantic poets reached out for the myth of Prometheus, who emerged, as it were, as the ideal model of a rebel whose motivations are humane.

---

2   Vyacheslav Ivanov, "Invocation of Bacchus" ["Vyzyvanie Vakkha"], in: *Sobranie sochinenii*, eds. D.V. Ivanov & O. Deschartes (Brussels: Foyer Oriental Chrétien, 1971–87), vol. II, p. 368; first two lines after: Pamela Davidson, *The Poetic Imagination of Vyacheslav Ivanov* (Cambridge: Cambridge University Press, 2009), p. 118.

3   For more information on topos theory see: Ernst Robert Curtius, *European Literature and the Latin Middle Ages*, transl. W. R. Trask (Princeton: Princeton University Press, 2013).

Following suit, writers working at the turn of the 19th and 20th century, and during the first quarter of the 20th century, have revived the myth of Dionysus. After all, antiquity constitutes an inexhaustible repository of themes, symbols, and myths suitable for many occasions – ones that have established themselves so well in European culture that they remain easily recognizable even after far-reaching transformations. Consequently, both Romantic poets, who expressed their rebellion through the figure of Prometheus, and modernists, who eagerly donned the mask of Dionysus, have retained in the myths they recycled a historically original component. It may even be said that these constructions were the outcome of the interaction between contents determined historically by the original form of the old myth, and new meanings that authors attempted to attach to elements hailing from an older tradition.

Therefore, the phenomenon of traditional themes and symbols, being lifted from the sanctioned fields of culture in order to infuse them with new meanings, is usually also a question of the attitude towards Greco-Roman antiquity, understood as the origin of most of them. It has been pointed out by Zygmunt Łempicki that myth acts as the link between antiquity and new literature. In his view, myth is something poetic rather than religious. "The longing for myth," he argues, "is one of the most characteristic manifestations of a deeply poetic nature."[4]

However, myth is not only about incorporating a pre-established theme, understood in either religious or poetic terms. What is in fact paramount is to endow it with a new meaning. Accordingly, the modernist myth of Dionysus draws on certain old Greek beliefs and stories about this deity. Nevertheless, writers from early 20th century were never committed to the reconstruction of this myth. They rather desired to utilize some of its components in an attempt to erect an entirely new edifice. Thus, the Dionysian myth acquired a new function determined by the cultural institutions operating at the turn of the 19th and 20th centuries.

Consequently, there arises the question of the function this myth could play, and whether it was still a myth. Perhaps, it just turned into a popular theme or a metaphorical story. What factors were decisive in determining its activity during that period? In order to answer these questions, it becomes crucial firstly to establish which elements present in the Dionysian beliefs from antiquity allowed this myth to be brought up to date, and secondly – and far more importantly – to focus on what exactly was it about the cultural situation at the beginning of the

---

4   Zygmunt Łempicki, *Demon antyku a kultura nowożytna* (Warszawa: Książnica Polska, 1933), p. 23.

20th century that affected this process or even determined its inception. This essay attempts to address these questions, taking as the point of departure the conviction that the modernist myth of Dionysus is a phenomenon of great significance, one that expresses the most characteristic tendencies of the discussed period.

At the foundation of the modernists' Dionysian creation there lies the phenomenon that could be termed "cultural equation." What these artists sought was to find similarities between their epoch and other times – a perspective from which it would be possible to survey their period. Regardless whether they acknowledged their times as an important stage in the development of culture, or criticized it, emphasizing its paltriness, they did seek those parallels.[5] They wanted to explain their times by drawing analogies that would throw light on what seemed novel by virtue of departing from the 19th-century model of culture, and testified to the crisis of a liberal mindset. They saw the unfolding of new phenomena, including the rise of mass movements and intense urbanization that turned cities into multi-million behemoths, which entailed a sharp increase in the dynamism of social life and the emergence of new forms of social existence. Modernists stood helplessly in the face of these transformations, especially if they attempted to retain the Romantic relationship between artist and society, confronting the "philistines" and "prigs" with a bohemian lifestyle. This helplessness was revealed by the caricatural rendering of the Romantic attitude by the decadent movement of the 1890s, which transformed the former's rebelliousness into a fascination with one's own powerlessness. However, this attitude was impotent with regard to the new phenomena that departed from the traditionally understood 19th-century bourgeois mentality, all the more so since the newly emergent realities turned out to be rather compelling. Writers are usually fascinated by dynamism and anxiety, especially after longer periods of peace and stabilization, which ossified bourgeois positions and mores. What attitudes were they supposed to assume in the face of a world whose contours kept changing? How were they to grasp the swift transformations? The Romantic tradition was still too strong for poets to step forth as eulogists of those standing behind those shifts, and to compose odes dedicated to those who impose a new order on the seemingly stable world. There was also one factor of particular significance. It remained uncertain what these changes were leading to, and what was their

---

5   As one critic claims, Nietzsche saw Greek mythology only as a parallel, never as an aim in itself; see: Erich Ruprecht, *Der Mythos bei Wagner und Nietzsche* (Berlin: Junker und Dünnhaupt, 1938), p. 65.

supposed goal. Even among those in favour of the new dynamic that determined contemporary life many were not optimistic. The world they faced evoked both joy and terror. It appeared mysterious and unpredictable, not allowing anyone to easily find out what turn things were about to take.

This was all the more confounding because modernists had little prospects of grasping the meaning of what was unfolding before their eyes. Therefore, they decided to explain the perplexing present by referring to well-known history, turning – as is often the case in such circumstances – towards antiquity. However, it was not the kind of antiquity envisioned by 17th-century classicists, representatives of the Enlightenment, or the ideologues of the French Revolution. Modernists would not invoke Homeric mythology, Greece under Pericles, the Roman Republic, or the first Emperors. What rather possessed them was – so to speak – the beginning and the end: the dark and still primitive centuries of antiquity, when the hallmarks of the classical period were not yet formed, and the final period of collapse, when different cultures mixed and diverse religious cults emerged around the Mediterranean. Both periods – the early and the late – were dramatic and full of anxiety, making them appropriate for this cultural equation.[6]

What modernists sought was not historical exactitude, all the more so because they saw history primarily as a kind of myth. Thus, even if they referenced antiquity's rise and fall, it was the mythical dimension that remained in the focus of their attention, with phenomena related to historically determinable social issues pushed into the background. Given such an approach, the similarity between the beginning and end of antiquity emerged as something obvious: both epochs were in fact far from Homer's calm and clear religion. Both favoured cults in which unruliness was combined with dynamism and metaphysical anxiety. Finally, both were distinguished by a marked intensification of the cult of Dionysus.

Thus, it was myth that acted as the bridge between the old and the new era. However, this was the case not only because poetically inclined natures long for it but also by virtue of cultural equations – ones that reveal similarities between

---

6   "When we speak of the Greeks," Nietzsche argues, "we involuntarily speak of today and yesterday: their familiar history is a polished mirror that always radiates something that is not in the mirror itself. We employ our freedom to speak of them so as to be allowed to remain silent about others – so that the latter may now say something into the thoughtful reader's ear. Thus the Greeks make it easier for modern man to communicate much that is delicate and hard to communicate." In: Friedrich Nietzsche, *Human, All Too Human*, transl. R.J. Hollingdale (Cambridge: Cambridge University Press, 1996), p. 264.

the present on the one hand, and the beginning or ending of antiquity on the other. These equations found expression in the structure of a myth that became remarkably lively during the periods of nascence and decline. Consequently, the myth of Dionysus carried references both to contemporary and historical times, in effect belonging to both modernism and antiquity. In this sense, it was an interpretation of both the present and the past. As Lévi-Strauss put it,

> a myth always refers to events alleged to have taken place long ago. But what gives the myth an operational value is that the specific pattern described is timeless; it explains the present and the past as well as the future.[7]

It is this "timeless" structure that allows making the myth eternally relevant, as long as the condition of culture favours this, and to ascribe new meanings to it on each such occasion. The said structure has also determined the significance of the modernist myth of Dionysus, enabling it to become, as it were, an embodiment of the cultural equation – a double-winged myth: one scooping the past and the other embracing new phenomena that became topical at the beginning of the 20th century.

Why was it this particular myth that came to embody the conviction that the modern world was so similar to antiquity in its initial and final stages, allowing to prove this equation right? Clearly, the fundamental reason was that modernism's cultural situation provoked the actualization of this particular belief. However, the very condition of this was related, to some degree, to the properties of myth itself. A crucial role was played by its ambiguity, which stemmed from the fact that already the ancients referred this belief to many phenomena, including primarily death and resurrection, and from the existence of many variants of this myth, which could be used according to the situation they would fit. To quote again from Lévi-Strauss, "[t]here is no single 'true' version of which all the others are but copies or distortions. Every version belongs to the myth."[8]

Therefore, Dionysus is simultaneously the god of joy and mourning, birth and catastrophe, beginning and end, appreciation of life and flight from it into grim mysteries and rituals. As a result, the myth of Dionysus facilitates embracing complex situations that involve contradictory elements and allows expressing conflicting attitudes ranging from blind joy at the present day to the terrifying vision of the fall of Europe and its culture. The synthetic nature of this myth was also decisive with respect to the value it had for the modernists, who expressed

---

7   Claude Lévi-Strauss, *Structural Anthropology*, transl. C. Jacobson & B.G. Schoepf (New York: Basic Books, 1963), p. 209.
8   Ibid., p. 218.

contradictory social attitudes oscillating between extremes. For the period of modernism – understood as a beginning towards the end of the 19th century – was a breakthrough one in which many cultural layers overlapped, resulting in chaos. It was only later that from this chaos emerged elements that crystallized in recognizable forms.

However, was the Dionysian theme really a myth during that period? The question is not entirely without merit if we stop perceiving myth as a story about issues one would be inclined to associate with this or that mythology, and view it as a cultural force organizing the actions of those who bring this myth to life. Modern theoreticians of myth such as W.F. Otto and Karl Kerenyi emphasize that myth is fundamentally different from folk tales or stories about phenomena in which people once believed because it remains closely connected with social action and cultic practice. When it becomes merely a folk tale, it ceases to be a myth and becomes part of the tradition of art.

Strictly speaking, the Dionysian theme is not really a myth insofar as it is not linked to any cult understood as religious in nature. Nor does it constitute an established topos or a simple mythological story, even if we see it as one endowed with a met-aphorical meaning. Thus, it stands apart from such mythological themes as those developed by dramatic poets in tragedies staged at the court of Louis XIV because those writers saw them merely as conventionalized vehicles for narration. During modernism, on the other hand, myth came to perform an organizing function. It is not only the subject of works, expressing a particular attitude, but also the model of an attitude that exceeds literary categories, encroaching on social matters and thus becoming an element of "life" as a cultural experience in itself. The Dionysian theme is further illuminated by the deliberations of Bronisław Malinowski, who defined the role of myth in primitive societies in these terms:

> Myth as it exists in a savage community, that is, in its living primitive form, is not merely a story told but a reality lived. It is not of the nature of fiction, such as we read today in a novel, but it is living reality, believed to have once happened in primeval times, and continuing ever since to influence the world and human destinies. This myth is to the savage what, to a fully believing Christian, is the Biblical History of Creation, of the Fall, of the Redemption by Christ's Sacrifice on the Cross. As our sacred story lives in our ritual, in our morality, as it governs our faith and controls our conduct, even so does his myth for the savage.[9]

In order to ascertain that a given theme is not, during some period, a folk tale or a fantastic story, but in fact myth, it becomes necessary to present its real

---

9   Bronisław Malinowski, *Magic, Science and Religion and Other Essays* (Glencoe: The Free Press, 1948), p. 78.

relationship to the social reality. However, it cannot be a mirroring relation – it needs to be a shaping factor. Thus, we ought to ask what is it exactly that the legend of Dionysus contributed to modernism and what portion of that period's reality was affected directly by it. It seems that the Dionysian myth has become the model describing the poet's role in society. As Mircea Eliade remarks, "the foremost function of myth is to reveal the exemplary models for all human rites and all significant human activities – diet or marriage, work or education, art or wisdom."[10]

Thus, at the turn of the centuries, the Dionysian theme acted as a model for poets' attitude towards the contemporary world, offering a paradigm of the relationship between artist and society, replacing the former one, which originated in the Romantic juxtaposition of artist and philistine. The new model referenced authentic rituals practiced in antiquity by those following the cult of Dionysus. In these ceremonies, a crucial role was played by a democratically understood collective. The said cult functioned as the point of departure for many variations on the theme of Dionysus developed by writers in the years 1890–1920. This godhead was invoked for various reasons and given many meanings. At the hands of the modernists, Dionysus became radically ambiguous, while his transformations expressed intense changes in attitudes.[11]

1.2 In the circle of Nietzsche

Notably, the modernist myth of Dionysus does not owe its nascence simply to the fact that it allowed formulating answers to contemporary questions. Its rise to prominence was made possible by a long process that can be regarded as an evolution of the attitude towards antiquity – a process that occurred throughout the 19th century and involved the shedding of the image of the Greek world developed by the great Winckelmann. This process was largely undetected because the general approach displayed by scholars and artists who took interest in antiquity was shaped by Winckelmann's model, which consisted in favouring classicism along with giving preference for order and harmony. Curtius sneered at this, calling such view "the humanism of middle school professors." Despite

---

10 Mircea Eliade, *Myth and Reality*, transl. W.R. Trask (Long Grove: Waveland Press, 1998), p. 8. Eliade discusses this issue more broadly in the volume of essays *Myths, Dreams and Mysteries* (New York: Harper & Row, 1975).

11 For more information on the transforming meaning of symbols see: Stefan Czarnowski, "Warunki społeczne zmiany znaczenia symbolów literackich," in: *Dzieła*, vol. I, eds. N. Assorodobraj & S. Ossowski (Warszawa: Państwowe Wydawnictwa Naukowe, 1956).

being pushed into the background during the 19th century, new perspectives proved their cultural significance when Nietzsche became the most influential thinker in Europe. His stance towards the ancient world was not entirely original – it rather constituted the apogee of the development of ideas formulated at the beginning of the 19th century by scholars of antiquity associated with Romanticism.

One pioneer in this matter was Friedrich Creuzer, author of the work *Symbolik und Mythologie der alten Völker* (1810–1812), which was conceived as a sort of an antidote to Winckelmann. Creuzer was not interested in the merry Olympian religion, but in those ancient cults that functioned on its margins. He was the first researcher to note the distinct character of the Dionysian cult. His studies were influential among representatives of the last generation of German Romantics. Schelling, for example, refers to Creuzer in his deliberations on the philosophy of myth. In this way, Dionysian cults became a subject explored in religious studies and theory of mythology, as well as one debated among historians of antiquity. J.J. Bachofen, a philosopher of myth, focused extensively on this topic, while Burckhardt covered it during his lectures at the University of Basel.

> It was Burckhardt who has drawn attention to the entirely distinct figure among the gods – Dionysus, whose cult has many features that make it truly satanic. However, he does not consider the wild celebrations to be indicative of degeneration but views them as an untouched relic of religious feeling, one that does not originate in atrophy but in excessive growth and overabundant spiritual sensitivity, which have been recognized in modernist art.[12]

Nevertheless, the myth of Dionysus did not acquire cultural significance in the 19th century because of Creuzer, Bachofen, the ever-influential Burckhardt, or Nietzsche's peer and friend Erwin Rhode, author of the great work *Psyche*. It was the author of *Human, All Too Human* who contributed mostly to this process, even though he did not examine this myth through the lens of philological or religious studies. He achieved what others before him could only do partially: he brought the myth up to date, referring it to contemporary developments in the evolution of ideas, and treating it as an expression of new attitudes towards the world. This is visible already in *The Birth of Tragedy*, a book that manifests the

---

12 Stanisław Schneider, "Nowe poglądy na cywilizację grecką," *Muzeum* 1902, p. 3. Apart from this article by Schneider, the changes in the understanding of antiquity in the 19th century in relation to new theories of myth are discussed in two articles by Bogdan Suchodolski published in the magazine *Nauka i Sztuka* (1946): "Idea mitu" (no. 1) and "Filozofia mitu" (no. 5–6).

greatest aspirations among all of his works in scholarly and historical terms (which Nietzsche understood, by the way, in the spirit of Burckhardt, who would, in fact, bring history up to date).

What developments and attitudes are these? What new significance has Dionysus acquired, making him not just the object of interest for a narrow group of specialists in religious studies, but a figure captivating the "intelligent public," as 19th-century columnists used to say? In Nietzsche's philosophy, Dionysus ceases to be merely a parallel, limited to being a figure found in Greek beliefs. He emerges as a metaphor for something central to the oeuvre of the German thinker, or rather some *things* because this deity is not unambiguous like, say, the Prometheus of Romantic accounts. The meaning of Dionysus changed along with the evolution of Nietzsche's thought, ultimately denoting in his writings two entirely different things. The double symbolic nature of Dionysus makes him represent two disparate positions or worldviews: Dionysus I and Dionysus II, the former emerging in *The Birth of Tragedy* and the latter in later writings. Although the two have much in common – e.g. fascination with elemental forces, intoxication with life, and approval of the world in which humans exist – the two versions are fundamentally at odds. The former Dionysus is part of a collectivist myth, whereas the latter one belongs to an individualistic myth. The former references a collective ritual, while the latter – the *Übermensch*. The former is rooted in a homogenous and coherent collective, one that is simultaneously solemn and joyful, while the latter is based on an individual elevated above the crowd, full of hostility and disdain for it.

> This is the first effect of Dionysiac tragedy: state and society, indeed all divisions between one human being and another, give way to an overwhelming feeling of unity which leads men back to the heart of nature.[13]

This is how the Dionysus of the collectivist myth would appear. The one from the other, individualistic myth was Zarathustra, who would come down from the mountains to teach by dancing – an unmatched man, the king of life.[14]

Despite the fact that *The Birth of Tragedy* has been, since its publishing, among the best-known works of Nietzsche, it was not the collectivist myth that has come to attract wider attention. Later, his interest shifted towards the *Übermensch*,

---

13 Friedrich Nietzsche, *The Birth of Tragedy and Other Writings*, transl. R. Speirs (Cambridge: Cambridge University Press, 2007), p. 39.

14 That Dionysus can, in fact, stand for many different things in Nietzsche's philosophy was already pointed out by the first interpreters of his ideas, e.g. Ernest Seillière, otherwise a rather questionable thinker.

primarily in the form this concept was given in *Thus Spoke Zarathustra*. This seems easily understandable when we take into account the fact that both myths established actual references to the modern period. As is generally known, in *The Birth of Tragedy* this function was played by Wagnerian theatre, which was supposed to realize the ideals of a mythic-ritualistic art, thus unifying the public and the artist, the crowd and the priest. "Greek Tragedy," wrote Wagner many years before Nietzsche, "in its Chorus and its Heroes, combined the Public with the Art-work."[15] In this way, a single organism was born: approving art also meant approving the public, and consequently – the society.

Artists from the last quarter of the 19th century were not ready to accept a myth that carried such ideological consequences, regardless whether they were naturalists motivated by social passion to present the dark sides of life, Parnassian advocates of beauty arguing for *désintéressement* regarding current events, or rebellious poets like Rimbaud or Verlaine, who primarily chose negation.

The second myth – involving an individualistic Dionysus – perfectly matched the tendencies discernible in the practice of writers from that period. This was augmented by the continued persistence of the Romantic tradition, which principally favoured the individual component in confrontation with the collective. Furthermore, the Nietzschean teachings articulated by Zarathustra in the book, which quickly achieved the greatest popularity, exacerbated this conflict. However, at that point it was already a mere caricature of the Romantic rebellion, basically reduced to a misunderstanding regarding mores. In the last decade of the 19th century it was also a caricature of the rebellion of the kind represented by, say, Baudelaire or Verlaine. Who was involved in it after all? The philistine or the prig – an adversary defined in terms that did not allow for any serious struggle. Romantic rebellion became, at least for the time being, entirely farcical.

The literary reception of the individualistic variant of the Dionysian myth during the last nine years of the 19th century was also somewhat farcical. The legend of the superman was embraced chiefly by those who were most eager to speak about the illness eating away at the heart of the century, about the lack of adaptation to the world, and primarily – about their own weakness. This frail nature of theirs, however, was not something they would be ashamed of like proper Nietzschean thinkers. They were not offended by being referred to as "decadents," despite the fact that *décadent* is in Nietzsche's writings one of the worst insults. The term became widespread quickly; already in the 1890s,

---

15 Richard Wagner, *Opera and Drama*, transl. W. Ashton Ellis (Lincoln: University of Nebraska Press, 1995), p. 60.

basically everyone would be called decadent. Columnists who polemicized with Nietzsche (like Henryk Struve and Władysław Mieczysław Kozłowski in Poland) accused him of being a decadent, too. Writers, on the other hand, quickly accepted the role of decadents, finding in it their true vocation. Still, the supermen they created were only mediocre artists opposing the already legend-like philistines, and composing incantations praising nirvana or songs invoking death instead of hymns to life.[16] Thus, the Dionysian ideal of a great individual was reduced to an already existing schema. The result of this was so weird that it could not survive long, especially because a range of external phenomena also contributed to its swift departure from the literary stage.

Nor did it have a long life in Poland, where the reception of Nietzsche took specific forms as his ideas were employed to tackle local issues. Firstly, it was not belated in comparison to other countries, although some manifestations of his reception cannot be taken seriously. As early as in 1894 Ludwik Krzywicki ridiculed the "men of fashion" who tried to be home-grown Nietzscheans, con-cluding that they "treat great ideas and people simply as something to gossip about," albeit not attacking the philosopher himself.[17] Nevertheless, it was not only that specific breed of "men about town" who were interested in Nietzsche at the time. Usually, his thought was rendered correctly. In the decade when his works were not translated there did appear many longer articles or even books meant to introduce Polish readers to the teachings of the mysterious philoso-pher (e.g. works of Przewóska, Garfein or Daszyńska-Golińska). There were also polemical accounts that proved some of their authors to be misguided in their interpretations. One good example is a book by Henryk Struve, a Warsaw professor of philosophy, who offers in it such a dull argumentation – ignorant and irresponsible – that even today it could be called "philistine." On the whole, however, the initial years of contacts between Polish intellectuals and Nietzsche were rather informative.

At that stage, Nietzsche was inciting greater interest among columnists and philosophers rather than artists. On the other hand, the second phase – one marked by a fascination with the concept of the "superman" – belonged pri-marily to writers. It was then that the Nietzschean pattern overlapped with the moral rebellion against the philistines. It was also then that the superman ceased to be a mythical figure, embodied in Dionysus or Zarathustra, and became a concrete character in lyrical-psychological novels whose stories unfold in

---

16 Cf. Kazimierz Wyka, *Modernizm polski* (Kraków: Wydawnictwo Literackie, 1959).

17 Ludwik Krzywicki, "Nasz nietzscheanizm," *Prawda* 4 (1894).

a realistic setting. Fictional works of Stanisław Przybyszewski are perhaps most characteristic in this respect. They present the superman as an artist who does not heed generally accepted moral rules and unscrupulously violates them in order to demonstrate his superiority. At first glance, this approach corresponds to ideas developed by Nietzsche, whose *Übermensch* was born as a negation of bourgeois morality. However, this is in fact largely superficial insofar as it leads to a clear mystification. The superman's father never imagined him in a particular, historically determined reality. It was such a general idea that the only proper place of *Übermensch* would be in the mythological world. Even though it came into existence as a response to contemporary phenomena, it was – as Stanisław Brzozowski noted – "basically a vote of no confidence in the man he knew, the modern European."[18]

However, when this "vote of no confidence" – set in contemporary reality – boiled down to a programmatic praise of amorality and violation of established forms of social coexistence, it compromised, in fact, the concept of the superman. This was quite typical as is often the case when a very broad and general idea is given an individual and particular sense. This is also why this kind of a literary continuation of Nietzsche's idea led to a dead end. In consequence, after such transformation it could not prevail, and finally proved to be rather short-lived.[19]

Thus, a new attitude towards Nietzsche began to take shape already during the period of fascination with the superman. A premonition of this can be found for example in one of Brzozowski's earliest polemical articles:

> This man [Nietzsche] lived through the same plight as we, walking the same lonely paths – that is why we have grown to love him. For a long time, however, he was regarded merely as a master of "despair," "discouragement" and "anger." We did not comprehend his "laughing lion," his joy. Today, when it has become part of our souls, this joy is different although it is the same thing. It could not be anything else because, just like he did, we believed in the possibility to act, that we can create truth on our own and that we have to do so in order to act upon it later.[20]

---

18 Stanisław Brzozowski, "Filozofia Fryderyka Nietzschego," *Przegląd Filozoficzny* IV (1912), p. 499.

19 Even Stanisław Przybyszewski discovered this later in his career. In the introduction to the 1922 edition of *De Profundis* (Lwów: Lektor) he was quite convinced that he had never been a follower of Nietzsche and those who said so in fact insulted him. Moreover, he questioned the concept of the *Übermensch* and limited his enthusiasm for Nietzsche to a reverence for his great handling of German and a dithyrambic flourish. In this way, Przybyszewski has unconsciously written off his almost entire oeuvre.

20 Stanisław Brzozowski, "Echa artykułu 'My młodzi'. Replika," *Głos* 5 (1903).

The direction of changes is already signalled here: from despair to joy, and from individual discouragement to collective action. As a result, Nietzsche's ideas become not a means of reassuring one in individual rebellion, but of securing mastery over the world. The Romantically understood superman disappears from the stage, yielding to an attitude characterised by possessiveness about the world. This position is modelled – as in the case of Stanisław Wyspiański or Stanisław Brzozowski – on that of Nietzsche, although their references to him did not have a programmatic character. The thought of Nietzsche – creator of the Dionysian collectivist myth – impacted the intellectual life of his epoch so profoundly that it became, in fact, almost anonymous. Moreover, it became customary to associate him with the idea of the superman, which was already something others were moving away from. In this way, Nietzsche was becoming unfashionable. In the period preceding the First World War, many would openly deny any links to the philosopher despite the fact that – as it shall hopefully become clear – these ties were quite strong, though rooted not in *Also sprach Zarathustra* but rather in *The Birth of Tragedy*. Some would simply make a living on crumbs from the Nietzschean table. Nevertheless, protesting voices could be heard coming from many directions. Ludwik Hieronim Morstin – editor and main theoretician at *Museion*, a magazine that advocated Dionysian classicism – claimed that Nietzsche was already outdated and a thing of the past. He even confessed he did not understand the Dionysian phenomenon in spite of the fact that Dionysian musings found in *Museion* were a straightforward continuation of Nietzsche's ideas.[21]

Arguments formed in a similar spirit were raised by Kazimierz Filip Wize, probably the first Polish scholar to propagate the Belgian poet Émile Verhaeren, who was so influential throughout Europe. In fact, Wize defended Verhaeren from criticism levelled by a French commentator, who detected echoes of Nietzscheanism in Verhaeren's works.

> Nietzsche's superman is a step back for humanity, its downfall. On the other hand, Son of God and Verhaeren's humanism are progressive, offering an ideal or model to follow.[22]

---

21 Cf. Ludwik Hieronim Morstin, "Wpływ idei filozoficznych na współczesną twórczość literacką," *Museion* 11 (1911). Bronisław Biegeleisen argued similarly in an article titled "Pragmatyzm Nietzschego," in: *Museion* 12 (1912). Although the author observes that Nietzsche has, in general, become outdated, he does not refuse to acknowledge his value, questioning primarily that which has become the most popular aspect of the philosopher's work – the idea of the superhuman.

22 Kazimierz Filip Wize, introduction to *Obrazy życia* by Émile Verhaeren (Poznań: Leitgeber, 1913), p. 10.

Verhaeren's case is highly characteristic because he was a poet who developed, with utmost consistency, a collectivist myth, which accepted contemporary reality and gave it mythical approval, following Walt Whitman by elevating the modern civilization to the rank of ritualistic reality. Verhaeren's experience rapidly became one shared by the entire epoch, and Nietzsche's ideas were thereby revived in a hitherto unknown form.

1.3 Allegro barbaro

This brings us back to the phenomenon of cultural equation, which emerged in Nietzsche and became a universal value in the first decades of the 20th century as an attempt at interpreting the new situation that proved to be no longer explicable using old formulas. New phenomena in culture shook its very foundations, affecting the conviction about its stability and worth. Serenus Zeitblom, Dr. Phil., relates one of his conversations with the young Adrian Leverkühn in the following way:

> "But the alternative to culture," I interjected, "is barbarism."

> "Beg your pardon," he said, "but barbarism is the antithesis of culture only within a structure of thought that provides us the concept. Outside of that structure, the antithesis may be something quite different or not even an antithesis at all."[23]

The idea expressed by this literary character, a slightly odd composer, was not a rare one at the beginning of the 20th century. Like many convictions that circulated at that time, it can be found formulated *expressis verbis* in works of Nietzsche.[24] In general, it was a manifestation of the belief that the existing social institutions are in crisis, failing to respond to the emerging dynamics of life. This crisis consisted not in disintegration but apathy. Thus, there was an expectation that a boost of energy would be provided from those spheres that remained free from the reach of the fossilized culture. A new human model was in demand, one that would embrace elements of other cultures, both contemporary and historical, and lead European culture out of the crisis. The new man would be neither a rebellious Romantic poet, nor an intellectual captivated by learning about the world.

---

23 Thomas Mann, *Doctor Faustus*, transl. J.E. Woods (New York: Vintage International, 1999), p. 66.

24 It suffices to quote Nietzsche's radical proposition that "the domestication ('the culture') of man does not go deep – Where it does go deep it at once becomes degeneration (type: the Christian). The 'savage' [...] is a return to nature – and in a certain sense his recovery, his cure from 'culture.' " In: Friedrich Nietzsche, *The Will to Power*, transl. W. Kaufmann & R.J. Hollingdale (New York: Vintage Books, 1968), pp. 363–364.

It was an almost universal belief that all intellectual activity, regardless whether manifesting as art or philosophy, is meaningful only insofar as it leads to change. This idea retained relevance for everyone, including those who forgot about, or never even heard of Marx's claim that it is not interpretation that is at stake but change. In extreme cases, this position led to the negation of the cognitive dimension. Brzozowski, perhaps the principal representative of this tendency, argued point-blank that "humanity defines itself the goals of life, the reason for living. It is not about getting to know or interpreting destiny, but creating it."[25] In literature, this attitude stripped writing of former expressive or cognitive-contemplative functions, turning it primarily into a form of action, one that is dynamic and irrational. When he was still young, Julian Tuwim wrote that "poetry is the leap of a barbarian who felt God."

In this perspective, humanity shapes its own world. 19th-century intellectualism was thus relegated to the rank of a superstition that actually worked like an action-hindering shell. Architects of the new destiny were convinced that they would be able to form matter in whatever way they please, totally confident in their own powers. The whole globe appeared to be made of a plastic mass that could be freely modelled.

However, active humans committed to the realization of the irrational "Act" were not understood as guided by commitment to a community, as builders or "transfigurers" of a particular social reality. They would rather realize a generally understood *élan vital* (Bergson was the other thinker, besides Nietzsche, who hugely influenced the literature from the first decades of the 20th century).[26] Thus, they would, in fact, be mythological creations and subjects in the collectivist variant of the Dionysian myth. They would never embark on a solitary conquest of the world, but rather remain part of the flock. Experiencing elation when immersed in the crowd, they would participate in a Dionysian orgy, and feel – as Vyacheslav Ivanov, the leading theoretician of Russian symbolism put it in a cycle of studies titled *Hellenic Religion of a Suffering God* – "an ecstasy of unification and de-individualization."[27] Belonging to the flock is something that would define their essence. Here is revealed the new meaning of the mask of Dionysus donned by poets and thinkers during the first quarter of the 20th century.

---

25 Stanisław Brzozowski, "Filozofia Fryderyka Nietzschego," p. 464.

26 Bergson's impact on French literature is shown by Romeo Arbour in the book *Henri Bergson et les lettres françaisses* (Paris: José Corti, 1955).

27 Ivanov's study was printed in parts in the magazines *Nowyj Put'* (1904) and *Woprosy Żyzni* (1905). Quotation from: *Nowyj Put'* (February 1904), p. 74.

Dionysus – omnipresent in literature and invoked by the likes of Stefan George and Walter Pater, probably all Russian symbolists, as well as Wacław Berent, German expressionists and the Polish Skamander group – became expressive of an activist attitude, sanctioning it culturally and providing a foundation to rest upon. Dionysian cults were very dynamic in Greece, where their character was far removed from the Apollonian cults of the Olympians. Celebrations gathered entire populations, which would fall into ecstasy during the mysteries. Moreover, they were democratic in nature; the Dionysian procession in Athens would be formed in Kerameikos, the poor district of potters. It was already there that singers and dancers would come to the foreground as the ritual's protagonists fascinated by the celebrations.[28] An ecstatic reconciliation would take place, with groups of people forming a ritual choir that would praise the deity not through supplication or calm paeans, but in dithyrambs supplemented by dance, action and movement, with "the idea of a mystical identification binding the Bacchic group into one choral body: Dionysus."[29]

For writers active at the beginning of the 20th century, this identification acquired yet another meaning. It entailed the identification of contemporary world with the rituals of the Greek mysteries and the ancient *polis*, in which these mysteries were developed. Thus, a mystery-related dimension was given to the present – the sole focus of action-oriented people, many of whom felt as if they embodied Dionysus. Consequently, the cultural equations discussed earlier were given a new form. To reshape bourgeois culture, it was necessary to reduce it to an alien cultural formation. On the other hand, it was paramount to equate the postulated dynamic reality, i.e., the one that would emerge thanks to the efforts of the activists, with one of the aforementioned formations. History was therefore considered in presentist terms, especially those periods when the cult of Dionysus was a flourishing phenomenon in culture: the beginning and the end of antiquity. History was thus introduced – so to speak – into the present system. As Andrei Bely remarked,

> [t]hat which is really new, what fascinates us in symbolism, is the attempt to shed light on the deepest contradictions of contemporary culture by referencing various cultures. It is as if we were now experiencing the whole past: India, Persia, Egypt, Greece and the Middle Ages all come alive and march in front of us as if they were closer to us in time than other epochs. It is said that in crucial moments of life one sees, in one's mind eye, the whole life in a single sequence. Now, the entire history

---

28 Cf. August Mommsen, *Feste der Stadt Athen im Altertum, geordnet nach attischem Kalendar* (Leipzig: Teubner, 1898), pp. 428–448.

29 Vyacheslav Ivanov, *Hellenic Religion of a Suffering God, Nowyj Put'* (August 1904), p. 23.

of humanity unfolds before our eyes, which can mean that humankind reached an important moment. We do feel something new, but we experience it by framing the new in an abundance of old categories, or at least largely so. In this lies the novelty of so-called symbolism.[30]

This is how the concept of cultural syncretism was born. Those in favour of the mixing of cultures would refer to the times when this was a real phenomenon, namely the Hellenistic period and the last centuries of the ancient world. Stefan George's poem "Algabal" is set in the 3rd century CE and focuses primarily on how cultures permeate, just like Dmitry Merezhkovsky's *Julian the Apostate*, set in the same period. These phenomena also emerged in Polish literature. Stanisław Wyspiański systematically mixed cultural systems, introducing Demeter to a Warsaw garden, where she bids farewell to Persephone, identifying Christ with Apollo, or – on the other hand – making "Scamander glimmer with Vistula's bright waves." Antoni Lange was fascinated with the clash of the West and the East. In the drama *Attila*, the eponymous hero is not just the destroyer and vanquisher of Europe, but primarily a representative of a foreign culture that cannot offer much to the West. This tendency culminated in Tomasz Miciński's drama *Bazylissa Teofanu*, where Dionysus is invoked most often, and where basically every character, including the eponymous heroine, is to some extent an incarnation of this god. The 9th-century Byzantium emerges in Miciński's work as a cultural melting pot. Bazylissa's court is a place where various forms of Christianity meet with both pagan Greek beliefs and some representative of the East; moreover, there are brave knights from the North and the as yet uncivilized Slavic warriors. This congregation includes both those who had already achieved great things in culture and those who would reach this stage only later. Rome was also a highly attractive place, which – according to Jan Parandowski – "is, as it were, a meeting point for the entire world."[31] Finally, the Middle Ages could also accommodate diverse ingredients, forming a unique conglomeration, as in the opera *King Roger* by Karol Szymanowski with a libretto by Jarosław Iwaszkiewicz, where a Sicilian shepherd is transformed into Dionysus.

Cultural syncretism can be also traced in other places than the cultural equation involving the present and the past. It surfaces in the juxtaposition of presently existing national cultures with other ones, especially those whose representatives had a strong sense of identity and wanted to retain it, all the while remaining part

30 Andrei Bely, *Simwolizm* (Moscow: Musaget, 1910), p. 50.
31 Jan Parandowski, *Juwenilia* (Warszawa: Państwowy Instytut Wydawniczy, 1960), p. 250.

of the European civilization understood as a totality. The juxtaposition of North and South emerged among Scandinavian writers already in the 19th century. It was intended to emphasize differences and similarities of both psychological and cultural nature (cf. Henrik Ibsen's play *The Burial Mound*, which is characteristic in this respect). However, this phenomenon emerged in clearest form among Russian symbolists, for whom the problem of West and East was perhaps of crucial significance, recurring both in theoretical writings and literary works. Still, this juxtaposition was not developed in the spirit of the Russian tradition because the symbolists did not take the side of either "Westernizers" or "Slavic enthusiasts" because they saw this conflict as irrevocably belonging to history. They did not idealize either imitation or isolation. It was the synthesis that they sought, desiring to be both authentically Russian *and* sincerely European. This idea recurs in writings by Merezhkovsky, Bryusov, Bely, and Ivanov. They would often even exacerbate the matter by assuming the guise of uncouth Easterners – the wild Scythians. These people have kept appearing in Russian literature since Vladimir Solovyov, for whom they represented the dark forces of the East (they appeared in this role earlier in Arthur de Gobineau). They were ambiguous as a symbol: on the one hand, they would be perceived in negative terms, in line with Solovyov's views, i.e. as enemies of Russia and Europe; on the other, however, they would embody the Russian spirit. Alexander Blok emphasized this ambiguity in the work titled *Scythians*. In turn, Sergei Prokofiev's *Scythian Suite*, written shortly before the start of the First World War, broke away from the period's musical conventions and foregrounded barbaric rhythms, but it was also the product of a specific tradition present in the history of Russian art.

The concept of cultural syncretism, sometimes equated with the idea of saving culture from becoming fossilized by injecting barbarism in it, found its fullest expression not in reflections on the identity of national traditions, but in considerations of the relationship between Christianity and paganism. "Have I been understood?" Nietzsche asks categorically, answering: "*Dionysus versus the crucified…*"[32] This idea, which kept recurring insistently in his late writings, became the epoch's obsession. Importantly, however, probably no one assumed such a radical position. The point was to iron out differences rather than to emphasize them. This was the direction pursued by Tadeusz Zieliński, whose scientific studies and popularizing essays, printed before the First World War in Russian literary monthlies, had a strong influence on symbolists from Moscow

---

32 Friedrich Nietzsche, *Ecce Homo*, transl. J. Norman (Cambridge: Cambridge University Press, 2006), p. 151 (emphasis preserved).

and St. Petersburg. Emphasis of similarities between paganism and Christianity also permeated Ivanov's cycle of studies on the Dionysian religion, written before Zieliński's works on this subject.[33] Ivanov claims that the main similarity rests in the concept of God's sacrifice made in the name of the people.[34]

The concept of synthesis proved to be particularly fascinating to Russian symbolists, who displayed unmatched attraction to religious issues among various literary formations from the beginning of the 20th century. Naturally, they were not interested in historical matters. They regarded religious syncretism as a contemporary problem, which aided them in finding their identity and served as a means of expressing their attitude towards the world. It was an expression of their attachment to the Christian tradition and its institutions, but simultaneously revealed their negative stance on certain implications of this tradition. In particular, they criticized asceticism and contemplative life. In this, they would also depart from the Christian underestimation of the body and life in its earthly fullness. Such issues are visible, for example, in Merezhkovsky's works. For many people living at the onset of the 20th century, religion was meaningful insofar as it supported an activist attitude, allowing to present the contemporary world as an object to be acted upon. Traditional Christianity could not perform this role because it was too institutionalized and too dogmatic.

Religious syncretism – visible not only among Russian symbolists but also in Stefan George, his disciples, and certain Polish artists – was in equal measure a means of reforming Christianity in the name of new ideas in philosophy and poetry, and an attempt at adopting a new perspective on antiquity. This was discussed already by Walter Pater, who anticipated modernist syncretism and was himself fascinated with the mixing of cultures. He studied

> certain Italian scholars of the fifteenth century [who wished] to reconcile Christianity with the religion of ancient Greece. To reconcile forms of sentiment which at first sight seem incompatible, to adjust the various products of the human mind to one another in one many-sided type of intellectual culture, to give humanity, for heart and imagination to feed upon, as much as it could possibly receive [...].[35]

---

33 Zieliński was an enthusiast of Ivanov's Dionysian studies, which he saw as combining the latter's philological expertise with philosophical and poetic talent. Cf. *Eos* 1926, pp. 208–209.

34 This view is certainly correct from a historical perspective, which is confirmed for example by works in religious studies, including James G. Frazer's *Adonis Attis Osiris* (1914), which examines pagan cults widespread in Christianity's formative years.

35 Walter Pater, *The Renaissance. Studies in Art and Poetry* (Berkeley: University of California Press, 1980), p. 23.

Pater – who also penned an essay on Dionysus[36] – was a true literary idol in
Europe (also in Poland), contributing to the development of the discussed syncretism, which was not only conceptual but also materialized in a system of
particular literary symbols. In most general terms this is embodied in the previously mentioned image from an opera by Szymanowski: the metamorphosis
of a Shepherd into Dionysus on the background of Christian Sicily during the
Middle Ages. It was Szymanowski who expressed this idea more strongly than
any other Polish artist. Iwaszkiewicz recalls that

> Sicily under King Roger is some kind of an abstract Kythira, or rather – to put it
> more properly – the terrain of the composer's soul, where various philosoph-
> ical systems battle for influence, the two major adversaries being Christianity, in
> which Szymanowski was raised, and paganism in the form of Dionysian cult, a reli-
> gion of life, which would not be victorious but rather transform itself into the power
> and joy of Polish people, finally emerging triumphant in *Harnasie* and Symphony
> No. 4.[37]

Szymanowski's lost novel features the fairly widespread comparison of Christ
and Orpheus.[38] This theme gained considerable popularity as many works liken
Christ to Eros, Dionysus or Orpheus, e.g. Miciński's *Bazylissa*.[39] This comparison
was accurately captured in the poem "Eros" by Józef Jedlicz, a writer who has
rather unfairly fallen into oblivion:

> On a grey hill, at the crossroads
> Under the leaf of a silver birch
> A stone Christ bows down
> And looks upon the wide world:
> Whether the crops sprout in fields,
> Whether wetlands are strewn with flowers—
> He rests his divine face in his palm,
> Not troubled with any worries,
> In boundless holy silence.

---

36 The essay, titled "The Study of Dionysus: A Spiritual Form of Fire and Dew" (1879),
    was published in *Greek Studies* (London: Macmillan, 1895).
37 Jarosław Iwaszkiewcz, *Książka o Sycylii* (Kraków: Wydawnictwo Literackie, 1956),
    p. 56. Iwaszkiewcz's reminiscences of Szymanowski are generally of crucial importance
    for the presently discussed matters.
38 This is discussed for example by Stefania Łobaczewska in her monograph on
    Szymanowski (Kraków: Polskie Wydawnictwa Muzyczne, 1950).
39 This also has historical grounding because Jesus was presented in this way in
    early Christian art. Cf. Vojeslav Molé, *Historia sztuki starochrześcijańskiej i
    wczesnobizantyjskiej* (Lwów: K.S. Jakubowski, 1931).

> When flowers bloom in May,
> And Sunday's charm falls on the fields,
> He stands joyful in the green thicket
> In a circle of colourful, lush climbers—
> And when a golden blaze glows down
> From the flowing expanse of mists
> And the dew shines with miraculous brightness,
> Christ turns into Eros
> And smiles at the radiant daybreak...[40]

Christ turned into Dionysus, Orpheus or Eros ceases to be a God who suffers for humanity in solitude, but rather becomes the leader of a group united through religious bonding, in which the distance between him and his followers is diminished. Both the deity and its worshippers are members of one magnificent mystery, which did not just occur at some point in a distant past, in mythical times of direct contact between man and god, but keeps repeating itself, also in the present. Hence the vision of Christ-Dionysus heading the march of rebellious soldiers, or living in a modern city amidst "executors, hanged men and prostitutes" (an obsessive motif returning in early poems by Tuwim).

As a result, literary forms of rites were transformed, with dancing substituting prayer. In this way, dance ceases to be merely playful and rises to the rank of a symbol expressing human activity: possessive, irrational, and dictated by an otherwise unmanageable momentum of life. References to ancient religious dancing, made already by Nietzsche, provided a certain ritualistic justification to this. The dancing crowd, joyously or convulsively gesturing to the accompaniment of a pipe and tambourine, would come to express an activist attitude since the group would also use movement to convey its dynamic worldview. Nietzsche wrote about "doing philosophy by dancing" or even of "dancing out philosophy."

As many as twenty years after Nietzsche gave vent to his fascination with dancing, Blaise Cendrars wrote the programmatic poem *La danse*, in which he uses dance to explain poetry, viewing it as a permanent state of all reality, including the poet who has found himself inside it ("I am not interested in the landscape, but in its dance"). Similarly, Paul Valéry compared poetry to dance, although in a slightly different sense than the one discussed here. He based his view on the conviction that words in a poem, just like dancing steps, are disinterested – brought forth not for any practical reason but for their own sake. The motif of dancing recurs in works of other poets as both something sanctifying

---

40 Józef Jedlicz, "Eros," in: *Nieznanemu Bogu* (Warszawa: J. Mortkowicz, 1912), p. 88.

and sanctified. Stefan George even published a poem (in the volume *Das neue Reich*) about Christ dancing with his followers, triumphing and redeeming through joy.[41] In a well-known poem by Tuwim, Socrates is philosophizing by dancing. Many more examples could be provided.

However, the point is rather to grasp the very meaning of dancing since its position in the modernist dialogue between barbarism and culture is highly ambiguous. Dance refers not only to ancient ritual, but also becomes a sign of primitivized art, one that appeals to humanity's simplest reactions, and abandons the canonical conventions of European art. This tendency culminates in the period preceding the First World War, when artists were attracted to naively deformed figures of African deities and enthused over the most uncouth artistic products of folklore. Moreover, it was the time when jazz arrived in Europe. The so-called Fauvism should be used in reference not only to the painting from that period but also to certain tendencies in literature and music. What else is at stake in the consciously primitivized cries of the Futurists, even if they praised airplanes and new models of automobiles? What else are we dealing with in the second decade of the 20th century, which sprouted "geographical poetry" born out of fascination with the cultures of those peoples who have not yet reached the European level of refinement?

This tendency is most clearly discernible in music, perhaps because it made such a sudden and explosive entrance, differing so starkly from what was dominant at the beginning of the 20th century, i.e. from the neo-romanticism of Richard Strauss and the subtly weaved impressionism of Claude Debussy. To Igor Stravinsky and Béla Bartók, who codified those new tendencies, the styles in question belonged to the past. Instead of pathos and subtlety they favoured brutalism based primarily on the foregrounding of rhythm and referencing folklore. In Stravinsky's early ballet works we find elements of folk music, which were unknown to Russian composers of the 19th century who were, after all, very close to the folk tradition. Moreover, he made the idol Pan lead the pagan crowd in *The Rite of Spring*, in which the assembly holds the ceremonial function it had in ancient Rus. Bartók, on the other hand, wrote in 1912 a short piece for piano, which heavily foregrounds rhythm, titled *Allegro barbaro*. This term could summarize the overall tendency in European art at the beginning of the 20th century. Ideas developed by Stravinsky and Bartók met with a favourable response in the West. Even the mature master Maurice Ravel turned to exotic

---

41 Cf. the analysis of this poem in the monograph of Claude David: *L'oeuvre poétique de Stefan George* (Abbeville: F. Paillart, 1952), p. 345.

and primitive folklore, for example in the cycle *Songs of Madagascar*, while the young Darius Milhaud introduced Brazilian themes in many of his works. At the same time, the first jazz stylizations were created. A new phenomenon emerged, which could be called populist music, consisting in the adaptation of street melodies and rhythms, as in *Boeuf sur le toit* by Milhaud.[42]

The examples taken from the field of music demonstrate that artists were leaning towards a refined barbarity in two distinct ways: either by reaching out to exotic art, mainly African, or by turning, if possible, to local folklore and "national primordialism."[43] Naturally, it was the second option that became dominant in Poland, where works about dancing Africans – which so irritated Karol Irzykowski – were rare. Primitivized folklore is perhaps expressed most fully in works of Polish Futurists (Stanisław Młodożeniec, Tytus Czyżewski), but it had some forerunners among the early modernists of the so-called Young Poland. Anyway, in both cases, it functioned as part of cultural equations, though this was certainly not a conscious effort among the Futurists. For example, Młodożeniec employed folk songs and adapted them into lofty and exuberant dithyrambs. In an early drama by Czyżewski, titled *Death of a Faun* [*Śmierć Fauna*], a Greek idol appears in the Polish countryside, which has been captured in all its diversity. Fauns also make an appearance in *Marcolf* [*Marchołt*] by Jan Kasprowicz, where the eponymous character is to some degree an incarnation of Dionysus since the poet emphasizes certain similarities between them – for example, the fact that the birth of the fat and lewd Marcolf caused his mother to die.[44]

However, the spiritual father of the tendency to weave Greek and Polish motifs, including even Polish peasant folklore, was Stanisław Wyspiański. Following his example, this phenomenon crystallized in the form of the poetic-mythological drama. A large number of such works were written in the period preceding the First World War. Cultural syncretism was expressed in them through the transplantation of Greek themes into Poland (one characteristic example of this is the oeuvre of Radosław Krajewski, a literary wannabe who published several dramas in this style) or through the development of Slavic legends and myths about early Polish history, which were treated in a fairy-tale-like spirit, much like

---

42 It is worth mentioning that Dionysian themes feature, during the first quarter of the 20th century, in works of many composers: Debussy (*Epigraphes antiques*), Roussel (*Bacchus et Ariadne*), Stravinsky (*The Rite of Spring*) and in several works of Szymanowski.

43 This has been pointed out by Kazimierz Wyka in a discussion of folk themes in works of Tytus Czyżewski. Cf. Kazimierz Wyka, *Rzecz Wyobraźni* (Warszawa: Państwowy Instytut Wydawniczy, 1959).

44 Cf. the essay by Jan Józef Lipski: "O poezji Tytusa Czyżewskiego," *Twórczość* 6 (1960).

Greek myths and dramas. The primevally lustful nature of the Slavs was supposed to contain a rejuvenating potential capable of breaking down chains. In this particular case, cultural syncretism carried direct political connotations. Dionysus, as shall be expounded later, would become the symbol of regeneration.

1.4 The historiosophical metaphor

Cultural syncretism, however, was first and foremost an attempt to answer the question about the nature of contemporary times by imagining the past. It could be said that – contrary to the Latin proverb – history is no longer life's teacher but the other way round: life is history's teacher. Cultural syncretism was never an antiquarian stance. Even if it directed attention to the past, history was endowed with a degree of topicality. In this perspective, the past can always return, revealing its hitherto unknown aspects: "The wheel of being rolls eternally." Persephone, abducted and taken to the underworld, returns every year. Dionysus-Zagreus dies torn into pieces by the Titans, but his limbs come together again so that the suffering deity can return in its original form. In Dionysian myth, just like in many primeval systems of belief, a specific idea is revealed – one of eternal return, which Nietzsche made the cornerstone of his philosophy. Thus, Dionysus acquires a new meaning as he becomes the symbol of eternal transformation, in which nothing dies but only temporarily ceases to function, returning at some point with redoubled strength, ready for action. As a result, Dionysus emerges as the symbol of history's course, understood as eternal transformation and eternal return. In this history, as Iwaszkiewicz writes,

> Everything that is bound
> Becomes unbound.
> Like the tangled shots
> Of climbers at cemeteries.[45]

The present is therefore just a brief moment in the unceasing process of binding and unbinding, a moment in which many things begin and end. However, which things are in their initial phase and which at their final stage? The interest in antiquity emerges in a different light then, especially the focus on its early and late periods. Naturally, given a circular vision of history, such notions as beginning and ending have only relative significance. For Nietzsche, who is the predominant originator of these ideas, the categories of decline and renaissance, decadence

---

45 Jarosław Iwaszkiewicz, "Piosenka dla zmarłej," in: *Wiersze* (Warszawa: Czytelnik, 1958), p. 383.

and power, were also quite relative. It was already Burckhardt who, in his early work on Constantine the Great, demonstrated that there does not exist anything like the period of absolute decline, and that late antiquity was not merely a period when former ideas of civilization were degenerating but also a time of spiritual transformation. The great scholar of the Renaissance stated that "Der Geist hat Wandelbarkeit, aber nicht Vergänglichkeit."[46] Consequently, renaissance and decadence could occur simultaneously. Nietzsche criticized his times because he saw in them primarily a decline, but he did also discern a possibility for changes in the direction he proposed. He would thus not consider his era as a closed one. Although Dionysus departed during the first centuries of historical Greece, he would return to spread his teachings. Similarly, during the Renaissance Christian asceticism was supplanted by a pagan intoxication with life, and the model of the penitent was substituted with the one of a person who subdues the world in a joyful effort, renouncing the spirit world in the name of becoming an earthly conqueror.

Nietzsche indicated those historical points he found particularly significant – literally, the turning points marking beginnings and endings, declines in power and onsets of decadence (or vice versa). According to him, one such negative point was the rise of Socrates in the ancient polis, the first decadent figure in history. With the emergence of his teachings, the original Greek spirit began to decline – the one that found expression in the cult of Dionysus and related mysteries. One positive point, on the other hand, was the start of the Renaissance in 15th-century Italy, which involved the cult of life at its fullest, and of earthly beauty. These ideas permeated literature and artistic consciousness. For example, Merezhkovsky's novel *Julian the Apostate* describes a pivotal moment in the 3rd century, when two forces clashed: on the one hand, the spirit of humility and asceticism, and on the other – the reverence for life's fullness as expressed in older Greek beliefs. The scene in which Julian reopens the temple of Dionysus, previously closed by Christians, is clearly symbolic in this respect.

The critical point that provoked the most heated debates was the Renaissance. Following the lead of Nietzsche and Burckhardt, many perceived it as the last great epoch in the history of European culture. "Renaissancism" became an autonomous tendency in German literature at the end of the 19th century.[47] Polish literature also fell under this spell as is confirmed by the early works of

---

46   After: Edgar Salin, *Vom deutschen Verhängnis. Gespräch an der Zeitenwende: Burckhardt-Nietzsche* (Hamburg: Rowohlt, 1959), p. 50.

47   Cf. Zygmunt Łempicki, preface to: Jacob Burckhardt, *Kultura Odrodzenia we Włoszech* [Polish translation of *The Civilization of the Renaissance in Italy*] (Kraków: Spółka Wydawnicza Polska, 1930), pp. xvi–xvii.

Leopold Staff. Przybyszewski, however, argues in the above-mentioned preface to *De Profundis* that the Renaissance

> [...] was, from the perspective of a naked soul, the wildest kind of madness to have ever haunted humanity, a monstrous and lecherous destructor of the progress undertaken on a grand scale by the human soul in the Gothic style [...] it is nothing more than a hellishly barbaric step backwards [...].[48]

The argumentation employed by Przybyszewski to support this decisive verdict is representative insofar as it is related to phenomena from the area of visual arts. It was the group of theorizing painters who protested most vigorously against the Renaissance, e.g. Leon Chwistek or Stanisław Ignacy Witkiewicz. Both considered Italian art of the Renaissance to be at the root of the tendency to copy reality, which they considered deadly for art.

Still, the tendency to grasp the present by approaching the past did not reach full potential in the domain of art. It rather defined a general perspective on history, one that was heralded in Romanticism. As Maria Janion put it,

> [f]or generations of Romantics the idea of eternal recurrence was, as usually, both a progressive and traditionalist path leading simultaneously towards catastrophe and evolution; moreover, it was combined with Christian teachings on Fall and Redemption. Krasiński certainly sought that formula too – one that would both justify revolutionary cataclysms and establish the law of transformative evolution as an inviolable principle.[49]

The difference would consist in the fact that the place of the motivation stemming from Christian dogmatism was taken by a vision originating in the culture of antiquity. What proved to be lasting was the very problem of "evolution and catastrophe," the ambiguity inherent in the course of history, although instead of evolution Nietzsche and his followers would rather speak of what has been termed above as "critical points." This Dionysian vision of history could lead in many directions, justifying the present state of affairs or directing attention to the total annihilation of civilization.

Nietzsche did not assume either of the two extreme positions. Negating the present, he believed – as shown above – in the possible return of Dionysus. However, already in his times people would lend certain ambiguity to the issues that he clothed in the antiquity-derived metaphor of Dionysus's retreats and returns. They would either fully approve of the present, which brought previously unimaginable

---

48 Stanisław Przybyszewski, *De Profundis*, p. 24.
49 Maria Janion, "Twórczość Krasińskiego do roku 1836 a problematyka ideowa romantyzmu," in: *Zygmunt Krasiński. W stulecie śmierci* (Warszawa: Państwowy Instytut Wydawniczy, 1960), p. 215.

advances in civilization, or grow terrified at the destruction to which the developing civilization seems to sentence itself. Already at this point, two distinct attitudes would emerge: the optimistic one, which found expression in some literary works from the first quarter of the 20th century, i.e. ones fascinated with "city, mass and machine," and the catastrophic one, which discerned the contradictions of civilization more clearly than its development, seeing the former in terms of forces that might split it from within, at the same time noticing external forces threatening this civilization from outside. Among Nietzsche's contemporaries, catastrophic ideas were articulated most strongly by Gobineau in his 1881 article titled "Ein Urteil über die jetzige Weltage" in connection with his lunatic racial theories. The above-mentioned cultural equations acquire in his case a new meaning. Gobineau compares 19th-century Europe, facing danger from all directions, to the Europe of the 4th century, the time of antiquity's final decomposition.[50] Although catastrophic ideas could be sometimes lost among the lofty dithyrambs in praise of the present, they constitute a significant phenomenon in literature from the beginning of the 20th-century, especially in the Russian prose, works of Merezhkovsky, Bryusov's poetry, and Ivanov's essays. Their catastrophism, however, did not have the kind of absolute character found later in novels by the likes of Roman Jaworski or Witkiewicz. Articulated most often by employing the metaphor of Dionysus (as in the historical trilogy by Merezhkovsky), it was not final and allowed to hope for possible rescue, even if it were to come far in the future.

Hence the typical juxtaposition found in the literature of the epoch: the old versus the young, or – in other terms – the ones ascending onto the world's stage versus the ones descending from it. Hope would be typically expressed in the concept of the mysteries, during which the antagonistic forces meet in an ultimate confrontation deciding the fate of the universe. Mysteries should be understood almost literally, not only because certain works were given this particular form, which in itself alludes to certain religious ceremonies, but primarily because mysteries are often the subject of these works (in most cases dramas) and actually occurred on the stage. In Polish literature works that feature such elements include *King Roger* by Szymanowski and Iwaszkiewicz, *Bazylissa Teofanu* by Miciński and *Euphorion* by Władysław Kozicki, a now-forgotten propagator of classicism before 1914. In Kozicki's drama a conflict emerges between the senile Origen, a fanatic proponent of Christian asceticism, and the young, beautiful Euphorion, who embodies the Greek approval of life and the charms of thriving bodies. Euphorion triumphs in the mysteries, aided

---

50   Cf. Michał Sobeski, *Kwiat złoty. Gobineau redivivus* (Poznań: Fiszer i Majewski, 1925).

by Dionysus, who metamorphoses during the ceremonies from a decrepit old man into a wonderful young one. Through his transformation culture is saved.[51] Even though the mysteries are happily resolved, they testify to a certain anxiety, a sense that the present is faced with "storm and stress." After all, such themes do not emerge in times of stabilization. Moreover, mysteries would involve other references as well.

The modernist perspective on the present and history stemmed from reflection on life's dynamic character, its movement and transformations, which impose themselves on people at every step. It is highly paradoxical, however, that this view of history brought to life classicist tendencies in literature. It remains puzzling even if it is understandable how the mediating factors operated: on the one hand, negating the Romantic rebellion against history, while on the other – conceiving of that history through the mythological theme of Dionysus. This appears paradoxical because in the past the striving for classicism in literature was motivated entirely differently. Sartre discusses this matter in relation to French literature from the 17th century:

> As a result, classicism emerges when the society assumes a relatively stable form and becomes saturated with the myth of its eternal nature, i.e., when it mixes the present with the eternal, and historicity with traditionalism [...].[52]

However, it is hard to find any of the characteristics described by Sartre in the culture of the first quarter of the 20th century. After all, writers from that period were fascinated with social fluidity and dynamism, which emerged with such great force. Moreover, they were preoccupied with the question of the disappearing – or transforming, at best – of the kind of cultural formation they came to inhabit. Further, mixing the present with the eternal was replaced by making links to epochs characterised by fluid boundaries – ones that have not crystallized or ones that have lost their form, e.g. the beginning or ending of antiquity. Thus, Dionysian classicism does not originate in the conviction that culture has a stable nature.

It is not without significance for this kind of classicism that Nietzsche, whose ideas shaped the epoch, adopted mythological costumes to express his ideas. In this way, he imposed his mode of thinking and his language on other writers. He expressed himself in literary forms that usually related in some way to literature from antiquity. The main reason for this may be the fact that the Romantic view of the relationship between the poet and the society had run its course, making

---

51 *Euphorion*, subtitled "A dramatic dithyramb," was written in 1914 and published in 1919 in Lviv.
52 Jean Paul Sartre, *Situations II* (Paris: Gallimard, 1948), p. 138.

the Romantic type of individualism appear to modernist writers as an unsuit-
ably weak position in the times of great changes and conflicts. The present as
the era of the crowd was discussed for example by Antoni Lange in the extraordinarily interesting essay "Cupid and Faun" ["Amor i Faun"].[53] He claims that,
since the French Revolution, Faun is the tragic leader who cannot ever fulfil his
ideals. In the world designed by Faun it is impossible to cling to such attitudes as
the ones embodied by Werther or Byronic loners. Poets cannot just oppose the
crowd by disagreeing with it; they must enter into contact with it and become its
part. Thus, the need was born to recall those ancient forms of literary expression
that facilitate bringing the artist and the ceremony-performing crowd together,
establishing ritual communication based on concord.

1.5 Poetry and the agora

In *Doctor Faustus*, Serenus Zeitblom confesses:

> I am an old-fashioned man, stuck in certain romantic views dear to me, among which
> is the heightened drama of an antithesis between the artist and the bourgeois. Adrian
> would have coolly contradicted any statement like the foregoing – that is, if he had found
> it worth his trouble to contradict. For he had extremely level-headed – and in response
> to others, often caustic – opinions about art and being an artist, and was so averse to the
> "Romantic fuss" the world at one time enjoyed making about such matters that he did not
> even like to hear the words "art" and "artist," as was evident from the face he would make
> when someone spoke them. It was the same with the word "inspiration," which one defi-
> nitely had to avoid in his company – if need be, by substituting a phrase like "fresh idea."[54]

In Mann's novel, a fictional biography of a modernist artist, the attitude of Adrian
Leverkühn is exemplary. In terms of ideas and aesthetics he was educated at the
beginning of the century, assimilating the period's prevalent concepts. He is a model
not only because the juxtaposition of artistry and the bourgeois seems to him a
Romantic anachronism but also due to the conclusions he draws from negating
it. Resigning from the pattern of artistic rebellion developed long ago, he does not
become inclined to accept the aesthetic values approved by the bourgeoisie and
remains an avant-garde creator who does not meet with much understanding.

---

53 This essay was published in the short story collection *W czwartym wymiarze*
    (Kraków: Książka, 1912). Perhaps for this reason, it was completely forgotten. As a
    side note, it is worth mentioning that in many works the functions ascribed to Dionysus
    were performed by members of his procession, especially Faun and Pan. Therefore, such
    works (e.g. Kasprowicz's *Marcolf* and Czyżewski's *Death of a Faun*) belong to the mod-
    ernist vein of the Dionysian current. I was guided to Lange's essay by Jacek Trznadel.
54 Thomas Mann, *Doctor Faustus*, p. 28.

Mann's Leverkühn flees from the world's hustle and bustle, in fact bearing certain characteristics of a hermit. This makes him different from the actual artists working at the beginning of the 20th century, who let Romantic models slide into the past but did not become hermits themselves, attempting rather to conquer the world. However, they embarked on this mission with the consciousness that they are members of great modern societies. The collectivist variant of the Dionysian myth thus acquired a new meaning. It became both the expression of – and motivation for – the shaping of a new relationship between the poet and the world, one that would emerge from a negation of Romanticism. By abandoning the juxtaposition of the poet and the philistine, which we know to have been still dominant in the last decade of the 19th century, poets would not assume the latter's position, becoming like petit bourgeois or nouveau riche reading novelettes and decorating drawing rooms with kitschy landscape paintings. They would not share such tastes, habits or social ideals. By approving of reality and relishing in that which is new and dynamic in it, they would divest it of one particular dimension, thus fabricating an almost ideal pattern. Or – in other words – they would reduce it to myth by employing cultural equations.

The Dionysian motifs surfacing at the beginning of the 19th century displayed a clearly mythological character, becoming – to use Eliade's term once again – an "archetype" of the artist's attitude towards the modern society. This seems to have been their primary function, developed as a result of assimilating Nietzsche's idea, but also going beyond it. For the German philosopher, the Dionysian world belonged to either the past or the future. He never writes about it in terms of the present. Nevertheless, poets from the beginning of the 20th century saw this kind of world around them and began to praise it, extolling simultaneously reality and myth.

Such mythologization was certainly heralded in 19th-century literature, even in those passages which might initially seem to be far removed from this practice. Mann wrote about the mythological themes present in novels by Émile Zola, creator of *Les Rougon-Macquart*, paradoxically juxtaposing the great French novelist with Wagner.

> Who is this Astarte of the Second Empire, named Nana, if not a symbolic and mythological figure? How come she is bearing that name? It is a primordial sound, humanity's early babbling. Nana was the nickname of Babylon's Ishtar. Did Zola know about this? It would be all the more worthwhile and characteristic if he did not.[55]

However, mythologization was given here a different meaning than the one developed by the realists of the 19th century because it did not only cast a network of

---

55   Thomas Mann, *Leiden und Grösse der Meister* (Frankfrut: Fischer-Bücherei, 1957), p. 218.

symbols over the world, but also constituted a form of taking action, and led to the determination of the artist's place in the world.

By mythologizing, artists would determine their roles and actions, turning themselves into *dithyrambists* – hence, into participants in contemporary mysteries. The role of the dithyrambist in the Dionysian ritual was always precisely defined: that figure would be the first singer, the coryphaeus of the ritual's choir. Though immersed in the ceremony, he would remain the guide who neither praises nor reproves, but rather cooperates. Acting as a priest, he would nevertheless avoid looking at the faithful from the perspective of the elevated pulpit and stand among them. He was the function of the crowd, just like – at least partially – the crowd was the function of his priestly actions. Still, he would not dissolve among others and his face – one among thousands – would not lose its individual features. Similarly, he would not renounce his traditional aesthetic tasks, fulfilled since time immemorial.

> [...] aesthetic and religious forms unite in the mysteries: on the one hand, we encounter a synthesis of universal forms, but on the other, the form experienced in the mysteries is a form in which the individual manifests.[56]

Those aesthetic forms would be understood in a way far removed from the approach of the Parnassian authors. Beauty became the domain of action and former aestheticism had to be abandoned. In a characteristic declaration found in the Russian monthly *Apollon* we read:

> However, we do not wish to flee to the forest, where Satyrs roam, or to Mars, but rather desire to make beauty once more alive and social, not just to pay tribute to things that are beautiful but dead.[57]

The aim of the dithyrambist would be thus to praise and, by doing so, to sanctify the surrounding reality. The dithyrambist is not only an individual, whose role is confirmed by the crowd, but himself becomes a synthesis of this crowd and also its medium. He turns towards it and simultaneously articulates its arguments. This perspective has been most fully developed by Ivanov in his "Thoughts on Symbolism." In it, he views symbolism as a specific form of contact between poet and society, one that leads to the establishing of harmony between creator and audience. According to Ivanov, "symbolism works like magnetism" and the two sides that attract each other are the writer and the addressee who has lost former passivity.[58] Ivanov points to the counterpoint developed in the above relation.

---

56 Andrei Bely, *Simwolizm*, p. 108.
57 Alexandre Nikolayevich Benois, "W ożidanii gimna Appolinu," *Apollon* 1 (1909), p. 10.
58 Vyacheslav Ivanov, "Mysli o simwolizmie," *Trudy i Dni* 1 (1912).

This counterpoint would be realized in a clearly defined place, in a specific setting. The poet-dithyrambist would enter the agora of a modern city in order to continually remain in touch with those whose presence gives poetry meaning. For in this view poetry is naturally a dialogue, just like elements of dialogue appear in authentic ancient dithyrambs – the kind that modernist lyricists could acquaint themselves with since the discovery of Bacchylides's dithyrambs in the last decade of the 19th century. It was a sensation not only among professional philologists but also among writers. In the newly found ritualistic dialogues, the soloist and the choir come together in articulating their thoughts.

As a result, the city emerges as a ritual setting; furthermore, it becomes incorporated into the ritual. What follows is a specific praise of the agora as the most fitting place for rituals reconciling the poet with the society. In this way, the urban theme accompanies the Dionysian one. The former god of wild nature becomes a city god as the urban environment rises in the eyes of the epoch's poets to the rank of nature, humanity's immediate surroundings, crucial insofar as people have themselves created this milieu. Enthusiasm for the city also involves excitement about humanity's efforts materialized, which surfaced already in mid-19th-century. As Sartre claims, it was Baudelaire,

> […] after Rétif, Balzac and Suem, who greatly contributed to the expansion of what Roger Caillois has called the "myth of the big city." It means that the city equals eternal creation: its buildings, smells, and hubbub always belong to the kingdom of humankind. In it, everything is *poetry* in the strictest sense of the term. It is in this sense that ca 1920 the admiration of young people for electric advertisements, modern lighting and cars is deeply Baudelaireian in character. The big city reflects the chasm of human freedom. Ultimately then, even Baudelaire, who hates people and the "tragedy of the human face," becomes a humanist through his cult of human work.[59]

In one of his early poems, Julian Przyboś wrote of grand buildings by comparing them to "mountains packed with human toil."

Praise of the city inhabited by Rimbaud's "*les Bacchantes des banlieues*"[60] is also praise of life's dynamism – of *everyone*. The collectivist myth clearly takes a democratic turn here. The ideal of freedom and life's fullness becomes embodied in the figure of the tramp, who does not sanction accepted habits, living in the city and yet remaining, as it were, a "natural man." The tramp made an appearance in Staff's poetry but was given a more socially precise dimension in early works written by authors associated with the Skamander group. The first years of the 20th century

---

59 Jean Paul Sartre, *Baudelaire* (Paris: Gallimard, 1947), p. 50.
60 From the prose poem "Villes I."

were a time of programmatic democratization of poetry – a phenomenon that affected entire Europe. In France, it manifested in the emergence of a number of literary groups whose main goal was to extol the modern city as the essence of life, not without the influence of Bergson by the way.[61] In Russia, this was articulated in the programmes of the symbolists, who lent a ritualistic dimension to the present and the masses that created it, in this way expressing their approval of it.[62]

In Poland – as is generally known – these tendencies surfaced with some delay but were equally strong. Walt Whitman became the new literary patron – a poet whose fascination with urbanization was quite unique during the period he worked in. He owes this position to the fact that he was the first to assume the role of the bard of the big city masses and of the modern civilization. Also, he championed the realization of the communal spirit in the context of urban crowds, linking it to literary values by addressing his poems – as Tuwim notes in a programmatic article – "to anyone, to the random passer-by."[63] Thus, Whitman's spirit hangs over the many literary manifestos published at the beginning of the interwar period. It suffices to quote the following passage from one such programmatic piece by Jan Nepomucen Miller, which is particularly characteristic due to its fresh language, confirming the fact that in the discussed period the approval of reality had mythological and ritualistic properties:

> The work of an artist becomes a work of art in the full sense through the great act that brings together the creative individual and the group (or the initiated community), who are joined in creation and form a mystical union, which makes everyone, dressed in white robes and approaching the Lord's table of "mysteries," come together, constituting one *Spiritual Communion* [...].[64]

Although this "spiritual communion" is formed by encompassing the poet and the city crowd, it acquires a much more universal dimension, becoming a communion that rejoins the artist and the crowd with the world at large. A metaphysical projection

---

61 Cf. the relevant chapters from Marcel Raymond's *De Baudelaire au surrealism* (Paris: José Corti, 1952), as well as the article by Zygmunt Czerny "Rozwój poezji francuskiej po 1900 roku (Szkic informacyjny)," *Nowy Przegląd Literatury i Sztuki* 1 (1921), pp. 111–159. Bergson's influence on the development of the said tendencies was demonstrated by Arbour in his above-mentioned book.

62 Cf. e.g. B.W. Mikhailovsky, *Russkaja literatura XX wieka* (Moscow, 1939).

63 Julian Tuwim, "Manifest powszechnej miłości (Walt Whitman)," *Pro Arte et Studio* 8 (1917). Quoted after: Julian Tuwim, *Pisma prozą*, ed. J. Stradecki (Warszawa: Czytelnik, 1964), p. 183.

64 Jan Nepomucen Miller, "O twórczość bezimienną I komunę duchową," *Ponowa* (1931), p. 66.

of concord arising between the artist and the community is found in pantheistic theories. Everyone, including the maker of aesthetic values, is inscribed in the universe, which always constitutes the highest value of all. It is God. As one of the expressionist manifestoes argues, "God is born again from all directions."[65] Dionysus becomes the apostle of harmony, the god of unity, causing human heart – as Kasimir Edschmid claims in the quoted manifesto – to "beat according to the same rhythm as that of the world." Following Whitman – who approved of the world in order to express his friendship to a coachman driving a carriage on New York's cobbled streets – as well as the pattern of pantheist thought linked to civilization-related issues, poets would construct bridges joining every detail to the universe. Such pantheism was not merely an expression of optimism but had more far-reaching implications. It stemmed from the approval of totality, and it is this totality that would bring sense to everything that is in itself malevolent and meaningless. One could say that the value of something is determined already by the fact that it exists, as in the poem "Song for a Deceased Girl" ["Piosenka dla zmarłej"] by Jarosław Iwaszkiewicz:

> In great love
> Is everything conceived
> And everything – meaningless –
> Is nevertheless entirely holy.
>
> You who lay in coffin,
> Among the flowers,
> Know that Dionysus
> Is praying for us.
>
> Know that the holy one will come,
> Take us in his arms,
> Explain all torment
> That has been endured.

The poet unites with the world, discovering that he is inscribed in it, and discerns in this situation the basis of his own strength, as in Émile Verhaeren's "Drunkenness":

> I have united with the world, through love of things
> So simple and strong that I was almost ready
> Not to feel my own heart otherwise than in the changes
> Of all things around me and their unstable state.[66]

---

65 Kasimir Edschmid, *Frühe Manifeste* (Hamburg: C. Wegner, 1957), p. 21.

66 Sometimes the situation is different: the world is – as it were – inscribed in the poet: "Vous existez en moi, fôrets et monts, / Et vous encore, mais vous surtout,

The ritual beginning at the modern agora would conclude with the approval of everything that exists, thus reaching out to cosmos. This view was especially typical for the expressionists. Love for man and nature (nature understood as everything that surrounds us) would be expressed symbolically both in Dionysus, drunk with life, and in the humble St. Francis. The modest saint from Assisi became, as it were, one of the many incarnations of the exuberant deity with two faces like Janus.[67] Both of these symbols expressed the renunciation of rebellion in favour of approbation. The meaning of this was accurately captured by the Russian commentator of Nietzsche, N.J. Abramowicz:

> Rebellion against life is senseless not because the philosopher recommends silent reconciliation and meekness, but because it would be an uprising of the small against the much larger.[68]

Thus, the literary hero of the epoch found his place by renouncing any aspirations to oppose the cosmos with his own ego, although he would certainly not disavow anxiety. Nietzsche's words about the "cheerful and trusting fatalism"[69] became a universal value in literature.

In this way, art was stripped of its rebellious functions just as it lost its cognitive and descriptive dimension, at least to the extent to which it was possible. It was thus framed differently, as if it were the factor that intervenes in the very interpersonal reality. This emerged as its main function, bringing literature's role back to that of a ritual art, which was not an alien idea to Nietzsche, especially in the early stages of his philosophical career.

> What do all our art of artworks matter if we lose that higher art, the art of festivals! Formerly, all artworks were displayed on the great festival road of humanity, as commemorations and memorials of high and happy moments. Now one uses artworks

---

villes puissantes, / Où je sens s'exalter les cris les plus profonds / D'âge en âge sur la terre retentissante" (Émile Verhaeren, "L'Or") ["You exist in me, rivers, forests and mountains, / And you, above all, the grand cities, / Where I feel that the deepest cries are launched / From epoch to epoch over the resounding earth"].

67 One especially characteristic example of this is Leopold Staff's introduction to *Little Flowers of St. Francis* [*Kwiatki św. Franciszka*] (Lwów: B. Połoniecki, 1910), where he uses his reflections on St. Francis to formulate ideas that would be usually expressed with the help of Dionysian metaphors.

68 N.J. Abramowicz, *Człowiek buduszczego (Oczerk filosofskoj utopii Fr. Nietzsche)* (no date and place of publication), p. 50.

69 Friedrich Nietzsche, *Twilight of the Idols*, transl. J. Norman (Cambridge: Cambridge University Press, 2006) p. 223.

to lure poor, exhausted, and sick human beings to the side of humanity's road of suffering for a short lascivious moment; one offers them a little intoxication and madness.[70]

Ritual art ceased to be a form of entertainment and an individual occupation. Its significance would then boil down to providing meaning to actions of those gathered at the agora, who wish to celebrate their holiday or, as a matter of fact, on any other day too.

In this view, ritual art is not created by the priest, but by the one who comes to understand the dynamics of life in full, along with its "cheerful fatalism." It was the poet-joculator, recalled so often by Wacław Berent in *Living Stones* [*Żywe kamienie*], a poet who saw no contradiction between rituals rooted in mythology, and pure games, or even – if we keep in mind certain traditions from antiquity – between ritual and ribaldry.[71] Approbation of the world, linked to the pantheistic belief in its divine nature, led to the negation of traditional hierarchies of values. In a ritual, everything can have equal significance because everything that is has the most important property: existence. Therefore, Dionysus could be equally a symbol of the entire world, and of its least significant elements. Ritual art developed under his aegis could sanctify an infinite array of situations, attitudes, and things.[72]

1.6 Dionysus in place of Tyrtaeus

The development of the above attitudes, manifesting symbolically in Dionysus, occurred not only during the "time of great reconstruction" (Jerzy Stempowski's term) but also in times of great conflicts. However, the "Act" invoked by poets and intellectuals took the kind of shape that most of them found abhorring. The adored "group" morphed into a battalion of soldiers, while the momentum of life would find expression in grenades thrown into enemy trenches. Few followed in the steps of Gabriele D'Annunzio by donning

---

70 Friedrich Nietzsche, *The Gay Science*, transl. J. Nauckhoff (Cambridge: Cambridge University Press, 2007), p. 89.

71 Even stately Aristotle allowed this combination in *Politics*: "The official must therefore be careful that there may be no sculpture or painting that represents indecent actions, except in the temples of a certain class of gods to whom the law allows even scurrility" (transl. H. Rackham [Cambridge: Harvard University Press, 1959], pp. 629–631).

72 The idea of ritual art usually occurred in discussions of drama and theatre. Most often it would crystallize under the influence of the theory and practice of Wagner, who was overwhelmingly influential at the time.

the mask of warlike conquerors. Nevertheless, the war did not basically pro-
voke songs of lament.

Historical transformations have triggered changes in the semantics of the
Dionysian motif. It became not only a symbol of attitudes considered in very general terms but also of various social tendencies. This is especially clear in Polish
literature, where Dionysus emerged as an expression of national aspirations.
Before 1918 these ambitions would revolve around the country's rebirth, motivated by the concept of eternal return, but after 1918 they were channelled into
the joy of what was achieved. In extreme cases, a specific understanding of the
metaphor of Dionysus could condition the interpretation of an entire work, as
was the case with Berent's *Snowy Crop* [*Ozimina*].[73] In the final vision, deleted by
the author in later editions, Dionysus was not the "leader of the wedding" but a
champion of the hope that what is buried must return to life, an idea developed
earlier by Wyspiański: "What is to live must die first."

After being introduced into the sphere of national matters, Dionysus
assumed a specifically Polish form, which nevertheless slightly differed in the
two periods of its rise. In both, however, he was linked to an anti-Romantic
position that involved a negation of traditional forms of patriotic literature.
Dionysus took over the role of Tyrtaeus, the poet who wrote calls for combat.
During the time of the First World War various writers authored a large number
of lyric appeals, militant poems, and lofty proclamations in verse. Heaps of
such works have fallen so deep into oblivion that it is even difficult to fathom
the scale of the phenomenon. They met their fate because their role was, after
all, rather slight. The poet-legionnaires left the literary scene as quickly as they
entered it, even if some of them went on writing for much longer. Their poetry
performed a quite narrow practical function and never made it into the canon,
although the contexts with which it was associated were considered to be of
huge importance. It was probably the first time in Polish history that, despite
favourable conditions, this kind of poetry found itself in a social vacuum. This
happened certainly not only because it was of low literary value but also, and
above all, because it followed models that were anachronistic already at that
time. By contrast, *Songs of Janusz* [*Pieśni Janusza*] by Wincenty Pol was not a

---

73 That this was so is confirmed by two contemporary critical accounts of the work. In the
    first, Gustaw Olechowski even accuses Berent of treason (*Przegląd Krytyki Literackiej
    i Artystycznej* 39–41 [1911]). In the second, Kazimierz Bukowski emphasizes the role
    of Dionysian metaphor and interprets the work in an entirely different spirit (*Sylwetki*
    [Lwów: Księgania Polska B. Połonieckiego, 1914]).

masterpiece too, and yet it remained very much alive in Polish national consciousness throughout the 19th century. The discussed kind of poetry, however, became anachronistic momentarily.

In fact, what the public expected from literature was something different than the performance of the function it had when Poland was partitioned. Poetry was expected to be "normal," to be *only* literature. The fact that poetry could just as well be simply itself was also the manifestation and consequence of Poland having regained independence. Tyrtaean lyric brought memories of the old, while the Dionysian kind confirmed the new, giving expression to universal optimism. Silhouettes of poets were stripped of Konrad's coat, which the society applauded. These tendencies were clearly articulated by Adolf Nowaczyński in an article on the Skamander poets, which could be quoted *in extenso*:

> Mainly due to the favourable postwar historical context, the Skamander galaxy is the first literary group that orients itself towards the future rather than the past like its predecessors. The moment when Poland's national boundaries were sketched on the map of Europe there was no longer any need or room either for the Konrad-Gustaw type, or for Orcio, Irydion as well as domesticated Werthers and Hamlets. Poetry was liberated from the obligation to rule and lead in the domains of historiosophy and politics. Skamander was the first movement to enter the literary world fully conscious of the axiom that in an independent country creators of poetic, literary and artistic values cease to be responsible for "politics," "economy" and even the nation's culture and education. In works produced so far in the Skamander circles it clearly transpires that they are painfully aware that, for example, the question of Upper Silesia cannot be shifted onto a new political track with a sonnet on Huta Laura, an ode to the river Odra, or a drama "after Wyspiański" in which Konrad-Gustaw, surrounded with masks of Silesian princes, would deliver a lengthy monologue on the mightiness of coal (that cokes well too). Therefore, if the Skamander writers were able to emancipate themselves from the role and mission of bards and shamans, prophets and arch-priests, at the same time not isolating themselves in ivory towers and not rolling out banners heralding *"l'art pour l'art,"* we should praise them, be grateful and revel in their glory![74]

Thus, it was the "truly Dionysian group of Skamander-dervishes" (as Nowaczyński called them elsewhere in the quoted article) that was responsible for the most direct answer to the new "social demand." This certainly decided about their success.

Moreover, this quality also shaped the image of Dionysus. It distinctly differed from the vision discussed earlier, not only because it was decidedly hedonistic or even primitivized due to its emphasis of such tendencies. It was original

---

74 Adolf Nowaczyński, "Skamander połyska, wiślaną świetlący się falą," *Skamander* 7–9 (1921), p. 301.

insofar as it gave new meaning to anti-Romantic elements. It is already clear that in the discussed period the entire motif was contradictory to Romanticism. In Poland's early years of its second independence, it all boiled down to cutting away ties with the most sanctified tradition, not only in the literary sense but also in terms of ideology. The anti-Romantic trend emerged with obvious clarity. The paradox of this situation manifested in the fact that, previously, invocations of Dionysus were in all literatures a manifestation of a specifically understood engagement with the course of history, but in Poland after 1918 they became an expression of renouncing this engagement, despite the fact that for over a century this seemed to be the inherent quality of all artistic creativity. Naturally, such anti-Romanticism was a short-lived, or even ephemeral phenomenon, especially in the case of Skamander poets. As Stempowski accurately diagnosed,

> [...] great literary traditions cannot be immediately abandoned after calling a constitutional parliament.[75]

The Dionysus of the Skamander group, the most joyous and the least problematic of all incarnations of Dionysus, was the god of conformism, expressing not the idea of approbation of the world and its inexorable rhythm, but rather approval of what was reborn and came to constitute – as it initially seemed at least – the most beautiful of all possible worlds.

1.7 Epilepsy

Optimism, an activist attitude, and all that was expressed in the symbolism of Dionysus proved to be related not only to social life and history but also to art, which developed in accordance with the increasingly mighty world. Under the sign of Dionysus, the god of life and rhythm, avant-garde movements were entering the arena. As Przyboś remarked,

> [...] it seems that such an unrestrained belief in the brave new world, as well as the triumphant optimism, did not pay attention to the origins of any specific movement. The great innovative current of the first decades of the 20th century sparked a wave of optimism so immense that it did not break during the war and lived through it, becoming even more intense after the declaration of peace. The innovators proclaimed the *unique character of the epoch*, its grandness incomparable to any other period in history. They believed in its undefeatable potential to work wonders.[76]

---

75 Jerzy Stempowski, *Literatura w okresie wielkiej przebudowy* (Wilno: Kurier Wileński, 1935), p. 16.

76 Julian Przyboś, "Cele i trafy Awangardy," *Życie Sztuki* (1939), pp. 31–32.

However, this wave was slowly diminishing when the accompanying idea of great reconstruction began to take shapes that its propagators among artists and intellectuals found unfamiliar, i.e. when its proponents included people from the social margins, who in fact wanted to destroy culture. They were authentic barbarians, not the mythical ones. Moreover, at the same time evident signs of crisis emerged, signalling that the world which seemed to be stable and indestructible could be in fact shaken. As Anatol Stern put it, Dionysus lost his former vitality and strength:

> [...]
> O, how terrible is Europe's death!
> O, the blessed one!
>
> The epileptic Dionysus
> Is leading them
> the women
> with floating breasts,
> holding the trembling, naked body
> of a torn radio receiver,
> mechanical Orpheus;[77]

The epilepsy-struck Dionysus from this expressionist poem is, in fact, the last vision of this deity. It bids farewell to the literary god of the first quarter of the 20th century: to all that came to be associated with him, and to what he hid inside himself. Dionysus had to depart when all things postulated by the poets who donned his mask became dangerous and ominous, when barbarity became a real threat, and when market squares in a certain Central European country were no longer a place where poets could seek reconciliation with the crowd that comprised the new civilization, turning rather into bleak places witnessing the burning of books. Dionysus had to depart when writers suddenly discerned with great terror the liabilities of the modern civilization and abandoned all desire to compare it to the beautiful Greek world, even that of the times which cannot be called the classical periods of Hellenic culture. Dionysus had to depart when writers renounced the role of dithyrambists and began to seek a new place for themselves in the modern world, a place that would allow them to retain their dignity. Thus, they would become either clerks or catastrophists: the former if they argued that proclaiming humanistic values can be preserved as

---

77 Anatol Stern, "Europa," in: *Wiersze dawne i nowe* (Warszawa: Czytelnik, 1957), p. 104. Already before that poem was written in 1925, the Futurists claimed in the almanac *Gga* that "the great rainbow ape called Dionysus is long dead and stiff."

long as intellectuals do not interfere with the unfolding of history in a barba-
rized world, or as long as they hold on to their attitude in this world, and the
latter if they perceived the "great reconstruction" as the first step towards a great
fall, the kind that cannot be appealed against and shall not allow anything to
arise from it. The dwarfed Dionysus departed forever, becoming useless – also
as a metaphor – in the face of the new shape of the world. Moreover, his history
in the literature of the end of the 19th century and the first quarter of the 20th
turned into a history of a certain intellectual formation, embracing its hopes
and delusions, its rise and fall, and finally – its demise.[78]

---

78 I have worked on this essay in the years 1960–61 and originally published it in *Twórczość*
    11 (1961). Since that time, several works on this topic were published, further elaborating
    on the symbolism of Dionysus in 20th-century literature. In the Polish context, it is nec-
    essary to mention Jerzy Kwiatkowski's *Eleuter* (first printed in 1966 and later included
    in the book *Poezja Jarosława Iwaszkiewicza na tle dwudziestolecia międzywojennego*
    [Warszawa: Czytelnik, 1975]), in which a separate chapter is devoted to the role of
    this motif in the early poetry of Iwaszkiewicz. The critic even goes beyond the subject,
    making his remarks more general (e.g. in important considerations of the relation-
    ship between the symbolism of Christ and Dionysus). Dionysian themes in paintings
    by Jacek Malczewski are discussed by Kazimierz Wyka in the book *Thanatos i Polska*
    (Kraków: Wydawnictwo Literackie, 1971). As far as foreign studies are concerned, I wish
    to recall an earlier work by J.H.W. Rosteutscher, which I nevertheless was not aware of
    at the time of writing this article, titled *Die Wiederkunft des Dionysos* (Bern: A. Francke,
    1947), and which analyses the history of this motif in German literature from Hölderlin
    to Mann. Among later works, I was not able to acquaint myself with M.L. Baenmer's
    "Das Dionysiscche – Entwicklung eines literarischen Klischees" (*Colloquia Germanica* 3
    [1967]). One notable work is M.K. Spear's *Dionysus and the City. Modernism in Twentieth-
    Century Poetry* (Oxford: Oxford University Press, 1970), whose second chapter, "The
    nature of Modernism: Dionysus" is devoted entirely to the present subject. The author
    demonstrates in it the role of this theme in 20th-century art, viewing it as an expression
    of certain characteristic attitudes related, among other things, to the crisis of the kind
    of humanism that was developed during the Renaissance. The study contains a lot of
    information about the history of the Dionysian motif in English language poetry. For
    example, Spears quotes the following stanza from Ezra Pound: "Christ follows Dionysus,
    / Phallic and ambrosial / Made way for macerations; / Caliban casts out Ariel." Another
    lengthy study on Nietzsche's influence on literature was penned by J.B. Foster. However,
    in the introduction to *Heirs to Dionysus. A Nietzschean Current in Literary Modernism*
    (Princeton: Princeton University Press, 1981), he makes the reservation that this work
    does not limit itself merely to what Nietzsche saw as the Dionysian quality, but wishes
    to use this figure to embrace many aspects of writers' fascination with this deity; he even
    goes on to suggest that it could by the mask of Nietzsche himself, who actually began to
    sign his letters with this name soon after descending into madness (p. 15).

2 Narcissus and his reflections

2.1 "A song that runs through the ages"

Let us consider two paintings depicting Narcissus. Despite the fact that in chronological terms they are separated only by several decades, they are miles apart as far as the eponymous character's representation is concerned. The first work – ascribed to Caravaggio – presents him as the painter's contemporary: a young man dressed in clothes typical for early-17th-century Italy, a vagabond who prefers to quench his thirst rather than contemplate his reflection in the spring, which is clearly visible in the work. Lack of a mythological setting makes the antique theme quite de-mythologized here: only the main character is left, and if he did not notice his countenance in the water, he could not be named Narcissus. The second painting – Poussin's *Narcissus and Echo* – is entirely different. It presents an elaborate scene, which abounds in elaborate mythological detail. Narcissus is not only accompanied by Echo and Cupid, but also surrounded by lush nature, entirely neglected in Caravaggio's work. The protagonist appears as a mythological hero – backed by a long-standing tradition and deliberately evoking specific connotations.[79]

These two hugely disparate depictions reveal the various possible ways of transmitting the myth, indicating that it has been subject to diverse interpretations, which allowed to emphasize its various elements without effectively exhausting the theme. It was impossible for these renditions to cover the myth's entire scope also because visual arts do not constitute a field in which the subject of Narcissus would be of particular importance. As Hubert Damisch claims, it emerges relatively rarely (excluding Pompeiian painting), at least in comparison to other myths. Wacław Kubacki observed that "it was not a particularly visual theme. […] Its reproduction has been rather the task of literature."[80] This diagnosis seems to be right – there can be little doubt that it was literature which has recorded, over the ages, the most significant variations on this classical theme.

"Classical" may be too broad a term, and hence inadequate, when it is possible to precisely indicate the source of this theme. This is somewhat unusual

---

79 The comparison of these two works is influenced the exquisite essay "D'un Narcisse l'autre" written by Hubert Damisch and published in an issue of *Nouvelle Revue de Psychoanalyse* devoted entirely to Narcissus (No. 13, 1976).

80 Wacław Kubacki, "Motyw Narcyza," in: *Lata terminowania. Szkice literackie 1932–1962* (Kraków: Wydawnictwo Literackie, 1963), p. 323.

yet highly helpful. The many variations written during the last hundreds of years are based neither on dispersed versions of the myth, transmitted through tradition, nor on shreds preserved in more or less intact form in this or that mythographer. Most versions rather prefer to return directly to the account provided in Ovid's masterpiece: *Metamorphoses*. Therefore, the story of Narcissus belongs to those myths that, if not created late, were recorded late. To be sure, Ovid drew on tradition, but the myth was notably recorded already in a highly developed literary form. When it became available, it already had the character of a story or a tale rather than constituted an account that would be, strictly speaking, believed in.

Ovid formed the myth's model version, but other ones emerged too. The Greek prose writer Konon, Ovid's contemporary and author of fifty tales, pre-served a variant in which the place of the nymph Echo is replaced by that of a beautiful young man named Ameinias. A more thoroughgoing reformulation was penned by Pausanias in the ninth book of his *Description of Greece*, which is devoted to Boeotia (the place where Narcissus was supposed to originate from). Narcissus fell in love with his reflection in this account because his countenance reminded him of his beloved sister who died young. By introducing the theme of incest to the story, Pausanias provided psychological justification to what did not have to be substantiated in the early versions. According to commentators, these transformations testify to the fact that in the 2nd century CE, when Pausanias was active, the story of Narcissus was not considered to be mythical or linked to any religious beliefs. It was rather an ordinary tale that demanded some explana-tion to make it more credible.[81]

However, these versions known to erudite people cannot compete with the account established in the popular imagination by Ovid, who developed the basic form of this "song that runs through the ages."[82] As a result, Narcissus now belongs to the group of characters from the Mediterranean pantheon of imagina-tion, whose names have been permanently affixed to that of Ovid.

By creating a certain vision of a hero, developing and consolidating his idea, Ovid nevertheless did not impose it on all those who later turned to Narcissus. This was so not just because the story about the unfortunate boy from Boeotia

---

81 The history of the theme of Narcissus in European literature is presented by a Swedish scholar Louise Vinge in her dazzlingly erudite book *The Narcissus Theme in Western European Literature up to the Early 19th Century* (Lund: Gleerups, 1967).

82 This is emphasized by all authors of works devoted to the theme of Narcissus. See for example: Julien Eymard, *Ophélie ou le narcissisme au féminin* (Paris: Lettres Modernes/ Minard, 1977).

became popular only centuries later, but mainly because Ovid's account is so rich, varied and complex that it opened a range of diverse possibilities. What is highly characteristic, those who reached out to this theme would be least interested in what motivated the incorporation of this story in *Metamorphoses* – its epilogue, where, after "preparing / The funeral pile, the bier, the brandished torches," the mourners want to bury Narcissus,

> But when they sought his body, they found nothing,
> Only a flower with a yellow centre
> Surrounded with white petals.[83]

Thus, the metamorphosis itself would be neglected, despite the fact that this theme ranks among those that have been always firing poetic imagination.[84] Given the attitude allowing "Narcissus be Narcissus, and the hero in love with himself – a waterside flower," this metamorphosis failed to attract attention.[85] Its symbolic potential was relatively slight, even though it seemed to be of such importance in the first and, as it were, canonical version of the myth. However, giving canonical authority to one version of the myth does not necessarily entail the exact same distribution of accents, or the assumption that it ought to be followed in absolute terms. Only the main outline of Narcissus's story would, in fact, come to be preserved. Even though not significantly transformed, it would be saturated with different, often deeply contrasting meanings. The metamorphosis itself, on the other hand, did not really bother anyone: neither those who saw the story as an exemplum recalled to instruct ordinary people nor those who imposed on it other webs of allegorical meanings. Moreover, the story did not seem to attract poets, who were inclined to identify with Narcissus and experience his drama in their own personal dimension, interpreting it in their own specific ways. Anyway, the drama ends with death, which makes the final metamorphosis a rather insignificant addition introduced solely as a way of conforming with the tradition.

The story of Narcissus was creatively taken up in Europe only towards the end of the 11th century, when *Metamorphoses* was rediscovered, becoming part of Christian literary canon. A new epoch in mediaeval culture commenced,

---

83 Ovid, *Metamorphoses*, transl. R. Humphries (Bloomington: Indiana University Press, 1983), p. 73 (book III, lines 509–511).

84 See: Pierre Brunel, *Le mythe de la métamorphose* (Paris: Colin, 1974).

85 Nevertheless, Hegel did treat Narcissus primarily as a hero undergoing metamorphosis. See: G.W.F. Hegel, *Aesthetics. Lectures on Fine Art*, vol. 1, transl. T.M. Knox (Oxford: Clarendon Press, 1988), p. 393.

sometimes called *aetas ovidiana*.[86] The great work's third book, which contains the story of Narcissus, proved to be a rich and diverse source for imagination. As is well known, Ovid composed something more than just a catalogue of myths – he gave us a literary narrative invested with meanings that must have been alien to the "purely" mythological versions (if they existed at all). If we adopt a historical perspective to consider Ovid's version of the myth, bearing at the same time in mind its important later variants, it could be argued that his account somewhat prefigures them all, indicating potential transformations and thus constituting one of those themes that culture ceaselessly recycles, producing ever new variations. The face of Narcissus is reflected not only in the waters of the Boeotian lake, but also in mirrors of cultures from subsequent centuries, making him the hero of a "song that runs through the ages," a song taken up in different times and contexts.

However, initially Ovid undoubtedly functioned as the main point of reference, perhaps because he tells the story of Narcissus in two ways. On the one hand, Narcissus is treated like a typical antique hero who lived – "once upon a time" – in a world that had already gone, although remaining part of the narrator's cultural heritage. This kind of story is already closed and its contents are well known. On the other hand, however, the story is told from the inside, with Narcissus appearing as a real hero of a drama, one who is thrown in a specific situation and wishes to learn about it, emerging – as it were – as the subject of a soliloquy:

> You reach out arms when I do, and your smile
> Follows my smiling; I have seen your tears
> When I was tearful; you nod and beckon when I do;
> Your lips, it seems, answer when I am talking
> Though what you say I cannot hear. I know
> The truth at last. He is myself! I feel it,
> I know my image now. I burn with love
> Of my own self; I start the fire I suffer.
> What shall I do? Shall I give or take the asking?
> What shall I ask for? What I want is with me,
> My riches make me poor.[87]

---

86 See: Louise Vinge, *The Narcissus Theme…*, as well as other valuable works: Frederick Goldin, *The Mirror of Narcissus in the Courtly Love Lyric* (New York: Cornell University Press, 1967); Jean Frappier, "Variations sur le thème du miroir, de Bernard de Venradour à Maurice Scève," in: *Histoire, mythes et symboles* (Genève: Librairie Droz, 1976).

87 Ovid, *Metamorphoses*, pp. 71–72 (book III, lines 458–468).

In this guise, Narcissus could be not only the protagonist of an instructive tale demonstrating uncritical self-absorption, but also a tragic hero who investigates the nature of his fate and struggles with destiny. He could be both a beautiful yet silly man unable to see anything besides himself, as well as a hero whose main passion is primarily to learn something about himself. Ultimately, Narcissus is all of those things in Ovid's account since the Roman poet not only provide the theme but also suggested its multiple variations. To employ yet again a musical metaphor, the theme chosen by the composer as the basis for variations does not immediately decide about their character because their course and structure are equally determined by the composer's conscious choices and the epoch's style. This is exactly what has happened to the many variations on the theme of Narcissus composed across the centuries.

The greatness of Ovid's model also lies in the fact that his text is particularly dense, featuring themes that suggest various symbolic interpretations. Some of them would inevitably turn out to be irrelevant for continuators. The principle of choice prevails here too. One such theme from Narcissus's pre-history is his hunting ("driving deer / Into the nets"[88]), but it did not interest anyone. Surely, Ovid mentions this in passing only, without attributing much significance to it, but this did not have to automatically determine later literary choices.

Narcissus's name became a term used to denote a specific type of one's relationship to their "I." This happens not only in works that focus on this subject alone, but also in other places where the term is used casually, for example in an aria from Mozart's *The Marriage of Figaro*, which begins with the words "Non piu andrai; Narcissetto, Adoncino d'amor" uttered by Figaro in reference to the Cherub. Sometimes this term is encountered in works of art or literature, where it acquires a metaphorical meaning.[89] Obviously, this is not all. It suffices to recall the career made in the 20th century by the concept of a "narcissistic personality."[90] It became a symbol from the domain of psychoanalysis, which perhaps contributed most – along with its popular versions addressed to the wider public – to the spread of this concept, more than anything else really, even literature. However, the present essay shall not explore the psychoanalytic version of

---

88 Ibid., p. 68.

89 See, for example, the chapter "Narcyz przed sztalugami" in Joanna Guze's *Twarze z portretów* (Warszawa: Państwowy Instytut Wydawniczy, 1974), or Jean Rousset's *Narcisse romancier. Essai sur la première personne dans le roman* (Paris: José Corti, 1973).

90 Vinge and Eymard discuss the shaping of this term, which emerged towards the end of the 19th century. Freud did not invent it, of course, but he certainly made its use common.

Narcissus's story since this would mean straying too far from its chief subject –
the literary variants of this myth.

In simplified versions, which reach back to the old allegorical tradition,
Narcissus is usually associated with images of vanity. However, if this were to
exhaust the meaning of this story, it would be reduced to a pathetic and limited
example of obtrusive didacticism. The reason why it is otherwise has been aptly
diagnosed by Walter Hilsbecher:

> We pose questions to the myth and its gallery of characters. We explicate, guess and
> comment not just to bring it back to life, but to dissolve it *within ourselves*, in the contours
> of our own mysterious face. What else could explain the decision to take interest in such
> a meagre story like the legend about the young man Narcissus than the painful, unre-
> solved problem contained in the nagging questions "Who am I?" and "What is being?"[91]

These are indeed the most fundamental questions. Thus, we move from Mozart's
happy-go-lucky Narcisetto, still very young, to the basic questions about human
existence. Did the mythological Narcissus try to find answers to them, at least in the
version of the story provided by Ovid? Certainly, no such attempts at arriving at a
solution can be found there. However, the protagonist undoubtedly found himself
in an extreme situation. It is impossible to assess today whether Ovid was aware of
such references in the myth. One can nevertheless safely argue, without any risk of
interpretative excess, that – importantly – this was evident to others who have taken
up this myth, sought hidden meanings in it, or lent it such senses. Significantly,
this is not limited to later continuators. The myth of Narcissus was employed by
Plotinus, who interprets it metaphysically in the first *Ennead*, arguing that the
fate of Narcissus reminds us of the fact that the body and the sensual world are
only a mere reflection of a much broader, richer and fuller reality. In this account,
Narcissus would be overcome by the partial, imperfect reality instead of guiding
his eyes towards the vast horizons of the One.[92] Following Plotinus, Ficino saw
Narcissus as "symbolical of the poverty characteristic for those who forget about the
beauty of the soul, prioritizing instead the sensual."[93] Kierkegaard linked Narcissus's
predicament with the problem of suicide.[94] Louis Lavelle discerned in that figure

---

91 Walter Hilsbecher, "Apologia Narcyza," in: *Tragizm, absurd i paradoks*, transl. S. Błaut
    (Warszawa: Państwowy Instytut Wydawniczy, 1972), p. 63.
92 I base my discussion on an essay by Pierre Hadot titled "Le mythe de Narcisse et
    son interprètation par Plotin" from the aforementioned issue of *Nouvelle Revue de
    Psychoanalyse*.
93 Ibid., p. 103.
94 Søren Kierkegaard, *Either/Or*, vol. 2, transl. D. F. Swenson & L. M. Swenson (Garden
    City: Doubleday, 1959), p. 236.

a general metaphor of humanity's existential situation, claiming that "Narcissus needs to achieve certainty with regard to his existence. He doubts it and this is exactly why he desires to see himself."[95] Herbert Marcuse interpreted Narcissus as a figure reconciling Eros and Thanatos, seeing in him the overcoming of the opposition between man and nature, between subject and object.[96] Gaston Bachelard claimed that Narcissus, who contemplates his own image in the spring, becomes the centre of the world, while his experience becomes universalized, transforming into a "cosmic narcissism"; as proof he approvingly quotes a sentence from the novel *Narcisse* by Joachim Gasquet: "The world is a giant Narcissus thinking himself."[97]

This catalogue could be certainly extended and supplemented with opinions voiced by writers. Obviously, though, these statements would usually not have such a direct character, because the myth of Narcissus is not developed in such cases conceptually, even if the questions posed are philosophical. Altogether, it is quite astounding to see the variety of meanings surrounding Narcissus and the abundance of senses that have come to be associated with him. He has been the protagonist of moralistic tales, and a negative character of "erotic rhetoric": the fate of the young man from Boeotia supposedly turned out so disastrous because he rejected Echo's love and badly reacted to every amorous kind of interest in his person, thus offending Eros; therefore, Eros punished Narcissus.[98] Allegories and instructive stories – abundant from the Middle Ages to the baroque – are among the banalest and thus the least interesting incarnations of Narcissus, even though they are the most popular. Since the middle of the 16th century, Narcissus began to appear in numerous emblems – the artistic form of expression bordering on literature and visual arts, highly characteristic for the Renaissance and the baroque; moreover, he would be the hero of certain religious dramas, in which his fate illustrates Christian issues.[99]

---

95 Louis Lavelle, *L'Erreur de Narcisse* (Paris: Bernard Grasset, 1939), p. 16.

96 Herbert Marcuse, *Eros and Civilization* (London: Sphere Books, 1969), Chapter 8: "The Images of Orpheus and Narcissus."

97 Gaston Bachelard, *L'Eau et les rêves. Essai sur l'imagination de la matière* (Paris: José Corti, 1942). The myth of Narcissus is discussed primarily in the first chapter (pp. 29–62) and the quotation from Gasquet is on page 36.

98 The theme of Narcissus as the opponent of Eros is discussed by Marcuse in *Eros and Civilization*, p. 137.

99 See the relevant chapters of books by Vinge and Eymard, as well as Roland Derche's essay "Narcisse" in: *Quatres mythes poétiques* (Paris: Société D'édition d'Enseignement Supérieur, 1962), pp. 78–82. The religious Narcissus is the hero of Calderon's drama *Eco y Narciso*, as well as the drama written by the mid-17th-century nun Juana Inés de la Cruz, titled *El Divino Narciso*, which is a classic of Mexican literature, highly praised by Octavio Paz.

Anyway, the baroque Narcissus is not limited to religious mysteries. According to Gérard Genette, Narcissus constitutes a primarily intellectual problem as he ponders on his uniquely tragic situation and becomes an abyss to himself.[100]

This is because Narcissus became, to himself, the other; having fallen in love with himself, he takes on roles meant for different figures.[101] Hence his close relationship with two important images or themes: the double and the reflection, which are closely linked with each other insofar as both feature redoubling as their primary component. This has been especially strongly emphasized by Otto Rank in his classic yet astonishingly topical study about the double and role played by this figure in human imagination.[102] The situation of Narcissus is one of a person who has a double. Loss of one's double means perdition, even more so in this case than in other stories. It cannot be otherwise since the double emerges in the reflection. This leads towards a theme that holds special significance in the case of Narcissus: that of reflections and mirrors. The fact that he discerned himself on the surface of the water was not something neutral; on the contrary, this event was one of the factors that shaped and defined this theme's trajectory, determining its continuations and transformations. The phenomenon of reflection and mirror has been naturally quite fascinating regardless of Narcissus; it captivated minds at least since the Middle Ages.[103] Entire volumes have been devoted to the role of mirrors in the history of culture.[104] The mirror has always been more than just a practical tool. By allowing

---

100 Gérard Genette, "Complexe du Narcisse," in: *Figures* (Paris: Seuil, 1966). The baroque Narcissus is also mentioned by Jadwiga Sokołowska in the book *Dwie nieskończoności* (Warszawa: Państowy Instytut Wydawniczy, 1978), pp. 94–97.

101 This did not always have to be the case, as is pointed out by José Ortega y Gasset in a disquisition that may seem paradoxical on the background of the tradition surrounding Narcissus, but nevertheless could be in some ways accurate: "The majority of those primitives had not seen themselves and, consequently, did not recognize themselves. In the looking-glass they saw precisely... another man. It is from here that we should have to start if we would rightly understand the myth of Narcissus, which could not originally have consisted in a boy's delighting in nothing but contemplating his own beauty mirrored in a fountain, but in the magical and sudden appearance of another man where there was only one – the I that was Narcissus. The original Narcissus did not see himself but another, and lived with him in the magical solitude of the forest"; in: *Man and People*, transl. W. R. Trask (New York: W.W. Norton & Company, 1957), p. 126.

102 Otto Rank, *Don Juan et le Double* (Paris: Payot, 1973), especially pp. 75–88. See also: Robery Rogers, *The Double in Literature* (Detroit: Wayne State University Press, 1970), especially Chapter 2: "The Mirror Image."

103 See the aforementioned great book by Frederick Goldin.

104 Mieczysław Wallis, *Dzieje zwierciadła* (Warszawa: Wydawnictwa Artystyczne i Filmowe, 1973).

one to see his or her reflection, it would incline them to reflect, both psychologically and metaphysically. Thus, the mirror has acquired numerous metaphorical meanings. One contemporary sociologist focusing on the analysis of the contemporary "system of objects" argues that "mirror is a symbolic object."[105] In this respect, nothing has changed since ancient times.

The symbolic order revealed itself also when Narcissus contemplated his reflection in a Boeotian lake – a natural mirror. He became enchanted by the beauty of his own countenance, but this has not always been the point. External beauty could be – as was often the case in the Middle Ages – merely a material symbol of the soul's beauty, its outer expression, so to speak. Mirrors, however, can also reveal ugliness. This happens, for example, in La Fontaine's fairy tale titled "L'homme et son image" ("Man and his reflection"), where a hideous man – ironically called "our Narcissus" – puts the blame for his bad looks in the mirror, although it actually testifies to the truth. The reflection of ugliness is even clearer in Baudelaire's prose poem "The Mirror."

Although a mirror reveals to people their physical nature, it also suggests problems because any reflection is subject to interpretation, raising questions concerning one's identity and position. It becomes particularly pressing what one actually sees in the mirror. Ronsard wrote, paraphrasing Ovid, that:

> Je suis mesme celui qui me mets en fureur,
> Je suis mesme celui, celui mesme que j'aime,
> Rien je ne voi dans l'eau que l'ombre de moi mesme.[106]

What we deal with here is full-blown narcissism or at least one stage of its development. The reflection reassures one about his or her identity, allowing to overcome its problematic nature. This matter is put in very original terms by Cyprian Kamil Norwid in one of his letters to Agaton Giller:

> Socrates taught that *one ought to look into the mirror from time to time*. We trust that he did not recommend this for the sake of satisfying one's vanity, but rather viewed it as a warning, deducted from the very nature of the human being. After all, *no one is able to see their profile* in any natural way... This is the measure of the extent to which humans are destined to be part of society.[107]

---

105 Jean Baudrillard, *The System of Objects* (London: Verso, 1996), p. 22.

106 After: Louise Vinge, *The Narcissus Theme...*, p. 153. "I am the one who pushes me into madness / I am the one whom I love / In these waters I cannot see anything but my own shadow."

107 Cyprian Kamil Norwid, *Pisma wszystkie*, ed. J.W. Gomulicki, vol. 9 (Warszawa: Państwowy Instytut Wydawniczy, 1971), pp. 408–409 (letter no. 706).

By contemplating our countenance in the mirror, we reject for a moment the social order, bracketing it (it was not in vain for some to have interpreted the myth of Narcissus as a story comprised not by a continuous time flow but rather constituted by particularly important moments in the development of the protagonist's consciousness). Reflection introduces a moment of suspension, allowing one to be in his or her own presence only. However, is that really the case? As Sartre argues, when Narcissus wishes to touch his own reflection, he meets only an abstraction, an empty form of nothingness.[108] In this situation, Narcissus demonstrates that for him the reflection ceases to be just a reflection, i.e. he treats it as something material and concrete, wishing to move from contemplation to action. His tragedy, however, rests on something else. The reflection only seemingly allows to suspend all social relations; in fact, it constitutes another form of these relations. Even in this case, a social microcosm is born, along with rules of "social interaction."

There are different "styles of reflecting," which are linked to different ideas and ways of shaping the figure of Narcissus. Is it possible to agree with the apodictic judgement that "societies change but Narcissus does not"?[109] He certainly does not insofar as we consider "change" to pertain to possible transformations of the myth's core, the outline of its story and its crucial images. However, if we were to reduce the myth to those components, we would greatly impoverish it and render it ahistorical, investing it with a once-and-for-all significance that resists the passage of time. Therefore, the claim that "Narcissus does not change" is not fully true. In fact, he does change along with the society because despite focusing on his own image Narcissus is a sensitive indicator of society's evolution and transformation. Narcissus's self-interest points – as we know – towards various attitudes, and he could be invested with diverse meanings throughout history. This also guarantees the longevity of this myth, or – as Juliusz Słowacki put it – of this "song that runs through the ages." The reflections of Narcissus capture and record the different shapes of the reality in which he has been discussed.

It is impossible, however, to sketch a single-track evolution of the myth, one that would meet the requirements of a strictly diachronic perspective. In no epoch is Narcissus an unambiguous character, even in the Middle Ages, an epoch that seemed inclined to make meanings uniform. He belongs to the group

---

108 Jean Paul Sartre, *Saint Genet comédien et martyr* (Paris: Gallimard, 1952), p. 225.
109 Robery Emmet Jones, *Panorama de la nouvelle critique en France de Gaston Bachelard à Jean-Paul Weber* (Paris: Seuil, 1968), p. 196.

of those mythological figures that have survived.[110] Or at least he survived after a slight pause, i.e., since the times that mediaevalists refer to with the term *aetas ovidiana*. Narcissus survived as one of the figures that populated the allegorical imagination of the period.[111] However, he also did survive in different ways: in courtly love lyricism written by troubadours, trouvères, and *Minnesänger*. In this way, Narcissus became a hero of the intimate world, which did not fall under the jurisdiction, or at least not the complete control, of the rules of the allegorical game. As a consequence, in mediaeval culture he played a role similar to that of St. Augustine: he was the one trying to penetrate his own identity and determine it, to achieve the consciousness of his own "I."[112] Therefore, he is – in a way – a symbol of aspirations usually ascribed to later epochs.

Ambiguity has decided about the existence of Narcissus in the history of culture. Even at a time when certain types of meanings came to be – as it seemed – utterly dominant, others would still reveal themselves. Therefore, since the time Narcissus resurfaced along with a rekindled interest in Ovid's *Metamorphoses* in the Middle Ages, he has been a figure abounding in diverse meanings. In his comprehensive study, Louise Vinge claims that the former concepts of Narcissus broke down at the turn of the 18th and 19th century, which was primarily related to the crisis of allegory. However, Vinge also argues – quite rightly – that this crisis, entailing the inability to continue the tradition in its former shape, became the factor that allowed Narcissus to reappear on the literary stage towards the end of the 19th century. Thus, he had to retreat in order to make a comeback later on, taking a new shape and carrying a novel set of meanings.

2.2 The symbolist Narcissus

Questions that people ask about the discussed myth have changed in the course of history, but the core of its story has remained unchanged.[113] From this perspective, the myth constitutes a set of meaning-possibilities, and constitutes – to a certain degree at least – pure potentiality. Interpretation of myths is one of the components of literary evolution; an indicator of the occurring changes and,

---

110 Jean Seznec, *The Survival of the Pagan Gods. The Mythological Tradition and Its Place in Renaissance Humanism and Art* (Princeton: Princeton University Press, 1972).

111 See: Rosemond Tuve, *Allegorical Imagery. Some Mediaeval Books and Their Posterity* (Princeton: Princeton University Press, 1966).

112 I base my argumentation here on the book by Frederick Goldin.

113 See for example: William Righter, *Myth and Literature* (London: Routledge & Paul, 1975).

at the same time, a factor in these transformations. The myth of Narcissus was differently read by mediaeval poets, for whom the universe of images inherited from antiquity was precious only insofar as it facilitated proclaiming the truths of their religious beliefs, whereas poets from the turn of the 19th and 20th centuries would not seek any direct truths hidden in the myth, nor subordinate that myth to any truths coming from outside, imposed on a more or less arbitrary basis. Naturally, the latter also contribute certain meanings to the myth, but in a different manner, treating it primarily as a mask that helps to express their own attitudes, or – if one prefers so – as a symbol of those attitudes. It is impossible to draw a strict boundary between symbol and allegory, but the very idea of such differentiation belongs to Romantic heritage, which proved to be so lasting and influential. This distinction was also embraced by the symbolists. Therefore, the myth of Narcissus was liberated from any clear-cut interpretation: instead, it was meant to direct readers towards deeper meanings by suggesting them. This does not mean that these meanings were supposed to be particularly complex, tangled or hermetic. On the contrary, they are considerably clear, even among such poets as Valéry or Rilke.

For writers working at the turn of the 19th and 20th centuries Narcissus became the symbol of an artist, their *porte-parole*.[114] Sometimes this was done overtly (these are the cases discussed here) and sometimes by way distant comparisons and allusions. This is the case in the numerous works written at that time about artists and art, the famous model being Oscar Wilde's *The Portrait of Dorian Gray*.[115] Artists are by their very nature selfish and obsessed with their creative endeavours; thus, whatever happens in the field of their vision and reflection, it acts like a mirror. Whatever the source they pore over, they see themselves.

Certainly, the fascination with Narcissus is related to the programme of "art for art's sake." However, this idea was formulated much earlier before Narcissus's grand entrance into the works of major authors during the last decade of the 19th century. How could this be explained? It seems that there exist two fundamental versions of this aesthetic concept. The first – let us call it "Parnassian" – focused on the work alone, i.e. on the object or artefact. Its ideal was a perfectly

---

114 It was already August Wilhelm von Schlegel who wrote: "Dichter sind doch immer Narzise" (after: Charles Baudouin, *Psychoanalyse de l'art* [Paris: Alcan, 1929]; passage 132 from "Athenaeum").

115 Sometimes Narcissus would become the hero of works about people alienated for different reasons. See for example the anthology *Sexual Heretics* edited by Brian Reade, who also wrote a lengthy introduction to it (London: Routledge & Kegan Paul, 1970), which features examples from Victorian literature.

made product (also in terms of craftsmanship), which would often go beyond the boundaries of good taste at a given period, but would not necessarily express rebellion against it. This product would be to a certain extent separated from the artist, and thus objectified. In this account, the artist understood as a creator of beautiful objects could not be the subject of an easy analogy to Narcissus. In the second version – let us call it "symbolist" – the concept of art for art's sake might not be even directly formulated, but would refer primarily to artists themselves, their activities and attitudes. In this account, the work would not become fully autonomous, and would not emerge as separated from its creator even after beginning its own existence. It is thus always treated as an act of expression, invariably tied to the creative "I." It is in this account that circumstances facilitate making references to the myth of Narcissus.

If these references were to be limited merely to the idea that artists have to concentrate on themselves, because this is demanded by their situation or social role, it would be a purely programmatic and essentially trivial call. However, this assumption was just a point of departure, further enriched with various subplots deciding about the character of the myth. This happens in the case of at least two great writers: André Gide, author of "Le traité du Narcisse" (1891), and Paul Valéry, who explored the theme of Narcissus throughout his creative years: from the early poem "Narcisse parle" (1891), to the crucial "Fragments du Narcisse" from the volume *Charmes* (1922), and the late "Cantate du Narcisse" (1938).[116]

Works of Gide and Valéry were not isolated incidents in their time: "It is the myth of Narcissus that we keep stumbling upon in the history of French symbolism."[117] One could even risk formulating a thesis that this theme became quite widespread, appearing in works of Henri de Régnier, Joachim Gasquet, Saint-Georges de Bouhélier, Jean Royère and many other authors who have by now fallen into oblivion.[118]

---

116 "Le traité du Narcisse" is quoted here after: André Gide, *Romans. Rècits et Soties* (Paris: Gallimard, 1969). Works of Paul Valéry are quoted after: *Oeuvres*, ed. J. Hytier, vol. 1 (Paris: Gallimard, 1968).

117 Guy Michaud, *Message poétique du Symbolisme* (Paris: Nizet, 1951), p. 34.

118 Let us list the following works, bearing in mind that this catalogue could not be comprehensive and perhaps can also include some random pieces: Camille Mauclair, "Narcisse," in: *Eleusis. Causeries sur lat cité intérieure* (Paris: Perrin et Cie, 1894); Joachim Gasquet, *Narcisse* (Paris: Librairie de France, 1931); Saint-Georges de Bouhélier, *Discours sur la Mort de Narcisse ou l'impérieuse métamorphose* (Paris: Vanier, 1895); Jean-Marc Bernard, "La Mort de Narcisse," in: *Oeuvres* (Paris: Le Divan, 1923 [1904]); Eugène Marsan, "L'Agonie de Narcisse," in: *La Plume* 359 (1904); Jean Schlumberger, "Le Narcisse," in: *Ecrits pour l'Art* 6 (1905); Jean Royère, "Soeur de

The point of departure for these works was usually the most common version, the one most deeply embedded in culture, i.e. Ovid's. However, symbolists transformed this myth in various ways, albeit preserving that which decides about its essence, identity, and recognisability. One of the fundamental differences was noted by Kubacki:

> The Narcissus of antiquity was a naïve realist: he thought an illusion is something real. The modernist Narcissus, on the other hand, has read some Schopenhauer, and reversed the problem, taking reality to be an illusion. [...] Recently it became possible to observe the return of former, Romantic symbols of shadow, mirror and reflection. Currently, poets employ them to express the duality of being: things and appearances, waking reality and dream, life and death; in short, the tragic complication of being.[119]

I shall not venture into the dense regions of symbolist imagination, which is related to Narcissus in one way or another. However, it is of fundamental significance here that the symbolists defied tradition by reshaping the relationship between the person looking and his or her reflection. Narcissus is no longer a victim of illusion, naivety or false optics. He has become aware of the game he is engaged in. By looking at himself in the mirror, he projects himself into the world. He does so not because he is a consistent solipsist who would like to form the universe after himself and his own image. Even if he were, his ambitions would never extend so far.

Narcissus is a poet. Although this idea was formulated long before by A.W. Schlegel, it was the symbolists who embraced and appropriated it. Narcissus is a poet wherever he may find himself: not only in his native Boeotia, but also in heaven, as in Gide's work. Narcissus is a poet fascinated by the beauty found in all forms, regardless of how it manifests, and in what.[120] As a poet, he not

---

Narcisse nue," in: *Soeur de Narcisse nue* (Paris: Editions de La Phalange, 1907). These works are of different character and value. The most interesting one is undoubtedly the novel by Gasquet, which has the form of a diary kept by a mentally ill man writing down his biography at a hospital. In the course of the narrative, the main protagonist identifies with Narcissus. The novel was highly praised by Bachelard. Moreover, in the last quarter of the 19th century all forms of intimate literature were viewed as a manifestation of "writing under the sign of Narcissus." For example, Paul Bourget made the following comment on Amiel: "His lengthy diary [...] feels like a never-ending monologue of some psychological Narcissus ceaselessly poring over his own consciousness in order to discern in it his own changing image"; "Henri-Frédéric Amiel," in: *Nouveaus Essais de Psychologie contemporaine* (Paris: Lemerre, 1886), p. 271.

119 Wacław Kubacki, "Motyw Narcyza," p. 332.
120 This dimension of the Narcissus myth was particularly emphasized by Marcuse. M.K. Spears takes up and expands this theme in the book *Dionysus and the City* (Oxford: Oxford University Press, 1970), pp. 47–48.

only creates but also wishes to learn about himself in the process. His hunger for self-knowledge is not motivated by vanity ("Narcissus was not vain," claims Hilsbecher), but rather by the desire to find out who he is and how he exists:

> Mais moi, Narcisse aimé, je ne suis curieux
> Que de ma seule essence;
> Tout autre n'a pour moi qu'un coeur mystérieux,
> Tout autre n'est qu'absence.
> O mon bien souverain, cher corps, he n'ai que toi!
> Le plus beau mortels ne peut chérir que soi...[121]

A similar situation is encountered in Gide's "Le traité...":

> He finally wishes to know what form his soul is supposed to take; it should be – he feels – particularly praiseworthy [...]. Oh! Not to know when one is in love... Not to learn about one's beauty!

Being self-absorbed is, in this case, motivated by the cognitive fixation on the part of both the writer and – in a way – of art itself, since this is the condition of its autonomy and perhaps even of its existence. This fixation would allow one to break away from the mere appearances of phenomena, and reach the world of ideas. In comparison to them, the outer world seems like a largely uninteresting and banal garment (it is not a coincidence that commentators consistently point out the Platonism of "Le traité..."). In symbolist poetry, Narcissus is an artist, a hero of cognition, while his tragedy is a tragedy of cognition, albeit one that ends miserably.[122] It is a tragedy that takes place in a space that is highly characteristic for the poets working at the turn of the century: in the "mental mirror."[123]

Narcissus is a hero of cognition, a hero of contemplation. Still, he does not contemplate his own beauty – though this has fundamental meaning also for symbolists – but principally his situation in the world, reflecting on the boundaries of cognition: not only his own, but also those faced by the artist and perhaps even humanity in general. Lost in contemplation, Narcissus is doomed to loneliness. This is true for all variants of the Narcissus figure, but most of all – for

---

121 Paul Valéry, "Fragments du Narcisse II,": "But I, Narcissus, love and only am curious / About my own essence; / Everything else is a mysterious heart to me, / Everything else is merely absent. / O, my good lord, my dear body, I have only you! / The most beautiful of all mortals can praise only himself..."

122 Pierre Albouy generally refers to the myth of Narcissus as a cognitive one in *Mythes et mythologies dans la littérature française* (Paris: Armand Colin, 1969).

123 The term was developed by Jean Rousset in *L'intérieur et l'extérieur* (Paris: José Corti, 1968), p. 224.

the symbolist one. His solitude is both a twist of fate leading to catastrophe and a value in itself. "You have disturbed my solitude," Narcissus complains to the nymphs in "Cantate du Narcisse" and adds:

> Vous!... Mais je n'ai pour soif qu'une amour sans mélange
> Qui ses yeux dans ses yeux, s'enivre de l'échange
> Entre soi-même et soi, des plus secret souhaits…
> Je suis seul. Je suis moi. Je sui vrai… Je vous hais.

Valéry's Narcissus is fully self-aware; he not only avoids falling for the illusion or becoming surprised but also chooses his own fate:

> Nulle des nymphes, nulle amie, ne m'attire
> Comme tu fais sur l'onde, inépuisable Moi!…[124]

In this passage, Narcissus treats nymphs as if they represented the universally approved common sense and conventional social values, which the artist cannot accept if he is to remain true to himself. The inexhaustible and unfathomable "I" is the sphere of self-aware authenticity, which cares for its autonomy and inviolability, while the nymphs represent an incessant threat, a disturbing factor. The tensions between Narcissus and nymphs could be read as the Romantic conflict between the "I" and the world. The novelty of this situation consists primarily in the fact that Narcissus-as-artist openly opposes the world and society with his "I," which not only creates beauty but is also self-aware.

Such a treatment of nymphs proves that this conflict was expressed in the language of myth, as a result of which it was invested with new meanings. How is this captured by symbolists? Which of the two extremes do Gide and Valéry finally choose? Is it archival faithfulness to Ovid's original or full modernization, in which the ancient story becomes a more or less important point of reference or even just a pretext? They did not pose such questions because their views on myth precluded such extremism. In their opinion, the Narcissus myth did not cease to be a myth, i.e. a source text of culture marked by its origins, which have also contributed to the myth's meaning. However, as an expression of modern artists (and a commentary about them), it could not be reduced to this. Thus, bringing the myth up to date was absolutely necessary. Admittedly, when regarded in such general terms, this solution does not seem to be particularly original because it characterizes the assimilation of myths in all periods since the

---

124 Paul Valéry, "Fragments du Narcisse I,": "You!… I just crave love without admixtures / His eyes in his own, he is exhilarated by the exchange / between him and himself, the most secret wishes… / I am alone. I am myself. I am real… I hate you"; "No nymph, none of my friends attract me / As you do, the inexhaustible me!…"

days when people actually believed in them. However, one cannot deny the two writers' inventiveness – they refused to stop at the most general level and proved capable of backing their artistic choices with specific contents.

In "Le traité du Narcisse" Gide observes that "wherever Narcissus turns his eyes, there he finds the present." There is no distinction between the time of myth and the present: it becomes faded or is even entirely obliterated. The time in which Narcissus lives is both the past and the present. He lives in the time in which he speaks, or in the time in which he is spoken of. Myth renews itself because it can be retold – this decides about its range of potential meanings. In the introduction to this piece, Gide begins in a garrulous spirit:

> You know this story. However, let us recount it once more. All has been already said, but since no one is listening, we need to begin anew.

It is true: both Gide and Valéry tell the story of Narcissus like a well-known myth. As is clear from the quoted passage, Gide does so ostentatiously. When myth is told as a myth, one usually introduces a certain distance, necessarily opening a perspective that exceeds the myth's framework – typically a contemporary perspective. This is visible in the case of both writers, although they are distinctly moderate in this respect, refraining from dressing up the protagonist in a cape and making him drink absinthe. Furthermore, each of them develops a distinct approach.

In accordance with tendencies typical for the literature of the 1890s, Gide does not respect the unity of the myth. More than that – heeding cultural syncretism, so lively at the time, he combines the Narcissus myth with the story of Adam, also introducing the Yggdrasil tree from Nordic mythology. Extra-temporal myths can permeate and enter the present in such syncretic form, commenting on the position of the artist in the modern society.

In Valéry, on the other hand, the contemporary perspective manifests itself in what one scholar has termed "theatricalization"[125] (paradoxically, it does not refer to the later "Cantate...," which the poet himself called a libretto and wrote using a dramatic form). Both "Narcisse parle" and "Fragments du Narcisse" are

---

125 See: Jean Bellemin-Noël, "Le narcissime des 'Narcisses' (Valéry)," in: *Littérature* 6 (1972). See also another article by the same author titled "En marge des premiers 'Narcisse' de Valéry: l'en-jeu et hors-jeu du texte," in: *Revue d'Histoire Littéraire de la France* 5–6 (1970). Works of Valéry, especially "Fragments...," have been the subject of many interpretations. See for example: Pierre-Oliver Walzer, *La poésie de Valéry* (Genève: Cailler, 1953), pp. 271–290; James R. Lawler, *Lecture de Valéry. Une lecture des Charmes* (Paris: Presses Universitaires De France, 1963), pp. 95–116.

monologues of the main protagonist – forms close to the dramatic monologue or soliloquy. The "theatricalization" of the monologue indicates, as Bellemin-Noël underscores, the consciousness of referring to a myth. Let us also add to this that in this way the poet imposes such a consciousness on the reader. Theatricalization points to distance and modernization, at the same time exempting the author from admitting this directly. Narcissus speaks subjectively about himself as the hero of a myth. It is impossible to forget about this despite the awareness that this is simultaneously one of the masks donned by a contemporary artist.

2.3 The humble Polish Narcissus

And how does the Polish Narcissus look? One could write a learned monograph on the subject, titled *Narcissus in Polish Literature*, but I shall not attempt this task – I fail to find it tempting. This is not because of shortage of material to examine. The problem is that these works do not form a pattern from which clear-cut meanings would emerge. Lacking an overall coherence, they seem dispersed, isolated and independent.

Naturally, it would be possible to impose a uniform meaning on these literary works, thus presenting the theme's development since the 16th century, beginning with the poem "To Kasia" ["Do Kasie"] from the cycle published as *Anonymous Love Songs* [*Anonima Pieśni miłosne*] (a Zamojski family manuscript), which is probably the first work to take up the theme of Narcissus in Polish poetry. More importantly, however, it needs to be asked why this myth has not assumed in Polish literature the kind of place that other Greek myths have made for themselves, despite the fact that it must have been known among educated poets who were thoroughly versed in mythological matters. Obviously, such questions are meaningful only insofar as they are related to myths that create, in a particular culture, a specific sphere of potentiality, which means that they could have been adopted and developed, but actually were not. These questions would be entirely groundless if they referred to the myths of the Bororo tribe, or the Iroquois, which in Poland could only be the subject of ethnographical inquiry, or a purely exotic element. However, Greek myths have never been merely exotic in the country of the Vistula River.

It seems that the Polish imagination has understandably favoured those mythological heroes whom Marcuse called the heroes of culture: the ones that have become the foremost symbols of attitudes and actions determining the fate of the community, or – from a universalist perspective – of humankind. Prometheus is the prime example. Such mythological figures as Narcissus or Orpheus (and, to a certain extent, Dionysus) are the exact opposite of this because they do not create culture in a conscious act, but rather rebel against it. Things become much clearer if we exchange Marcuse's "culture" for "history." Narcissus did not create history; moreover, it remained beyond the scope of his cognition and reflection, not really being able to enter into his world in any way. One could rebel against history, or fulminate against it, but it was inescapable. However, taking up the theme of Narcissus would be interpreted as an attempt at fleeing into a territory that seems irrelevant from the perspective of society and nation. When Felicjan Faleński published a short poem titled "Narcissus" – undeniably a lyrical joke and not a programmatic declaration of an egoistic attitude – he was sharply admonished by the critics.[126] To them, the very fact of referencing Narcissus must have seemed a serious blunder. Therefore, one should not be amazed at the fact that he did not play a significant role in the poetry of the early modernists from the "Young Poland" movement.

The ahistorical nature of Narcissus explains his exile from poetry written in the period when Poland was partitioned.[127] But then, did things change in independent Poland, when such limitations and modes of resistance lost their power? Surely, the theme recurs not only in the aforementioned erotic poem "To Kasia," but also appears in an idyll by Bartłomiej Zimorowic. It is also present in the 18th century, in a poem by Elżbieta Drużbacka titled "On haughty Narcissus fleeing from the love of a nymph named Echo" ["Na pysznego Narcyza uciekającego od miłości nimfy Echo nazwanej"] – one of the best-known works in her oeuvre, reproduced in anthologies – and in an idyll by Adam Naruszewicz titled "Narcissus," a reworking of a 17th-century elegy by the French Jesuit

---

126 This is reported by Maria Grzędzielska in her introduction to: Felicjan Faleński, *Wybór utworów* (Wrocław: Zakład Narodowy im. Ossolińskich, 1971).

127 Nevertheless, this exile was not absolute. Romanticism followed certain general principles which Polish poets neither would nor could renounce (part of their greatness rests in this). As Maria Janion observed: "Romanticism was born along with the modern discovery of the 'I,' initially becoming an individualism that explores the experience of particular existence and the mystery of identity. Hence the overwhelming abundance of various takes on the theme of the double and the myth of Narcissus. Young Mickiewicz's interests also revolved around these subjects. Perhaps, the most remarkable outcome of this is the ballad of the 'enchanted young man transformed into rocks' from the first part of *Forefathers' Eve* [*Dziady*], where gazing into the mirror makes the looking person turn into stone, while the subject of the story is the double in the mirror, the reflection of Narcissus who is in love with his own image." See: Maria Janion, "Powrót romantyzmu i powrót do romantyzmu," in: *Odnawianie znaczeń* (Kraków: Wydawnictwo Literackie, 1980), p. 77.

Sautel.[128] That is not much, even if we assume that these works do not exhaust (which is probable) the list of works on this subject from the Old Polish period. One could assume, however, that the works not included here would not fundamentally alter the general picture. The baroque visions of Narcissus encountered in Polish poetry (both the poem by Drużbacka and Naruszewicz's idyll are still stylistically closer to the baroque) perfectly fit within the theme's boundaries as these authors do not venture beyond conventional and commonplace meanings, e.g., that Narcissus was punished for spurning Eros. What we encounter here, then, is a "didacticism of Eros" – he is bound to triumph in all situations. This is particularly clear in the poem by Drużbacka:

> Show me a hero who, in all his courage,
> > Would not fall for the triumphant hymns of love.
> There is no sword or steel that would not burst:
> > All armour and basinets vanish
> > As the work of Mars
> > Is transformed into courtship.[129]

Narcissus was not a very Mars-like hero, so the ideas developed here by the poet may seem to be only loosely related to the main subject; however, a connection does exist since, just like the story of Narcissus, these ideas can be seen as testifying to the power of Eros. Steeped in such thematic concerns, often didactic in nature, historical Polish poems about Narcissus were not focusing on questions of individualism and consciousness. This was perhaps due to the fact such interests did not really fit in the canons of culture at that time. To take them up would require overcoming barriers and questioning accepted patterns.

This, however, did not happen even when it became possible, i.e. at a time when full use was already made of all that was entailed by the Romantic revolution. This is confirmed by Cyprian Kamil Norwid's poem "Narcissus," the best lyric to tackle this subject in Polish history. However, is it really a poem about Narcissus given that the eponymous character becomes an expression of the attitudes of "collective bodies" (to employ Norwid's formula from the poem "Moralities" ["Moralności"])? The poem does feature the themes of reflection and self-absorption, but it fails to preserve the single element that has decided about

---

128 See: Julian Platt, *Sielanki i poezje sielskie Adama Naruszewicza* (Wrocław: Zakład Narodowy im. Ossolińskich, 1967), pp. 134–137.

129 After: *Świat poprawiać – zuchwałe rzemiosło. Antologia poezji polskiego Oświecenia*, eds. T. Kostkiewicz & Z. Goliński (Warszawa: Państwowy Instytut Wydawniczy, 1981), p. 30.

the myth's essence throughout the centuries: Narcissus's particularity, his individualism. He is simply the supporter of what the poet found most alien, i.e. national megalomania, an attitude combining in this case egocentrism and ethnocentrism. The later words of Freud can be read as fitting commentary to the poem:

> [...] the creations of art heighten his feelings of identification, of which every cultural unit stands in so much need, by providing an occasion for sharing highly valued emotional experiences. And when those creations picture the achievements of his particular culture and bring to his mind its ideals in an impressive manner, they also minister to his narcissistic satisfaction.[130]

Norwid's Narcissus – one who reaffirms himself or achieves satisfaction (to follow Freud's vocabulary) by way of the collective to which he feels attached – greatly departs from the mythological pattern. Moreover, it differs from later versions too. Narcissus expresses rejected opinions, while the Nymph formulates an argument that readers are supposed to accept as their own, unlike in Valéry's "Cantate..." Nevertheless, in certain terms Norwid's "Narcissus" does have a traditionalist dimension: it is, after all, a parable containing a clear yet indirect didactic message, despite the fact that it cannot be reduced to the type of texts that employ Narcissus as an instructive model, which have proliferated in Europe since the "age of Ovid." Norwid often turned to parable as a form, combining it with irony in his own characteristic manner.[131] His "Narcissus" – comprised of the dialogue between the main protagonist and the nymph Echo – is a perfect model of such practice, allowing irony to relieve didacticism of its persistence and explicitness.

What was the fate of Narcissus in 20th-century Polish poetry? No obvious pattern emerges in this period: the interpretations are dispersed and multidirectional. Firstly, let us draw attention to those works in which Narcissus does not make a direct appearance, but which are nevertheless understandable only when one considers their allusions to the myth. For example, poems by Bolesław Leśmian abound in images of mirrors and reflections, which play a huge role in them.[132] As is well known, he did not utilize themes from ancient mythology, making only one exception for Acteon, the main character in the poem titled after the protagonist. This hero shares one thing with Narcissus – he is the subject

---

130 Sigmund Freud, *The Future of an Illusion*, transl. J. Strachey (New York: Norton & Co., 1961), p. 14.
131 I explore this topic further in the essay "Norwida wiersze-przypowieści," in: *Cyprian Norwid. W 150-lecie urodzin*, ed. M. Żmigrodzka (Warszawa: Państwowy Instytut Wydawniczy, 1973).
132 See: Ireneusz Opacki, "Pośmiertna w głębi jezior maska," in: *Studia o Leśmianie*, eds. M. Głowiński & J. Sławiński (Warszawa: Państwowy Instytut Wydawniczy, 1971).

of a transformation. As critics have extensively argued, this theme occupies a crucial position in Leśmian's imagination; however, it is not the one which relates in his poems to themes revolving around Narcissus. In the process of shaping characters after Narcissus it is paramount – as the widespread tradition dictates – to focus on self-absorption. It would be difficult to find a better example than "Girl before a mirror" ["Dziewczyna przed zwierciadłem"].[133] It is a rare type of a poem, as far as Leśmian is concerned, because its form approximates a mono-drama. Unusually for this author, the very beginning brings to mind relationships with rhetorical poetry:

> O, my mirror, the fathomless stream,
> O, the crystal that reproduces secret confidences!

However, this apostrophe is misleading because the Girl's passionate mono-logue does not really share much with traditional rhetorical composition. Contrary to what appearances tell us, by turning towards the stream-as-mirror she does not praise the object; she turns to her reflection and, as a conse-quence, to herself. The monodrama turns out to be something like an internal monologue. The image of a reflection in water reinforces the relationship with the myth of Narcissus. In this way, the poem takes place – as it were – simul-taneously in two dimensions: in a natural setting and in the enclosed space of a room.

Another group of poems is comprised by a small number of works that have a humorous character and are driven by paradox. This tradition was initiated, it seems, by Faleński in the aforementioned little-known piece. In one quatrain by Maria Pawlikowska-Jasnorzewska from the volume *Kisses* [*Pocałunki*], we can observe a reversal of one of the fundamental elements of this myth:

> At a pond surrounded by deep blue rosemary flowers
> I kneeled, engrossed in my own youthful face,
> looking in it for the cause,
> explaining why others love and torment me.

The paradox is even clearer in a perfect sonnet of Leopold Staff titled "Lady Narcissus" ["Narcyza"] (from the volume *Smiles of Hours* [*Uśmiechy godzin*]). The portrait of a contemporary fashionable dresser is concluded with the following point:

---

133 The poet included this poem in the collection *Napój cienisty* [*The Shadowy Drink*] (1936), but the work was published first much earlier, in 1909, in a supplement to the periodical *Nowa Gazeta* titled "Literatura i Sztuka."

> Until she stood at the source, more glamorous than spring,
> And jumped into the deathly deep, desperate and jealous
> That there exists a miracle to match her: her own reflection.

Many works jokingly confirm that the theme of Narcissus was not the vehicle of thoughts and attitudes considered to be substantial, but rather constitutes an element of poetic play. Something approximating this is proved by one rhetorical poem by Jarosław Iwaszkiewicz, titled "To S.B." ["Do S.B."] (from the volume *Return to Europe* [*Powrót do Europy*]). Here, it is not Narcissus who is speaking; he is rather addressed from a distance in an oratory manner that reveals certain polemical themes. As Jerzy Kwiatkowski noted,

> What predominates here is an imperative tone, one of issuing an order or articulating a wish. Even "Narcissus" is addressed with the words "O, my lover, look more," as if he had to be told to be narcissistic.[134]

This compulsion is naturally highly ironic.[135]

2.4 A weird adventure

It might be possible to finish at this point if it had not been for a one more text that recounts the most exceptional of all the adventures Narcissus had in the history of Polish literature. It is certainly not the last one, because the word "last" does not apply to myths and their functioning in history. There emerged the Narcissus of socialist realism. Although this may seem improbable, it is quite true. This happened in a book by Jerzy Andrzejewski titled *A Successful War, or an Account of the Battles and Sorties against Snobs* [*Wojna skuteczna, czyli opis bitew i potyczek z zadufkami*] (1953), a work that revisits the old, deeply mediaeval and allegorical idea of the war between good and evil.[136] Among the

---

134 Jerzy Kwiatkowski, *Poezja Jarosława Iwaszkiewicza na tle dwudziestolecia międzywojennego* (Warszawa: Czytelnik, 1975), p. 243. For a discussion of the relationship between this poem and Valéry's poetry see p. 238.

135 Narcissus appeared in Poland also in other art forms. Karol Szymanowski wrote a piece for violin titled "Narcissus" (from the cycle *Myths*, op. 30, no. 2); allusions to Narcissus are also found in works of Jacek Malczewski – Kazimierz Wyka discusses them in the book *Thanatos i Polska* (Kraków: Wydawnictwo Literackie, 1971).

136 See the excellent analysis of Andrzejewski's work in the book by Jan Błoński titled *Odmarsz* (Kraków: Wydawnictwo Literackie, 1978), pp. 246–250. I discuss this further in the article "Niby-groteska," in: *Problemy wiedzy o kulturze. Prace dedykowane Stefanowi Żółkiewskiemu*, eds. A. Brodzka, M. Hopfinger, J. Lalewicz (Wrocław: Zakład Narodowy im. Ossolińskich, 1986), pp. 569–581.

enemies fought in this book we encounter Narcissus. The episode in question is introduced into the rather loose structure of the novel in an intermission-like story titled "A battle with Narcissus, a mighty snob" ["Potyczka z Narcyzem, zadufkiem krzepkim"]. Someone who does not know this piece might infer that Narcissus would be renounced for his egotism, for remaining an individual in times when a collectivist morality was ushered in. Admittedly, Andrzejewski greatly complicated his own task.

> Once upon a time, during the Trojan War, Zeus and Pallas Athena came down from the Olympus to Earth to do some divine fieldwork that would consist of inspecting. Wandering through the Greek country, they encountered Narcissus. The beautiful young man was kneeling at the shore of a forest lake and with great relish admired his own countenance in the transparent water.[137]

The divine inspectors did not approve of the actions of Narcissus because they were highly inappropriate in the historical circumstances. Heedless of the Trojan War raging around him, and of the struggling society, Narcissus focused on admiring his own beauty. He took this criticism to his heart, repented and decided to draw conclusions. In effect, be became a ragged and stinking tramp. However, this also met with the disapproval of the Olympian Superior when he descended once more to Greece accompanied by his divine train. Narcissus – now the epitome of scruffiness and ugliness – turned out to be overzealous. He overdid it and could not properly interpret the wise directives issued by the Olympian authorities. It is for this reason that he became the subject of allegorical satire.

It might be possible, yet again, to finish here if it had not been for… This time it is not a new text developing a novel interpretation of the Narcissus story, but a reprint of the short story discussed above. Andrzejewski sentenced the entirety of *A Successful War…* to oblivion save for one little passage – the story of Narcissus. He included it in his next book, a short story collection titled *Golden Fox* [*Złoty lis*] (1955) under the short and simplified title "Narcissus." The story thus reappeared in a different context: not one of war between right and wrong, but one of – to employ a phrase from the title of another story by Andrzejewski – "great lament of a paper head" ["Wielki lament papierowej głowy"]. The text was not changed at all, but the new context gave it a completely different meaning, becoming, in turn, a story about the world of absurdity. It is not only Narcissus who is absurd as an overzealous neophyte following orders, but also Zeus and his

---

137 Jerzy Andrzejewski, *Wojna skuteczna, czyli opis bitew i potyczek z zadufkami* (Warszawa: Czytelnik, 1953), p. 23.

divine inspection team. The latter absurdity rests in the fact that Zeus attempts to influence the sphere that cannot be regulated by any means. In the world of Narcissus reprinted in *Golden Fox* it is no longer clear which side the readers ought to take. What remains is a pure nightmare.

The shift of the meaning of this short story, which results from a change of context, indicates the capacity of the Narcissus myth to acquire various meanings. The "song that runs through the ages" has been made subject to multiple variations, changing its function and meaning. The bizarre adventure of Narcissus exemplified by Andrzejewski's story certainly was not the last. As has been already noted, the term "last" does not apply to myths, including that of Narcissus. The mythological stories that run through the ages are indeed always infinite.[138]

---

138 It might be worthwhile to add that apart from the socialist realist episode the myth of Narcissus also had a surrealist one in a publication by Salvador Dali titled *Métamorphose de Narcisse* (Paris: Éditions surréalistes, 1937), comprised of three images and a text, written partly in verse and partly in prose. Dali claims that this work was created as a result of "integral implementation of the paranoid-critical method."

3 That ridiculous Prometheus

> *Thou art a symbol and a sign*
> *To Mortals of their fate and force*
>
> George Gordon Byron, "Prometheus"

> *Look, these Prometheuses are the most pathetic creatures*
> *[...] who did not even get to fight gods because they were*
> *pinned down by their miserable lives. No eagle tears them*
> *apart*
> *– they were overrun with vermin, the most wretched, human*
> *vermin.*
>
> Wacław Berent, *Rotten Wood* [*Próchno*]

3.1 An ambiguous hero

For many decades Leopold Staff was a solemn poet who retained certain gravity even when preoccupied with fancy concepts and incredible paradoxes. It was only late in his life that he developed a predilection for poetic joking. Also, it was in that period that he penned the poem about Prometheus:

> Having once started his day off cloudy, the stern Jove
> Called a meeting of Olympian gods
> And said: "I've had enough! Let Hercules rise
> And immediately release Prometheus from captivity,
> Because whether you like it or not,
> I am sick and tired of this poser's liver,
> As well as of the chains, rocks etc."
> And so, Hercules took a hammer to free him,
> But Prometheus replied: "Oh no, you won't,
> Don't touch my shackles, don't even think about it!
> Can't you see how the Caucasus suits me?"[139]

---

139 The poem was published in the 1957 volume *Dziewięć muz* [*Nine Muses*]. Quoted here from: Leopold Staff, *Poezje zebrane*, vol. 2 (Warszawa: Państwowy Instytut Wydawniczy, 1967), s. 943. The theme of Prometheus in Staff's works is discussed by Władysław Madyda in *Motywy antyczne w poezji Leopolda Staffa* (Wrocław: Zakład Narodowy im. Ossolińskich, 1962), pp. 20–22. A lot of information about the theme of Prometheus in later Polish literature can be found in the book by Stanisław Stabryła titled *Hellada i Roma w Polsce Ludowej. Recepcja antyku w literaturze polskiej w latach 1945–1975* (Kraków: Wydawnictwo Literackie, 1983).

One could regard it as a mere jest deprived of any deeper meaning: yet another display of learned witticism playing with mythological themes, just one more burlesque take on a story known for ages or one last proof that myths have been devalued. After all, Staff reduces an important figure, ripe with symbolic meanings, to a vain youth who prefers superficiality over freedom. However, it is not vanity that gains prominence here but absurdity. This is achieved by presenting Prometheus as a figure bound to the mighty rocks not just with chains but also by his own sentimental attachment. Can the great suffering hero, humanity's benefactor and giver of fire, turn into a character from some bizarre comedy? And a *human* comedy at that? Appearing as a mundane person, he behaves as if he were not a god, even a degraded and cruelly punished one as a result of – let us not shun the political metaphor – an Olympian power struggle. The uniqueness of Zeus's punishment and the wrathfulness of his vengeance for disobeying him only confirm the magnificence of the divine rebel.

When writing an amusing as well as slightly ironic and grotesque poem about Prometheus the modern poet must have been aware of the meanings inherent in the myth he treated in such an unusual way, i.e. venturing far from any handbook takes on mythological themes, and from the canonical version adopted in Greek religious beliefs preserved for centuries in European imagination. Leopold Staff must have known the version passed down in grand literary form by Aeschylus, who tells the story of Prometheus in the famous drama. He was certainly aware of the myth's role in culture, or the fact – as Gadamer puts it – that Prometheus is still something more than a mere museum piece: a tragic hero of culture and protagonist in a myth that captures the destiny of the Western world, "a myth whose mute expression still reaches us."[140] Paradoxically, it reaches us even when Prometheus acquires certain comical features and relieves himself of the loftiness and solemnity that have accompanied him before. This is possible because we still retain his older forms: today's unheroic Prometheus would not be possible without his previous, valiant incarnations, as well as the less grandiose, mundane versions that emerged already in antiquity, even before the period entered into decline. In this poem, Staff plays with the heroic myth with full awareness that his audience recognizes the heroism of this character. In the 20th century, we observe the second degradation of Prometheus: no longer one involving a fall from divinity into damnation at the very edge of the world people knew at the

---

140 Hans-Georg Gadamer, "Prometeusz i tragedia kultury," transl. M. Łukasiewicz, in: *Rozum, słowo, dzieje* (Warszawa: Państwowy Instytut Wydawniczy, 1979), p. 165.

time, beyond which only lions lived, but one that entails the fall from pathos and solemnity into the domain of the grotesque and the absurd.

In order to make this possible (and worthwhile), the myth had to retain its significance – it had to be alive: ripe in meanings and rich in symbolism. After all, this is not a strategy adopted in relation to myths that have fallen into oblivion and now have only antiquarian value, remaining a mere reminder of a world that is already gone, or to myths that ceased to be anything more than vehicles for archaic images, today serving only as archaeological evidence. From the very beginning, the myth of Prometheus has been markedly ambiguous, provoking diverse interpretations.[141] Who was this god punished by gods? Even this relatively simple question cannot be easily answered. Certainly, this is not about the kind of information that is listed in passports, even if such documents were to exist in the world of ancient myths – it is not a question of classification or determination of place. When we ask about the identity of Prometheus, it is the symbolic dimension that becomes of primary interest. The question "Who are you?" is equivalent to "What meanings do you carry?"

Prometheus meant many things, even by way of his own paradoxical condition: although he never ceased to be a god, he was sentenced to interminable torments, far worse than any punishment given to the mortals. Thus, he became a hero not only because of his actions but also because of his suffering. In this way, he has become the embodiment of rebellion, one that is undertaken individually but with others in mind. Prometheus was the benefactor of humanity. However, according to other accounts, he was also the one who brought great misfortune upon people insofar as he disturbed the former shape of human existence, which may have been miserable and primitive, but remained in accord with the rhythms of nature and

---

141 There are literally hundreds of works on the subject. I have based my research on the following: Carl Kerenyi, *Prometheus: Archetypal Image of Human Existence* (Princeton, NJ: Princeton University Press, 1963); Louis Séchan, *Le mythe de Prométhée* (Paris: Presses Universitaires de France, 1951); Jacqueline Duchemin, *Prométhée. Histoire du Mythe, de ses Origines orientales à ses Incarnations modernes* (Paris: Belles Lettres, 1974); Aleksei Fedorovich Losev, *Simvol i realisticheskoe iskusstva* (Moscow: Iskusstvo, 1976). A separate position is occupied by Raymond Trousson in *Le Thème de Prométhée dans la littérature européenne* (Genève: Librairie Droz, 1964) – an overwhelmingly erudite history of the theme's literary uses. I owe a lot to Trousson as his book is a great guide to a vast territory. Among Polish works one should note Konrad Górski's essay "Przezwyciężenie prometeizmu w 'Dziadach'" published in the collection titled *Z historii i teorii literatury* (Warszawa: Państwowe Wydawnictwo Naukowe, 1959).

divine laws. He was the one who introduced humanity to Pandora's box, packed with all sorts of evils.[142] He was divine giver and thief, a sort of a noble robber from tales told by highlanders – one that takes away from the rich and shares with the poor – or even a Schiller's kind of highwayman. He sacrificed himself for others, suffering for them, which led many to compare him to Jesus in Christianity's early years. This was suggested by none other than Tertullian. This idea was later taken up by the Romantics and is still considered today by mythographers. Thus, he was god and demon, redeemer and evil-bringing tempter. Moreover, he was the creator and constructor of a new world. According to some folklore sources differing from the classical Olympian religion, it was Prometheus that created people by forming them in clay and then breathing life into them. Finally, of course, as the giver of fire, he is the creator of civilization, because he equipped humanity with means of transforming nature and becoming at least partially independent from it. "One short word sums up all you need to know: / all human arts derive from Prometheus."[143]

So many roles and achievements naturally elicit diverse assessments. It would be difficult to point out another mythological character that would be so absurdly ambiguous.[144] This ambiguity remains true even if we assume that individual versions of the myth functioned independently of each other (although it is widely accepted that this was not the case). There were no Prometheuses in the plural – mythological figures linked only by name and certain elements of biography (not even the crucial ones). However, Prometheus appears as ambiguous and vague already in Aeschylus's play. Classical philologists have been asking themselves since a long time how was it possible that the first genius of tragic drama, and a pious follower of the Olympian religion, created the figure of a great rebel and put Zeus in such unfavourable light. Answers

---

142 The history of this myth as a theme in the arts is discussed by Dora and Erwin Panofsky in *Pandora's Box: the Changing Aspects of a Mythical Symbol* (London: Routledge & Kegan Paul, 1956).

143 Aeschylus, *Prometheus Bound*, transl. D. H. Roberts (Indianapolis: Hackett, 2012), p. 24 (lines 516–517).

144 As Jan Kott observes, "Prometheus is the first absurd hero, the first one to negate the top-and-bottom structure, and made people like gods, giving them the blind hope that they could now, in turn, make gods into humans." Quoted from: "Tragedia grecka i absurd," in: *Zjadanie bogów. Szkice o tragedii greckiej* (Kraków: Wydawnictwo Literackie 1986), p. 273. Another essay from this volume – "Góra i dół albo o wieloznacznościach Prometeusza" – is one of the most important works devoted to this myth.

to this question vary: some claim that Aeschylus did not really write the play, while others argue that this tragedy was part of a trilogy whose later parts, now lost, were supposed to relieve the tensions depicted in *Prometheus Bound*. Naturally, this dilemma has never been solved. However, it goes beyond doubt that the blind chance allowing this tragedy to be preserved to this day turned out to be of immense importance for European culture, carrying numerous consequences.[145]

It is possible that this blind chance decided about the fate of this myth in Christian Europe[146] – a fate perfectly presented by Trousson. It is unique and much different from the stories of other famous myths. During the Middle Ages, Prometheus was virtually unknown. In that epoch, knowledge about myths was primarily derived from Ovid and Virgil, whose works barely mention Prometheus. During the Renaissance and the baroque, knowledge of myths was deepened, which makes it understandable why Prometheus re-emerged. However, unlike other great mythological characters, he belonged in the background, attracting the attention of thinkers rather than poets. The myth's inferior status finally changed in the 18th century, but not through efforts made by representatives of the Enlightenment but rather thanks to those poets and philosophers whose names came to be later associated with the budding aspirations of Romanticism. With respect to this, historians usually underline the significance of the achievements of two figures: Shaftesbury, who regarded Prometheus as a poet at the beginning of the 18th century, and Goethe, who made the mythological hero into a character of his famous poem and of an unfinished drama in the last quarter of the same century.[147]

This radically changed Prometheus's situation. He became a leading figure of the European imagination. An extraordinary transformation took place – one

---

145 See the argument developed in the commentary to the play provided in the Polish translation by Stefan Srebrny: Ajschylos, *Prometeusz w okowach*, in: *Tragedie* (Warszawa: Państwowy Instytut Wydwawniczy, 1954), pp. 149–150.

146 In the context of Prometheus and Christian imagery, it is necessary to quote the following deep remark by Karol Ludwik Koniński: "The Job-Prometheus is all the more tragic than the Greek Prometheus because the latter despised the cruel Zeus, whereas the former had tremendous humility before his mysterious oppressor. Prometheus was beyond Zeus, but Job carried Jehova inside himself as a tragic bug of doubt about his right to despair. It is good to despair!" In: *Ex labyrintho* (Warszawa: Pax, 1962), p. 272.

147 Already at the beginning of the 20th century (in 1910), a book was devoted to this by Oskar Franz Walzel, titled *Das Prometheussymbol von Shaftesbury zu Goethe* (München: Max Hueber Verlag, 1932).

that has no counterpart in the history of the reception of myths. The innovation of Shaftesbury and, primarily, of Goethe was not a mere actualization or
revival of the old myth. It was an entirely new version of such suggestiveness and
influence that allowed comparing it to classical, canonical texts. What is more,
the said canon has been since perceived from the perspective developed by the
Sturm und Drang poets and the Romantics. Trousson's book titled *Prometheus
Triumphant* is devoted to this particular period, while Kerenyi begins his monograph on myths with a consideration of Goethe's *Prometheus*. According to
Kerenyi, it was none other than Goethe who gave the myth a new meaning by
presenting Prometheus, not as a god or titan, but the model of man as a rebel, a
mutinous inhabitant of earth and its ruler – an anti-god.[148] Finally, we might add,
he has thus become the model of a creator, a poet who takes on roles hitherto
unknown in history.

However radical this remake of Prometheus may seem, it would not be
possible without the support of tradition. The discussed period was, after all,
a time when interest in Aeschylus's *Prometheus* was particularly intensified.
Previously, this drama failed to draw attention and was entirely misunder-
stood. This changed, however, into a great fascination. This does not seem to
be surprising if one takes into account the fact that Prometheus's monologues
can be regarded as a fine model of poetry praising rebellion, specifically one
set in motion out of the noblest motivations and in defence of humanity's crucial values:

> [...] But the wretched mortals
> were valueless to him, and so he wanted
> to annihilate the entire population
> and introduce another in its place.
> No one resisted him except for me:
> I had the courage, it was I who saved them
> from being crushed, from going down to Hades.
> For that I'm bent by agonies like these,
> painful to suffer, pitiful to see.
> I pitied mortals, and myself was judged
> unworthy of pity. Instead I'm disciplined
> without mercy, a sight to win Zeus infamy.
>   (l. 255–266, p. 13)

Creator and rebel – these were the traits discerned in the hero of the ancient drama.
As such, he was bound to earn a place in the Romantic imagination, turning into

---

148 Carl Kerenyi, *Prometheus*, p. 17.

one of those who – to refer to the title of a book by Maria Janion – were running a "Romantic fever." What is more, he became the model of a position that was crystallizing also when the myth was not being directly referenced: the aptly called "Prometheism." Thus, Prometheus became the archetypal Romantic hero – both in life and literature. It suffices to recall Shelley's *Prometheus Unbound* or Byron's poem "Prometheus," in which the said position was conveyed in a synthetic manner.

Creator and rebel – these were the traits discerned in the hero of the ancient drama. As such, he was bound to earn a place in the Romantic imagination, turning into one of those who – to refer to the title of a book by Maria Janion – were running a "Romantic fever." What is more, he became the model of a position that was crystallizing also when the myth was not being directly referenced: the aptly called "Prometheism." Thus, Prometheus became the archetypal Romantic hero – both in life and literature. It suffices to recall Shelley's Prometheus Unbound or Byron's poem "Prometheus," in which the said position was conveyed in a synthetic manner.

The Romantic Prometheus – creator and rebel, benefactor and tempter[149] – sometimes would even eclipse his ancient ancestor, thus defining – for at least another century – the fate of this hero and of this myth. This defining power rests not in the fact that this particular version of the theme, with those particular meanings, was continued a long time after, also by countless imitators. Its influence primarily manifests in the fact that all changes to the way in which the myth of Prometheus functioned – including some major ones – had to relate to what the Romantics achieved. The ambiguous and suspicious Prometheus of the 20th century was born largely in reaction to the Romantic Prometheus: an elevated rebel.

3.2 On Parisian boulevards

Trousson claims that authors from the first half of the 19th century contributed to the myth of Prometheus in four ways: (i) by treating Prometheus as a hero of progress; (ii) by identifying him with Christ; (iii) by reinforcing his myth as a symbol of Reason and Knowledge, confronting all kinds of darknesses; and (iv) by crucially adding to the myth a metaphysical dimension of rebellion, or

---

149 A rich and original interpretation of the Romantic Prometheus is contained in books by Maria Janion: *Romantyzm, rewolucja, marksizm* (Gdańsk: Wydawnictwo Morskie, 1972) and *Gorączka romantyczna* (Warszawa: Państwowy Instytut Wydawniczy, 1975).

generally speaking – a rebellion against powers of divine, political, social or religious nature.[150] Settembrini cautions Hans Castorp:

> [...] it is the body that is the evil, devilish principle, because the body is nature, and nature – as an opposing force, I repeat, to mind, to reason – is evil, mystical and evil. 'But you are a humanist!' Most certainly I am that, because I am a friend of humankind, just as Prometheus was a lover of humankind and its nobility.[151]

The old liberal from Mann's novel repeats one version of a specifically 19th-century illusion. Albert Camus, on the other hand, ordered Prometheus to come down into the hellish contemporary world. He did so in a 1946 essay, which constitutes a moralistic reaction to the events that changed the order of things:

> What does Prometheus mean to man today? One could doubtless claim this God-defying rebel as the model of contemporary man and his protest thousands of years ago in the deserts of Scythia as culminating in the unparalleled historical convulsion of our day. But, at the same time, something suggests that this victim of persecution is still among us and that we are still deaf to the great cry of human revolt of which he gives the solitary signal.[152]

Contemporary Prometheus is certainly a product of the existentialists rather than old-time liberals, at least because (as we shall see) he becomes the hero of diversely understood absurdity. Naturally, these two perspectives on Prometheus do not exhaust his 20th-century interpretations. Numerous continuations of traditional versions exist, referring both to antiquity and Romanticism. Usually, however, they fail to say anything original, despite the various modes of reviving those traditions. It seems as if they were all doomed to be imitations only. Therefore, with just a few exceptions, the original 20th-century Prometheus is a grotesque and absurd hero, both when sketched using a tragic palette and when comic forces prevail. As Jan Kott wrote, "Beckett's *Happy Days* are the ultimate version of the myth of Prometheus."[153]

This kind of a grotesque and absurd Prometheus appears in a novella by André Gide titled *Prométhée mal enchaîné* published first in the symbolists' magazine *L'Ermitage* in 1899, and later printed as a book. It was probably the first work by Gide to be published in Polish. The translation was done by Miriam; it was first printed

---

150 Raymond Trousson, *Le Thème de Prométhée...*, p. 385.

151 Thomas Mann, *The Magic Mountain*, transl. J. E. Woods (New York: Vintage, 1996), p. 246.

152 Albert Camus, "Prometheus in the Underworld," in: *Lyrical and Critical Essays*, transl. E. C. Kennedy (New York: Vintage, 1970), p. 217.

153 Jan Kott, *Zjadanie bogów*, p. 53.

in the magazine *Chimera* and then as a book.[154] This piece features the first 20th-century Prometheus, treated by Gide – as numerous commentators wrote, some without approval – quite offhandedly, without respect due to this noble figure or the myth that tells his story. Little is left of the traditional, Greek version, or the narrative shaped by the Romantics – only particular elements without which one would not be able to identify the myth at all, while the entire story of the hero's adventures in Parisian boulevards would be unmotivated or perhaps even unintelligible.

A crucial paradox is revealed here: no myth could be given a shape that would not be foreshadowed, even in slightest terms, by elements from the past. No myth could be entirely liberated from the burden of tradition. This is confirmed by Gide's original work. It is not the first grotesque account of Prometheus. As we read in Aeschylus's play,

> As it is, I hang here
> swaying in the air,
> my pain a delight to my enemies.
>   (l. 175–177, p. 10)

It turns out, however, that it was not only the enemies who would laugh at his torment. Grotesque accounts of this story date as far back as to antiquity, e.g. to Aesop's *Fables*, which offer a glimpse of folklore; to one scene from Aristophanes's *Birds*; and primarily, to three dialogues by Lucian (the most important one in this respect being "Prometheus in the Caucasus").[155] What Goethe and the Romantics found in the drama by Aeschylus, writers of the 20th century interested in the theme of Prometheus found in works of Lucian. Even Camus, who discusses a rebel thrown into the midst of the destructive whirlpool of modernity, took his motto from Lucian.

---

154 The Polish translation – *Prometeusz źle spętany* – was published in 1901 in *Chimera*, volume IV, nos. 10–12, and then as a book, with illustrations by St. Dębicki in Lviv (without date – probably in 1905). Miriam's translation is by all means successful and has retained literary value to this day. It is also distinguished by its faithfulness – the translator only changed the name of one character from the last episode titled "Historia Tytyra," replacing Angèle with Eulalia. The translation lacks, however, the several-sentece-long "Epilogue," which seems to have been added by Gide in later editions. Fifteen years after the original publication Gide also introduced a word denoting the work's form: *sotie*. The new Polish translation by Izabela Rogozińska, titled *Prometeusz źle skowany*, was published in the following edition: André Gide, *Immoralista i inne utwory* (Warszawa: Czytelnik, 1984). Nevertheless, from the perspective of literary history, Miriam's widely influential translation is of great importance.

155 This kind of comic Prometheus is discussed in Duchemin's study in a separate chapter titled "Prométhée populaire et Prométhée comique."

In folklore, grotesque visions of Prometheus were undoubtedly connected to matters of faith, though he certainly was not among the chief figures in religion. Certainly, however, these ties loosened in the 2nd century CE when Lucian was active; the liberty with which myths were treated at that time is a testimony to the fact that the Greek religious system was generally falling apart. Playful and learned wit, the de-heroization of gods, as well as treating them in a burlesque manner and putting in situations that do not befit divine beings – all of these had almost no polemical character left in them. Thus, the "unofficial" versions of the myth seemed peculiar insofar as its "official" form was rapidly losing significance. Gods, their deeds and ideas, could be only treated grotesquely. It is difficult, then, to consider works created in the period when mythology was decaying as manifestations of what Mikhail Bakhtin termed "carnivalization."[156] This concept assumes the existence of a system of institutions and beliefs that are treated with utmost solemnity and remain in effect, determining the shape of everyday life. However, in Lucian's times this system was already crumbling. Ridiculing it did not demand special sanction in the form ritual suspension. Any mockery was simply allowed, although grasping and appreciating it required a knowledge of classical myths.

The 20th-century history of Prometheus is similar. Grotesque accounts do not polemicize with classical ones stemming from faith, though the latter's significance needs to be kept in memory if the meaning of grotesque remodellings is to remain comprehensible. Still – let us emphasize once more – they do not polemicize with myths although they can – and often do – question some of the meanings carried by myths, along with certain symbolic values that have come to be associated with them. References to myths have a specific character – they do not send back to particular religious practices but to the kinds of stories that have survived for centuries in the European imagination, somehow ensuring its continuity. It is therefore of primary importance not to forge new myths but rather to develop a sort of a meta-myth, "myth squared," which would be more than its reiteration, even with changes. In fact, it would also include commentary on that myth and its contents. This leads us back to the work by Gide.[157]

It is not only the author and the reader that are aware of the protagonist's mythological nature – Prometheus himself seems to know this in this literary piece as he is thrown into the midst of a grand metropolis and entangled in a

---

156 Mikhail Bakhtin, *Rabelais and His World*, transl. H. Iswolsky (Bloomington: Indiana University Press, 1984).

157 *Prometheus Illbound* has been the subject of many studies. It is worthwhile to mention Kurt Weinberg's monograph: *On Gide's "Prométhée"* (Princeton: Princeton University Press, 1972), and the essay by Marcel Gutwirth: "Le 'Prométhée' de Gide," *Revue*

series of incredible and equivocal events. A profound feature of the contemporary, grotesque perspective is revealed here: regardless of the meanings attributed to him and of shifts of emphasis with regard to this notoriously ambiguous figure, this great rebel's biography would traditionally remain unchanged in terms of basic facts. It is precisely this aspect that is undermined in the grotesque account. Had Gide desired to stylize his *sotie* as a 18th-century work, he could just as well title it *Adventures of Prometheus*. Unexpected events replace the previously given, predictable and mythologically regulated ones. It is not a mere case of updating the myth so as to make it contemporary. After all, there are contemporary works that take up this myth and still reproduce the mythological story in its classic shape. What we encounter in Gide is a move that raises the stakes.

In previous versions of the myth, neither the actions of Prometheus nor those of his adversaries and tormentors were accidental. In the classic version, the protagonist acts consciously and suffers the consequences. In Gide's work, however, a specific "irregularity" is foregrounded – not only in relation to the widespread version of the story but also in much more general terms. As is known, the most persistent obsession that keeps recurring in Gide's works to a varying degree is the so-called *acte gratuit*, or a deed that is not motivated in any way, and thus free from any rational, psychological or moral justification. It is a deed that originates from an unknown source and entails further consequences, sometimes a real avalanche of events. *Prometheus Illbound* is one of the first works of Gide to feature this obsession, which emerges here with full force. The story begins with one such gratuitous deed: Zeus – now turned into a Parisian millionaire financier[158] – drops a handkerchief on a crowded street. When a polite passer-by picks it up, Zeus asks him to write any name and address on an envelope, sends five hundred francs to that address, and slaps the passer-by in the face. Therefore, the one who was supposed to impose an order on the world acts, in fact, in an unpredictable manner, against all accepted rules of behaviour. This early incident breeds further ones. Prometheus, who has just arrived in Paris, enters a restaurant in a boulevard that connects Place de la Madeleine and Place de l'Opéra. It is

---

des Sciences Humaines 1964 (fasc. 116), pp. 507–519. More or less space has been devoted to the issue by authors of the many monographs on Gide. One them contains a chapter that seems especially worth reccomending: William Wolfgang Holdheim, *Theory and Practice of the Novel: A Study of André Gide* (Genève: Librairie Droz, 1968), pp. 190–212.

158 Gide uses a slightly altered spelling – "Miglionnaire" – which gives the word the character of a proper name.

a peculiar establishment where the waiter sits guests at tables for three, ensuring that everyone has company during the meal, and facilitating conversation. Thanks to this, Prometheus meets Damocles, who has just received five hundred francs from god knows who, and Cocles, who has been punched in the face by a weird fat person perambulating down the boulevard. The three strangers recount their strange adventures, confiding in the waiter, who becomes in this account a sort of a master of ceremony, or a priest as Weinberg argues in his monograph on this work. The events that unfold next turn out to be incredible too; however, the point here is not to provide a synopsis of Gide's known work. The above account of the novella's beginning suffices to demonstrate the extent to which unexpected and unmotivated chance plays in this work, which is set in a peculiarly rendered Paris of the end of the 19th century (though any details are sparse). What is Prometheus doing in this world then?

He is entangled in the story of Cocles and Damocles – one that has no counterpart in any previous version of the myth. Nor does any account feature a speech delivered by a stranger from the Caucasus at a public meeting in Paris. Nevertheless, traditional themes do appear, although in contemporary guise. Prometheus is still the giver of fire, although in this version he is a producer of matches, one operating without an official permission. Moreover, there is an eagle that bites at his liver, but the changing relationship between the hero and the bird differs from the one preserved in Greek mythology. The eagle does not just blindly deliver the punishment in the name of Zeus. A dialectic of the executioner and the executed develops in the relationship between the bird and Prometheus, along with the mutability and ambiguity characteristic for this bond. The eagle makes Prometheus suffer but is also a friend, sometimes even favoured with an erotic fascination. This makes their last meeting all the more baffling: the protagonist finally decides to devour his tormentor-friend, thus liberating himself and taking control over the whole situation. Commentators rightly indicate that in this strange story the eagle can be interpreted allegorically (Gide suggests this himself). He might stand for the protagonist's moral problems or his conscience. Such a reading does not seem to be an overinterpretation that twists the meanings contained in this work. After all, this story, in which blind chance features so strongly, and is, in fact, the main subject, has also been interpreted as a polemic with Calvin's concept of predestination.

What we encounter in this novella is a play with myths, an off-handed and ironic[159] approach that questions traditional axiology. This playfulness welcomed

---

159 Irony is discussed by Holdheim.

many biting remarks long after the work was published.[160] Weinberg claims that Gide's *Prometheus Illbound* mimics and simultaneously parodies symbolism to a greater degree than his later works. By transposing myths, he prepares ground for the arrival of surrealism. Elsewhere, he argues that Gide anticipates the theatre of the absurd developed by Beckett, Ionesco, Albee and Pinter.[161] The protagonist of an originally heroic myth becomes an absurd man entangled in random events deprived of any greater significance, and acting in an unpredictable way. This seems to be of paramount importance here.

Still, one more aspect deserves to be underlined here. The unheroic and grotesque Prometheus is also an artist, or more specifically – a parody of the Romantic artist, who saw in the mythological figure the model of a creative attitude towards the world, associating Prometheus with various social roles. A vote of no confidence in the charismatic Promethean artist questions his leadership-related duties. Therefore, Gide's work could be regarded as strongly expressing an anti-Romantic reaction – one that began to crystallize at the beginning of the 20th century. An artist eagerly identifying with Narcissus could have nothing to do with the heroic Prometheus. Narcissus, as is known, primarily measured the world against his own "I."[162] In this sense, he would make positive proposals, ascribing particular goals to the artist. The degraded Prometheus inhabiting an absurd world would not be associated – especially in Gide's account – with anything positive: his life would be marked by the force of negativity. Gide questioned the ideas sanctioned by the Romantics, ones characterized by a broadness of scope and encroaching even on popular views on art. The grotesque adaptation of the myth was therefore a literary polemic too. The myth's protagonist – ambiguous from the very start – gave up the role of a saviour and benefactor, revealing his satanic nature. Himself of mythical origin, he nevertheless would destroy myths. Gide's role in reshaping Prometheus along these lines cannot be overestimated.

3.3 Un-Promethean Prometheus

The fact that Prometheus – a noble champion of human matters – was supplanted by a suspicious and grotesque variant, has acquired special significance in Polish literature. For a long time, it was supposed to perform Promethean tasks, even when the Greek hero would not be referred to in a direct manner. Within a

---

160 Gadamer mentions this work by Gide with open dislike (p. 176).
161 Kurt Weinberg, *On Gide's "Prométhée,"* p. 13 & 23.
162 See the essay "Narcissus and His Reflections" in this volume.

tradition that sanctioned both the impulse to rebel and the aspiration to lead, the hero's transformation into a bizarre or comic figure would necessarily turn into a literary polemic, introducing associations that were not crystallized in literature (including Romantic literature). Such a polemic would be first of all about literature, and only secondarily (and occasionally) a way of doing something, or quarrelling with God. This transformation of Prometheus in Polish literature indeed involved the overcoming of Prometheanism.[163] Czesław Miłosz has no doubts in *Treatise on Poetry* that the Prometheus descending from the Caucasus and assuming a traditional role would be purely anachronistic, even if he were to become the hero of a rationalist utopia:

> When the sky of Reason had grown blood-red,
> He gave his waning years to Aeschylus,
> Promised grandchildren the sight of
> Prometheus coming down a mountain in the Caucasus.[164]

As I have already stated, Gide's novella quickly reached the Polish audience thanks to Miriam's good eye for literary novelty. It did not pass unnoticed. Basically, in the 20th century, the grotesque Prometheus became much more attractive for Polish writers than the solemn one suffering for his noble deeds. Poland was to embrace Lucian's account rather than that of Aeschylus (the latter represented mainly in the 1973 drama by Jerzy Andrzejewski). This is also confirmed by Staff's playful poem discussed at the beginning of this essay. However, this epigram does not exhaust the subject.

In the literature of the early modernists from the "Young Poland" movement, the Promethean theme is revealed in many guises, as is proven by Kazimierz Przerwa-Tetmajer's early poem "Prometheus" – a dramatic monologue of the suffering hero[165] – or by Tadeusz Miciński's drama *Polish Thermopiles* [*Termopile polskie*], in which Prometheus is listed in dramatis personae and appears in an "Intermezzo" titled "Europe's Volcano."[166] Finally, one should not forget about

---

163 Cf. Konrad Górski, "Przezwyciężenie prometeizmu w 'Dziadach.'" See also Zofia Stefanowska's polemic about Polish Prometheanism in her review of Górski's book, published in *Pamiętnik Literacki* 1 (1962), pp. 249–251.

164 Czesław Miłosz, *A Treatise on Poetry*, transl. Cz. Miłosz & R. Haas, in: *New and Collected Poems 1931–2001* (New York: HarperCollins, 2003), p. 118.

165 Poem published in the second cycle of *Poezje* (1894). See: Kazmierz Przerwa-Tetmajer, *Poezje* (Warszawa: Państwowy Instytut Wydawniczy, 1980), p. 157.

166 Tadeusz Miciński, *Termopile polskie. Misterium na tle życia I śmierci ks. Józefa Poniatowskiego*, in: *Utwory dramatyczne*, ed. T. Wróblewska, vol. 3 (Kraków: Wydawnictwo Literackie, 1980).

Kasprowicz's translations of Aeschylus and Shelley. Prometheus appears in
Liberation [*Wyzwolenie*] by Stanisław Wyspiański, specifically in the dialogue
between Konrad and Mask No. 10, as well as in a statement made by the Director
in the third act:

> Advertisement! A necessary half-measure.
> This is the eternal order of all things:
> a moment on wedges and rest of time barefoot…
> The Promethean fire, stolen from the heavens,
> passes many hands and warms everyone,
> like parish fair holiness, it dwindles after distribution,
> but is indeed Promethean![167]

The Promethean motif is certainly treated here with clear distance. The grotesque Prometheus was to emerge quite soon. It is meaningful that this work
was published just before Gide's influence took hold: in 1908 Władysław Orkan
wrote the short story "The Wedding of Prometheus" ["Wesele Prometeusza"][168]
and published it one year later. It is a rather straightforward satire on an artist-
turned-philistine. Prometheus meets an affluent middle-class lady, marries her
and enters the world of bourgeoise, finally becoming the director of a bank and
forgetting about his heroic past. Orkan's story – in which the mythological hero
is thrown into the banal reality of the middle class[169] – is beyond doubt a grotesque work, but it lacks the rich meanings and original oddity that characterize
Gide's *sotie*. However, it is quite typical, primarily by the fact that Prometheus
is unambiguously made an artist, albeit a failed one who betrays his calling.
Further, the work is typical despite the fact that it is not Prometheus in general
who becomes the object of grotesque treatment but the false Prometheus – the
one who renounced Prometheanism. Still, turning Prometheus into a grotesque

---

167 Stanisław Wyspiański, *Wyzwolenie*, in: *Dzieła zebrane*, vol. 5 (Kraków: Wydawnictwo
     Literackie, 1959), p. 182.
168 Gide's influence on this work by Orkan is discussed by Stanisław Pigoń in the mono-
     graph *Władysław Orkan. Twórca i dzieło* (Kraków: Wydawnictwo Literackie, 1958).
169 A similar tone can be found in a poem by Kornel Makuszyński titled "Prometeida"
     ["Prometheid"] from the 1912 volume *Połów gwiazd* [*Star Fishing*]: "O Prometheus!
     Wise is the one who lays / A carpet on a rock when it feels too hard… / By Jove! I saw
     you in the magazine of prints, / Dying in the dust with contempt, / Behind a glass, in
     some museum on a stage; / You've never gazed so proudly, / Like you do today from the
     cliff, / Although you've just stolen a carpet from a cocotte, / And not a holy fire from
     anyone, / Your vulture is dead – from longing for brain." Polish text in: *Zbiór poetów
     polskich XIX w.*, ed. P. Hertz, vol. 5 (Warszawa: Państwowy Instytut Wydawniczy,
     1967), p. 426.

figure itself speaks volumes and marks a certain intellectual importance that introduces Orkan's work into a broader context. A grotesque treatment of Prometheus testifies to an evolution of ideas, which is not limited to literature alone. The de-heroization of Prometheus is symptomatic of a developing anti-Romantic tendency.

In 1909, when Orkan's short story was published, Stanisław Brzozowski wrote to Edmund Szalit, confiding in him one of his creative ideas:

> It would be fitting to write, as a pendant to Young Poland, a "Legend of Prometheus" that would criticize the entire European, radical and revolutionary psychology, covering Byron, Marx, Shelley, Ibsen, Nietzsche, and Tolstoy. [...] Napoleon III would have to be the last form and simultaneously caricature of messianism.[170]

As we know, Brzozowski never realized this project, but its concept seems significant. The Prometheus of such a legend could be only degraded and grotesque.

Let us consider one more expression of this spirit. Although it is slightly later and incorporated in a novel, its prose is specific insofar as the author did not shy away from employing ideological discourses, often not really considering whether the given character could actually formulate such thoughts. In Witkacy's *Farewell to Autumn* [*Pożegnanie jesieni*], Sajetan Tempe offers the following ideological disquisition:

> Enough of those Prometheanists who carry the torch of enlightenment – now in the form of electric torches – and visit the common people in their holes, returning later to their everyday heights (or rather spiritual lows). The masses will take what they want themselves without the often profitable mediation of the said carriers, and send their own people into the world.[171]

Passages like the ones quoted above from Brzozowski and Witkiewicz reveal the general, social and ideological framework in which the transition of Prometheus from one register to another occurred as he moved from heroism, tragedy and sacrifice towards the grotesque. In the era of mass social movements, the heroic Prometheus could only be anachronistic. The grotesque Prometheus, on the other hand, was certainly not flawed in this way. The point is not to indicate this context in the case of every poem in which Prometheus appears in order to trace such motivation in each individual work. What is worthwhile above all is

---

170 Stanisław Brzozowski, *Listy*, ed. M. Sroka, vol. 2 (Kraków: Wydawnictwo Literackie, 1970), pp. 245–246.

171 Stanisław Ignacy Witkiewicz, *Pożegnanie jesieni* (Warszawa: Księgarnia F. Hoesicka, 1927), p. 162. For a discussion of Prometheus's role in works of Witkacy, see the appendix to this volume titled "Richard III & Prometheus."

that in the poetry of the 20th century this mythological hero could not appear in the roles he was previously entrusted with. In each case, however, there is something that allows identifying Prometheus, i.e., the elements that establish references to tradition, without which this figure would be entirely deprived of all meaning.

This tradition, or its various components, is sometimes recalled by way of distant allusions or indirectly, in veiled form. The traditional vision of Prometheus as a suffering hero is found in a sonnet written by Lucjan Rydel during the First World War. However, even in this case the intention was not to reconstruct the myth but to bring it up to date. It matched the social moods of the time and was prone to a directly allegorical reading:

> The vultures crowd around him and tear at his entrails
> Until black blood icicles drip from their beaks;
> Crowing at him, fixing their dull eyes on his face…
>
> But in his agony, he does not even bat an eyelid,
> The immortal titan, though torn into pieces,
> Knows his immortality – believes in it… and waits![172]

All other perspectives departed from the traditional version of the myth, introducing into it elements hitherto unknown, and enforcing unexpected meanings on it. Surely, this was not always linked to the grotesque. One work that certainly does not have such a character is Mieczysław Braun's programmatic poem "The Prometheus of Work" ["Prometej pracy"] from the 1926 collection *Crafts* [*Rzemiosła*], in which the protagonist becomes the hero of hard physical labour, the patron saint of an effort to develop civilization:

> Over the villages, which listen in the morning to the chirping, croaking and clattering…
> Over the roads, cracked from rain and scorching heat…
>
> Over the cities, where toil is in full swing and lights are ablaze,
> Like the wind of spring you shall come – O, Poetry of Work![173]

Although Prometheus does not cease to be a hero here, his heroism is revealed in unexpected terms. Greek mythology also features gods who are patrons, not

---

172 Lucjan Rydel, "Prometeusz," in: *Polska pieśń wojenna: antologia poezyi polskiej z roku wielkiej wojny*, eds. S. Łempicki & A. Fischer (Lwów: Księgarnia Polska Bernarda Połonieckiego, 1916), p. 257.

173 Mieczysław Braun, *Wybór poezji*, ed. J. Maciejewski (Warszawa: Państwowy Instytut Wydawniczy, 1979), p. 90.

only of the beginnings of civilization (as the giver of fire) but of various crafts. However, Prometheus had no forge of his own, although in the above poem he does become a kind of Hephaestus, despite the fact that usually he would be portrayed as his opposite. "The fire of Prometheus was divine," Janion argues, "while that of Hephaestus or Vulcan was less pure and perfect but human."[174]

The prose poem "Prometheus" by Anna Świrszczyńska refers to a scene from Aeschylus's tragedy, specifically to the one with Io, thus elaborating on a theme that tended to be passed over in the history of the myth's reception.[175] Another very interesting poem was written by another author of Świrszczyńska's generation – Adolf Sowiński, who debuted in the 1930s but is now largely forgotten.[176] His "Prometheus" is a dream vision in which clear references to the myth appear towards the end:

> A page stood here. And here
> from the mushrooms, from screens on porches, from hills with smelling rubble,
> came crowds of spiders – household medusas –
> and chained him to the precipice in a spring
> with strings of dream. He didn't notice but the birds felt
> that captivity disturbs the dream, and crazed with darkness
> flew down the precipice as if it were a slit in a cloud.

The Prometheus we encounter in works of Wisława Szymborska, Gustaw Herling-Grudziński and Zbigniew Herbert is entirely deprived of heroic status. Depicted in everyday or suggestive situations, he becomes grotesque and a negation of himself. In "Written in a hotel" ["Pisane w hotelu"] by Szymborska, a historiosophic and moralistic poem streaked with irony as is typical for her, Prometheus is no longer the lighter of the world and a rebel, but the one who guards the everyday order of things and knows how to take delight in it:

> Day to day I trust in permanence,
> in history's prospects.
> How can I sink my teeth into apples
> in a constant state of terror.

---

174 Maria Janion, "Kuźnia natury," in: *Problemy polskiego romantyzmu (seria II)*, ed. M. Żmigrodzka (Wrocław: Zakład Narodowy im. Ossolińskich, 1974), p. 43. See also the comments made on this subject in: Maria Poprzędzka, *Kuźnia. Mit – alegoria – symbol* (Warszawa: Państwowe Wydawnictwo Naukowe, 1972).

175 Anna Świrszczyńska, *Liryki zebrane* (Warszawa: Państwowy Instytut Wydawniczy, 1958), p. 104.

176 Adolf Sowiński, *Wybór wierszy i przekładów* (Warszawa: Państwowy Instytut Wydawniczy, 1956), pp. 63–64.

> Now and then I hear about some Prometheus
> wearing his fire helmet,
> enjoying his grandkids.[177]

The elderly protagonist, now wearing morning slippers, is entirely different from figures encountered in an operetta by Offenbach, or in dramas presenting contemporary versions of the myth (in the style of Giraudoux), which were popular in the interwar period. His de-heroization acquires in this context diverse meanings that cannot be reduced to witty games of sharp intellect. Such a hero stands for distrust of civilization, its defenders and products; moreover, he also stands for distrust of all those who wanted to save humanity, often by force. In this way, Prometheus becomes a character in a specific dystopia. In a several-sentence-long parable, Kafka presented four possible legends of Prometheus.[178] Gustaw Herling-Grudziński added a fifth:

> According to the fifth legend (which Kafka did not know), Prometheus was a provocateur. After consultations with the gods, he revealed to people false secrets and then submitted himself to a staged comedy of punishment (as part of which he was chained to a rock in the Caucasus, where eagles would tear out his ever-regenerating liver) in order to direct people's attention away from the real secrets. Were they ever to become fully aware of this deception, and grasp that the Promethean myth about power stolen from gods was a provocation, it would be already too late. They could never press Prometheus against the rock and force him to confess the truth because the comedy's script assumed his melting with that rock after playing his assigned role: to deceive people and serve gods. It is possible that the condition of the human world will at that point make gods regret their provocation. However, it will be too late for them as well.[179]

This is precisely the kind of Prometheus – one operating in times when "it is already too late" – that we find in a prose poem by Zbigniew Herbert:

> He writes his memoirs. He is trying to explain the place of the hero in a system of necessities, to reconcile the notions of existence and fate that contradict each other.

---

177 Wisława Szymborska, *Poems New and Collected 1957–1997*, transl. S. Barańczak & C. Cavanagh (Orlando: Harvest, 1998), pp. 91–92.

178 Franz Kafka, *Konundrum: Selected Prose*, transl. P. Wortsman (New York: Archipelago, 2016), p. 73.

179 Gustaw Herling-Grudziński, *Dziennik pisany nocą (1973–1979)* (Paris: Instytut Literacki, 1980), p. 164. Herling-Grudziński's fifth legend brings associations not so much with Kafka, but with another Prague-based writer – Karel Čapek, author of a perverse short story titled "The Punishment of Prometheus," in: *Apocryphal Tales: With a Selection of Fables and Would-be Tales*, transl. N. Comrada (North Haven: Catbird, 1997), pp. 15–19.

> Fire is crackling gaily in the fireplace, in the kitchen his wife bustles about – an exalted girl who did not bear him a son, but is convinced she will pass into history anyway. Preparations for supper: the local parson is coming, and the pharmacist, now the closest friend of Prometheus.
>
> The fire blazes up. On the wall, a stuffed eagle and a letter of gratitude from the tyrant of the Caucasus, who successfully burned down a town in revolt because of Prometheus' discovery.
>
> Prometheus laughs quietly. Now it is the only way of expressing his disagreement with the world.[180]

The old Prometheus becomes laughable, but his heroic past does not cease to be ominous. Former factors in tragedy, and its accessories, become a mere decoration in a middle-class home. Traditional symbols lose their meaning and old values. The universe of acknowledged, generally approved symbols is dissolving as they transform into clearly negative ones. Prometheus leaves the stage of the world without glory, without any solemn epitaphs. The grotesque mode of presenting him, so successfully employed at the turn of the 19th and 20th centuries by Gide (and extending back to Lucian and Greek folklore), has reached its zenith. The time when literature would praise heroes is over. Heroes have become ambiguous, also in moral terms.[181]

---

180 Zbigniew Herbert, "Old Prometheus," transl. J. & B. Carpenter, in: *Gods and Mortals: Modern Poems on Classical Myths*, ed. N. Kossman (Oxford: Oxford University Press, 2001), p. 6.

181 This essay was the subject of debate during a seminar held by Roman Zimand in a cycle titled "Comparisons" ["Porównania"], held in April 1981 in the Institute of Literary Research at the Polish Academy of Sciences, Warsaw. While preparing this final version, I have taken into account some remarks made by Mirosława Puchalska and Roman Zimand.

4 A portrait of Marcolf

4.1 Superiority in inferiority

He was fat. He was rude. We know this much about him. We also know that he tried to outwit the wise King Solomon – and in this he achieved some notable successes. Here our knowledge of this rather strange and mysterious character usually falters. He appears in a medieval tale in which a folkish wisdom based on common sense triumphs over a dogmatic book wisdom founded on a set of claims accepted and endorsed by social consciousness. Yet this narrative does not exist only in amusing and mischievous tales by anonymous plebeian authors. It also continues to interest and disturb the 20th-century imagination, though no longer as an expression of non-conformism or authentic folk wisdom. Things have become significantly more complicated. For the moment, let us leave these concerns to one side. We shall deal with them in detail later in the course of these reflections. In the meantime, we shall focus our attention on the general outline of what we know about the strange figure of Marcolf "that right rude and great of body was."[182] Let us first examine his physical form more closely:

> This Marcolf was of short stature and thykke. The hede had he great, a brode forhede rede and fulle of wrinkelys or frouncys, his erys hery and to the myddys of chekys hangyng, great yes and rennyng, his nether lyppe hangyng lyke an horse, a berde harde and fowle lyke unto a goet, the handes short and blockyssh, his fyngres great and thycke, rounde feet, and the nose thycke and croked, a face lyke an asse, and the here of hys heed lyke the heer of a goet.

And so on and so forth. All the elements of Marcolf's physical form are depicted in the same deprecating manner.[183] Apparently he was not a legendary knight to

---

182 All quotations come from the online edition of the Middle English text edited by Nancy Mason Bradbury and Scott Bradbury, originally published as *The Dialogue of Solomon and Marcolf: A Dual-Language Edition from Latin and Middle English Printed Editions* (Kalamazoo: Medieval Institute Publications, 2012). Online: http://www.lib. rochester.edu/camelot/teams/bndsmfr.htm (accessed 26 April 2017). As proof of the interest inspired by Marcolf's story, we may point to a French reprint of "Dialogue de Salomon et de Marculfe" in the *Nouvelle Revue Française* 122 (1963). This is a translation into contemporary French of a version first published in Venice in 1550.

183 We find an astonishing description of a "boor" – alluding to the Marcolfian tradition and thus somewhat contradicted by this literary game – in Witold Gombrowicz's *Diary*: "I saw him again! Him! That boor! I saw him while having a nice little breakfast

inspire the dreams of maidens ensconced in castles from medieval tales. The story depicts Marcolf's wife in similar fashion ("His wyf was of short stature, and she was out of mesure thycke wyth great brestys, and the here of hyr hede clustred lyke thystelys"). So what does this all mean? Does it merely suggest that in medieval plebeian culture any faith in the strict parallel between wisdom or spiritual value and physical beauty had ceased to operate? Or could it rather suggest a reversal of the order, a conscious and predetermined disharmony, or even the perverse idea of an ugliness permeated with wisdom – since clothes maketh not the man (and here the "clothes" are the body)? According to Stanisław Grzeszczuk:

> Ugliness is an inseparable quality of the plebeian clown, the boor and the peasant. Authors of clownish literature have often provocatively emphasized this character- istic. Though Marcolf was "right rude and great of body," he was also "right subtyll." Consequently, ugliness – like birth in a state of slavery (peasantry) or poverty – is a mere appearance concealing entirely different contents and much deeper values.

Grzeszczuk goes on to discuss

> the antinomy of appearance and truth, which fits Marcolf's – and especially Aesop's – situation extremely well.[184]

Is this really the case? Surely, physical ugliness – so strongly foregrounded here with almost masochistic satisfaction – cannot merely be a question of appearances. We might guess at a much deeper significance. Anonymous plebeian

---

in the café suspended over the gardens. O holy proletariat! He (a fruit vendor who came in a wagon) was mostly dumpy and butt-heavy – but he was also stubby-fingered and chubby-cheeked and a stocky, ruddy, greedy gut straight from a good snooze in his bedclothes with a hot chick and right from the outhouse. I say 'right from the outhouse' because his butt was stronger than his mug; he was all butt. The whole was characterized by an incredible striving for boorishness, his liking and relishing of it, stubborn persistence in it, diligent and active transformation of the whole world into boorishness. Plus, the guy was in love with himself. […] but to find myself eye to eye with, not a boy but a peasant – and to have to bear him in his double ugliness of an aging boor. […] This adult boor torments and exhausts me. […] I cannot get away from him! That walking abomination!" (Witold Gombrowicz, *Diary: Volume Two*, transl. L. Vallee [Evanston: Northwestern University Press, 1989], pp. 75–76). Clearly, the author views this Marcolfian physicality from outside, though he does not spare himself either. Ultimately, this is a self-ironizing passage.

184 Stanisław Grzeszczuk, *Błazeńskie zwierciadło: Rzecz o humorystyce sowizdrzalskiej XVI i XVII wieku* (Kraków: Wydawnictwo Literackie, 1970), pp. 213–214. In connection with Aesop's fables, Maria Ossowska writes of the "persistent link of low birth with ugliness" (Maria Ossowska, *Ethos rycerski i jego odmiany* [Warszawa: ZGTUR, 1973], p. 56).

authors seem to view their plebeian characters through the eyes of participants in a cultural formation to which they themselves do not belong. Consequently, the characters themselves do the same thing in their own self-characterizations and self-assessments. Therefore, we are dealing here with a classic example of a situation in which a person views himself through the eyes of the other or in categories imposed by the other. Marcolf is able to represent himself (even to himself) only once he has begun to see himself as he appears to his partner in the dialogue – Solomon, who clearly belongs to a different cultural and social formation with different notions of the beautiful. In other words, Marcolf consents to a way of seeing himself through the other, endorsing this vision and adopting the role imposed upon him. This kind of approval does not necessarily – and ultimately does not – suggest any form of revaluation or the imposition of a new network of meanings and values. The caricatured figure is in no way ennobled. If this were the case, Marcolf would have to proclaim a new canon of beauty. He would have to elevate himself, attempting to fit the prevailing notions of the court in which he has somehow found himself by a strange turn of events. Yet he does not exhibit any such tendencies. Instead, we find a somewhat different mechanism at play.

Above all, this mechanism reveals that Marcolf's non-conformism has clearly defined boundaries, even as he takes the liberty of arguing with the ruler. For now, it will suffice to say that this non-conformism does not apply to the foundations defining the image of the world. By accepting his appearance – which we know derives from the gaze of the other – our hero endorses the value system of his dignified adversary in the dialogue. At best, he seeks his own place within this system. In principle, this does not necessarily coincide with the place Solomon might be inclined to grant him, though – as we shall see – things are somewhat more complicated since the system grants clowns a separate position. Imprisoned in this position and anchored in the dominant system of values, he still wishes to demonstrate his superiority over the figure who stands at the centre of the system and guarantees its stability – the ruler. He wishes to prove his superiority, while not throwing off his inferiority. Therefore, we might define the Marcolfian dialectic as superiority in inferiority. The plebeian with the misshapen physical form turns out to be wiser than the powerful and educated king who has devoured so many splendid tomes, though this intellectual advantage – as we shall discover – is rather peculiar in nature. As he achieves this dazzling success, he not only fails to throw off or overcome his inferiority, but rather he confirms it, almost programmatically demonstrating its virtues without transforming it into superiority. By proceeding in this manner, Marcolf is not a rebel. If he had become one, he would not have rooted himself in his inferiority. Instead, he declared "I am – like everybody else in my situation – different." The dialectic of vinferiority and superiority constitutes one of Witold Gombrowicz's key literary discoveries. He was the first to demonstrate its crucial significance with extraordinary profundity and suggestiveness in both discursive and strictly literary texts. As is generally the case when somebody formulates a new and interesting problem, we may very easily broaden its scope. In this way, fresh categories can serve to problematize phenomena sharing no direct connection with the objects to which these categories refer. We may also project them into the past in order to reveal new or previously undetected aspects. The Gombrowiczean idea of inferiority and superiority fused into a mutually complementary whole serves as a perfect tool for revealing certain features of the strange figure of Marcolf – and perhaps also of other bygone characters from plebeian literature.

4.2 The great debate

The main part of the story about Marcolf's encounter with King Solomon – as the title suggests – involves a debate between them. Not until later in the tale do we find accounts of how the wise and ugly clown acted towards the ruler, including various indignities to which he exposes the king by playing a series of practical jokes and generally making a mug of him. At the same time, this debate is peculiar, since we cannot equate it with any genuine discussion in the usual understanding of the term. This is not a battle of arguments. Neither is it a display of eristic skill as classical rhetoric has defined it. Mikhail Bakhtin makes the following observation about the Marcolfian stories:

> One of the main attributes of the medieval clown was precisely the transfer of every high ceremonial gesture or ritual to the material sphere.[185]

This applies to Marcolf's tale since in most cases the relation between the respective utterances of Solomon and Marcolf is precisely one that we might characterize as a form of translation. Almost without exception, Solomon takes the initiative, opening the dialogue as the first speaker. Marcolf himself is denied the

---

185 Mikhail Bakhtin, *Rabelais and His World*, transl. H. Iswolsky (Bloomington: Indiana University Press, 1984), p. 20. Bakhtin would return to this question on multiple occasions – for instance, in a section of *Forms of Time and Chronotype in the Novel* entitled "The Functions of the Rogue, Clown and Fool in the Novel" (See: Mikhail Bakhtin, *The Dialogic Imagination: Four Essays*, transl. C. Emerson & M. Holquist [Austin: University of Texas Press, 1981], pp. 158–167). Frances K. Barasch analyzes the development of the Marcolfian theme as an example of the formation of the medieval grotesque (Frances K. Barasch, *The Grotesque: A Study in Meaning* [The Hague: Mouton, 1971], pp. 43–44.)

right to speak when his utterances are not rejoinders to the king's words. He is defined by them. Ultimately, he has no right to choose. Examples of this type of "translation" appear in enormous numbers throughout the text:

S: "It is no frende that dureyth not in frendeshyp."
M: "The dung of a calf stynkyth not longe."
[...]
S: "As a man playeth upon an harpe, he kan not wele indicte."
M: "So whan the hownde shytyth, he berkyth noth."

There are very few deviations from this prevailing rule. One deviation is the Marcolfian parable, which in size and scope outstrips the problem – raised by Solomon – to which it responds. Two other types of expression function as complete exceptions here. We might define the first as a kind of explanation of behaviour. Here Marcolf does not make phrases parallel to the monarch's declarations, but instead explains his way of being and speaking, pointing indirectly to their "causes":

S: "God yave wysdam in my mouth, for me lyke is none in alle partys of the worlde."
M: "He that hath evyll neighborys praysyth hymself."

This clearly differs from another passage in which Marcolf juxtaposes Solomon's royal lineage with his own plebeian origins, proudly concluding his genealogical digression as follows: "Marquat gat Marcolphum and that is I." The passage in which he presents this genealogy is constructed as a parody.[186] In the other episode cited above, this element is clearly absent. Another exception is the format in which Solomon formulates a thesis, while Marcolf offers an example, replacing the king's generalized knowledge with concrete specifics:

S: "Evrything chesyth his lyke."
M: "Where a skabbyd horse is, he sekyth his lyke and eyther of thaym gnappyth othre."

We should note here that the thesis-example relation is closer than the behaviour explanation to the translation model since the explanations must by definition

---

186 Julian Krzyżanowski has emphasized the element of parody – especially biblical parody – in his commentaries to the Polish edition of the text (*Rozmowy, które miał król Salomon mądry z Marchołtem grubym a sprośnym*, transl. Jan z Koszyczek & J. Krzyżanowski [Warszawa: Państwowe Wydawnictwa Naukowe, 1954]). Bakhtin writes about the role of parodies of sacred texts in medieval culture in various places throughout his work on Rabelais.

go beyond the conceptual world imposed by Solomon. We must repeat that these are only exceptions. In the dialogical part of Marcolf's story, the principle of translation applies. But is he a faithful translator? To what extent does Marcolf include his own experiences and point of view in his paraphrases of the monarch's lines? It seems indisputable that he lowers the tone, introducing what Bakhtin refers to as "the material sphere." As the cited passages suggest, this often implies the nether regions of the physical body. Yet things are more complicated when we consider that Solomon does not always formulate his truths conceptually. Sometimes he also refers – in the style of proverbs – to concrete realities that supposedly convey the relevant knowledge. Therefore, we cannot reduce the differences merely to an opposition between an abstract wisdom derived from dogma or belief and a practical, spontaneous wisdom springing from experience and direct observation. In this regard, the juxtaposition of loftiness and baseness is more significant, since even the contrast between gravity and levity – or seriousness and mockery – does not always find expression. After all, Marcolf often expresses essential and binding truths in his bawdy and vulgar plebeian language. This is particularly true when he manages – following the example of his dignified adversary – to make general statements. Then the discussion comes closest to a debate in the contemporary sense:

S: "As verelye God helpe thee! In Gabaa, God appieryd to me and fulfylled me wyth sapience."
M: "He is holdyn wyse that reputyth hymself a fole."

Nonetheless, one thing seems certain. Marcolf's original contribution to the discussion is his own poor man's wisdom (or philosophy) – a wisdom that for obvious reasons remains outside Solomon's realm of experience. But is this contribution sufficient to guarantee Marcolf's intellectual freedom and independence from the rules, opinions, and views represented by the monarch in this clash between the clown and the king? This is the most significant question. Does the translation from the "high" to the "low," from the "spiritual" to the "physiological," constitute an intellectual innovation and thus an act of plebeian non-conformism against the ruler? If so, how? In slightly different terms, we might ask whether this kind of translation can overthrow or – more modestly – reshape the worldview of the person being translated. It would be difficult to answer these questions with a clear and decisive "yes." For it seems that the essence of the conversations between Solomon and Marcolf lies in the fact that both gentlemen – despite their different social conditions – largely verbalize the same set of opinions, though they do so in different ways and in different languages. Ultimately, this phenomenon should not surprise us, as it accords with what we usually understand as translation. By definition, a text that arises from an act of translation – even the most peculiar form of translation, as in this case – cannot defy or contradict the text that forms its basis. Marcolf's translation of Solomon's categories into the "low" and "physiological" does not break this rule. Indeed, we are essentially dealing with differences in expression rather than in conceptual universes. Marcolf hopes to outwit Solomon, but only in the realms of verbal expression and trivial life experience. He does not aim to overthrow the king's set of notions or to establish his own in its place. In this sense, Marcolf's world is closely dependent on Solomon's world. It has no independent existence of its own, but exists only as a response. This must be the case since in most instances a precise parallelism exists between the two utterances – and parallelism does not permit genuine discussion. At the root of this parallelism – as is often the case in folklore[187] – is a situation that we might describe as a contest, though the prize here is not the hand of a princess after many extraordinary deeds as predetermined conditions. Instead, the prize is simply to outsmart the opponent in the realm of expression without violating the existing system at all. After the verbal tournament, Marcolf and Solomon do not change their positions in society, since they both have pre-established roles. Furthermore, when a change of roles does occur – and we shall encounter precisely this situation when Marcolf seats himself on the royal throne – it does not transform the social order in any fundamental way, for in this order the role is more important than the person. The role is the defining element. After his unexpected promotion, Marcolf will perform the role of king, just as previously he has filled the role of clown. Clownish jokes are not essentially directed against the king, but rather they fit into the system. Our hero himself also becomes aware of this fact:

> Tho sayde Salomon: "Not so, but yeve hym wele to ete and drinke and lete hym than goo in pease." Tho spak Marcolphus goyng his weye to the king: "I suffre ynough what that ye have sayde. I shall alweyes saye, 'There is no king were no lawe is.'"

This is far removed from any non-conformism. After discharging his duty as a clown, Marcolf renders unto the king the things that are the king's. But why was the king willing to admit a person of such physical appearance and condition into his chambers in the first place – and even to enter into competition with him?

---

187 The echoes of the tale of Marcolf and Solomon still resonate in folklore. Jan Mirosław Kasjan analyzes one example in his book on Polish folk riddles. See: Jan Mirosław Kasjan, *Poetyka polskiej zagadki ludowej* (Toruń: Rozprawy, 1976), pp. 163–168.

4.3 The ritual clown

Pantagruel says to Panurge:

> Take heed, I have often heard it said in a vulgar proverb, the wise may be instructed by a fool. Seeing the answers and responses of sage and judicious men have in no manner of way satisfied you, take advice of some fool, and possibly by so doing you may come to get that counsel which will be agreeable to your own heart's desire and contentment. You know how by the advice and counsel and prediction of fools, many kings, princes, states, and commonwealths have been preserved, several battles gained, and divers doubts of a most perplexed intricacy resolved.[188]

The role of the fool or clown has become part of the political game, where he has turned into something like a state advisor, though he has no formal right to such a role. We do not learn whether Marcolf gave Solomon advice when the king found himself in military or political need. The medieval text says nothing on this point, though the problem does not cease to intrigue in this case. It remains interesting if only because the king has admitted Marcolf – a strange guest from the east – into his palace. Moreover, by entering into competition with him, he converses with him as one equal with another, only occasionally threatening him with sanctions or punishments. As a plebeian, Marcolf has attained an absolutely extraordinary position inaccessible to others of his class. He does not owe this honour only (or perhaps at all?) to his individual virtues. Events have taken this particular turn because he has become the incarnation of a role that already existed in the inventory of roles established by the archaic social system. Marcolf is necessary to the king and his court as one who is free to behave in a manner that clashes with the prevailing etiquette and free to say things sternly forbidden to others. In other words, his deviation from the system has been designed and interiorized by the system itself or inscribed within it. Marcolf reaps the benefits of this social device.

In his essay "The Priest and the Jester," Leszek Kołakowski makes the following observations:

> The jester is one who moves in the circles of high society, but does not belong to it and says impudent things to it. He casts doubt on everything that might seem obvious. He could not do so if he himself belonged to high society. Then he would be nothing but an acerbic salon wit, at best. The jester must be external to high society, viewing it from outside in order to reveal the unobvious nature of its obvious truths and the

---

188 François Rabelais, *Five Books of the Lives, Heroic Deeds and Sayings of Gargantua and His Son Pantagruel*, transl. T. Urquhart & P. A. Motteux (Electronic Classics), pp. 443–444.

unnecessary nature of its necessities. At the same time, he must move in high society in order to become familiar with its sanctities and have the chance to make his impertinent remarks.[189]

Marcolf was not the only one to assume this strange and highly ambiguous position. He had forerunners in various kinds of archaic communities. Sometimes even the most rigid societies – the most bound by rigorous regulations – in certain specific situations endorsed behaviour that ostentatiously departed from the norm and sometimes even constituted its prearranged violation. Yet here this departure from the norm has been foreseen and sanctioned by the norm itself. Ethnologists who have examined this question in their analyses of primitive societies often talk about these licensed violators of norms as ritual fools or clowns.[190] The ritual clown – and he alone – is free to break the taboo:

> Above all, we must consider the fact that even when this violation is practiced in the interests of the group, it can only be perpetrated individually, as a singular and exceptional fact. The social order, which is based on respect for taboos, would find itself in danger if the collectivity committed the violation or consented to it. At the same time, it is obvious that if the whole group were to violate the taboos, the magical value attached to their negation would be negated. Therefore, the violator must necessarily be imagined as somebody who acts alone, even if he does so in the interests of all. He must be conceived as "other," as somebody who opposes the group, even when he sacrifices himself for his comrades. This explains why clowns distinguish themselves through individual, independent and asocial characteristics as they participate in rituals.[191]

Therefore, the clown was accorded a special position in society. The fool's license became institutionalized. Indeed, this very sanctification became a condition if not for the existence then at least for the normal functioning of archaic society. Paradoxically, it became a function of the prevailing orthodoxy in multiple

---

189 Leszek Kołakowski, "Kapłan i błazen," *Twórczość* 10 (1959), p. 82. Elias Canetti has captured this problem equally well: "The court jester, one of those who possess the least, by the side of the all-possessor. He ceaselessly displays before his lord a particular kind of freedom, since in reality he is at the lord's mercy. The lord sees the freedom of the joker. Since the clown belongs to him, it seems to him that freedom belongs to him as well" (Elias Canetti, *Prowincja człowieka — Zapiski 1942–1972*, transl. H. Orłowski, [Warszawa: Czytelnik, 1977], p. 193).

190 Here I am basing my assumptions on an extraordinarily suggestive piece by Laura Makarius, "Clowns rituels et comportement symbolique," *Diogène* 69 (1970).

191 Ibid., pp. 56–57.

senses. Thanks to this license, various positions could express themselves that otherwise would have had no right to appear and thus would have been condemned to complete non-existence. Swept up from the surface of life, they could have survived in latent form and then emerged at a favourable moment to threaten the system, since they had all the attributes to break it down from inside. Therefore, the institutionalization of the fool's license fostered the consolidation of the system, while also guaranteeing a curious form of psychosocial hygiene. It fostered this consolidation because – as Larua Makarius has argued – the privileges of the clown were only accorded to selected individuals, who were distinct from the rest of society precisely through this very specific role. The rulers clearly could not grant the clown's insignia (and the associated rights) to any social group – to say nothing of the whole society (this would be tantamount to altering its structure). Neither could a guild of clowns exist. They could never form a trade organization, even one similar to those formed by the cut-throats and prostitutes – representatives of much more dubious professions. By the very nature of his function, the clown was a soloist, and never a member of a choir.

From the institutionalization of the fool's license, certain other advantages arose for the guardians of the prevailing laws in archaic societies. Above all, the scope of the license's jurisdiction did not have to be established once for all. Its boundaries could shift, widening or narrowing depending on the specific situation or on entirely random circumstances. The general rule seemed to dictate that the harsher the system, the more extensive the clown's domain. This certainly did not mean that the clown's real possibilities were greater when measured in absolute terms. Indeed, from this perspective, they were clearly diminished, impoverished and even more restricted. We should remember that no scenario defining the scope of the clown's action allows him to say absolutely anything. Even he must observe certain prohibitions. He may never pronounce certain truths. There are boundaries he may never cross (if he crosses them, he abandons the role of a clown and becomes a revolutionary). But let us return to the earlier question. In a harsher system, the clown's possibilities are relatively greater because the possibilities of the ordinary member of society have diminished. Issues and opinions that in other times and places might be expressed aloud in a normal manner are here saddled with various prohibitions. In the normal run of things – assuming the prohibition is not absolute – they become the domain of those who hold the fool's license.

We must also not forget that this institutionalization brings yet another benefit. Though the clown may have pronounced truths of the greatest importance, he does not cease to be a clown – and thus a suspicious, strange and ridiculous figure. Laura Makarius emphasizes that ridiculousness can be a fatal phenomenon in some tribal societies, where it is intolerable in normal social practice.[192] The clown has the right to express opinions incompatible with orthodoxy, allowing him to violate taboos. However, the community can always disavow, demean and disqualify his actions very easily. After all, nothing could be simpler than proclaiming to all and sundry that only a clown would behave in a manner at odds with the prevailing customs and beliefs, thus violating the sacred sphere. This argument has a strong chance of success with its intended audience, for why should any level-headed and loyal member of an archaic society take seriously a suspicious character who deviates from the norm? Indeed, he or she might even find the proper place for this person in the asylum for those who are said to be unbalanced or who disrupt the accepted order. Therefore, the clown might just as easily be a beneficiary of the king's good graces or a victim of royal disfavour – elevated or debased. Both possibilities form part of the scenario that defines his activities.

The Marcolf who comes to Solomon's palace personifies the clown's lot in all its ambiguity. The king converses with him almost as one equal with another, listening to his boorish expressions with an indulgent ear, though he might easily turn him out or throw him in the dungeon. The king understands that the clown never ceases to be a clown, even when he has been admitted to the royal chambers to take part in a debate. Indeed, his clownishness – and thus the very essence of his role – may well manifest itself even more clearly in the shadow of the monarch, and hence of somebody whose position makes him the highest guardian of the existing order. The king cannot entirely eliminate the clown's role, though – as we have seen – he can quite easily manipulate the boundaries of the freedoms accorded to those who hold the institutionalized fool's license. However, he is able to eliminate particular clowns – for instance, when a clown overestimates the scope of freedom accorded to him by tradition. Marcolf seems to be aware of these limitations. Ultimately, he does not test the boundaries, even when he wishes to prove his superiority to the king in debate. As we have already discussed, the debate takes place on the ground marked out by the monarch. Marcolf may not independently choose the subject or problem for discussion. His role is to debase and parody the lines pronounced

---

192 Ibid., pp. 99–100. Grzeszczuk informs us that "Catholics associated Protestants with Marcolf and Till Eulenspiegel, while Protestants associated Catholics with the same characters – mutually accusing each other of stupidity and a lack of moral principles supposedly personified precisely by this clownish pair" (p. 176).

by the king. The reverse situation of the king elevating or ennobling the clown's vulgar remarks would be unthinkable within the archaic culture. Admittedly, the king may sometimes be exposed to the clown's mockery, but he never loses the initiative. He can also permit himself all kinds of caprices towards the clown. If he so desires, he can treat him as an ordinary servant, dress him in a lackey's livery or order him to dance the mazurka on a banquet table for the amusement of the court rabble.

4.4 Marcolf on the throne

The clown is the shadow of the king.[193] But might another situation also be possible – namely, the clown as the king's successor, exercising power, seated on the throne and endowed with all the insignia of authority? At first glance, this would seem implausible. Nevertheless, the tale of Marcolf, who never really questions the king's rule, contains certain hints to this effect, though in a rather peculiar form. Indeed, we cannot include these hints under the familiar "peasant to king" motif of the folk imagination – a theme that continues to recur in literature today. In the end, the bumpkin promoted to monarch is not a clown, while the promotion itself usually occurs in a peculiar fashion, taking place through imagination or play – and often through the two elements simultaneously. In both cases, the criteria of reality are suspended, while ludic rules come into play. Here we find the development of what Bakhtin called "carnivalization." There are no true connections binding the peasant and the king. Instead, their only relation is a kind of dressing up. Either the peasant consciously pretends to be the king during the carnival festival or he is treated as a king by others during the same game. For a clown like Marcolf – who is the shadow of the king – this kind of dressing up is impossible. One cannot pretend to be the king in the king's presence,

---

193 In this article, I have examined only this particular side of the matter. We may also include the clown in various other oppositions. Sometimes he is depicted in juxtaposition with the priest, where the two are treated as representatives of different styles of philosophy – as in the above-mentioned essay by Kołakowski. Jean Starobinski examines the tension between the clown and the artist in his book *Portrait de l'artiste en saltimbanque* (Genève: Skira, 1970). It is also worth pointing out that the pair of king and clown is often expanded by a third figure – the executioner. The Czech satirists *Jiří Voskovec* and *Jan Werich* wrote a song in the interwar period entitled "The Executioner and the Clown." See: *A co básník: Antologie české poezie 20. století* (Praha: Mladá fronta, 1963). Professor Mojmír Grygar kindly drew my attention to this text.

even when normal social relations have ceased to apply thanks to carnival. Therefore, when Marcolf seats himself on the throne, he has no thought of treating his new role as the outcome of a game or the consequence of a temporary suspension of the world's prevailing laws. He was a serious clown and now he wants to be a serious king, though – as we shall see – he will never entirely renounce his devious ways, even when the fate of the world depends on him. This royal elevation of the clown has especially fascinated the poets of our own century. In this section of my reflections, I shall refer above all to two works – namely, to Jan Kasprowicz's drama, *Marcolf* [*Marchołt*, 1920], and to Antoni Słonimski's long poem, *The Judgment of Don Quichote* [*Sąd nad Don Kichotem*, 1963–1965], in which the equivalent of the clownish wielder of power is Sancho Panza.[194]

Marcolf – who for so long has been subject to the king's caprices – gets a taste of power and the possibilities it opens:

> And I have a great desire,
> though I be Marcolf and a boor,
> to seat myself upon the throne,
> Which is Power, which does not stand
> as if on a bog, as if it were sinking
> in a swamp! . . . A throne which in
> all its proverbial form is equal to
> the might of a stony mountain,
> not only in appearance, but in truth
> – this is the throne I want!
>
> (Kasprowicz)

He does not wish to be a mere make-believe king. He believes in his mission, and so he comes to bring order to the world. This order is harsh, both in conception and realization, unmitigated by any experiences from the earlier phases of his own biography, when he himself was in a miserable state – if not exactly hanging off the king, then always dependent on his monarchical whims. Marcolf's rule turns out to be populist only in the genetic sense, while it becomes functionally anti-populist. This state of affairs is not altered by the superficial preservation of certain popular customs, which we shall subsequently refer to as Marcolfian

---

194 I shall refer to the following editions: Jan Kasprowicz, Marchołt gruby a sprosny: Jego narodzin, życia i śmierci misterium tragikomiczne, in: *Dzieła*, vol. 15, ed. S. Kołaczkowski (Kraków: Meisels, 1930), pp. 157, 180, 224, 225, 155; Antoni Słonimski, *Sąd nad Don Kichotem*, in: *138 wierszy* (Warszawa: Państwowy Instytut Wydawniczy, 1973), pp. 229–240.

gestures. Its sole ideological foundation is faith in brutal and ruthless power. When he must part with the throne, Kasprowicz's Marcolf makes the following proclamation:

> I have turned away forever
> from that old hag,
> from that slut,
> who calls herself Mercy,
> but who like a strumpet,
> sucks the blood out of the weak
> down to the very last,
> and even turns the bravest
> into her vile prey…
> […]
> If today I were to sit upon the throne,
> if today my hands were once again
> to clutch the scepter,
> I would be just as harsh
> and just as cruel!

Leaving aside the Nietzschean terminology of this monologue, it remains crucial for us here. The important point is that it reveals what we might define as the consciousness of the charismatic clown – a clown convinced of his mission and refusing to shun any means that might lead to the realization of his stated aims. In Słonimski's poem, Sancho Panza – who now holds the reins of power in hands previously accustomed to other uses – declares:

> It is worth it, I say, for the sake of the altar
> To sacrifice a few generations of little shits.

In this interpretation, a "little shit" is anybody – besides the charismatic clown himself – who has sat on the throne. The clown has ceased to be a character with any moderate dreams of power. He does not abide by any rules stemming from noble human wisdom. Instead, he becomes the hero of an anti-utopia, the ruler of a world in which power and ruthlessness are the main regulating components. We are a long way here from the clownish banter with the king of the medieval tale or the simple opposition between folk wisdom and official wisdom. The common people will not find their representative in Marcolf the ruler or feel any kind of solidarity with him. "Autocrat!" they shout at him in Kasprowicz's drama. This clownish autocracy turns out to be just as difficult to abolish as the autocracy of the king who inherits a throne passed down from father to son from time immemorial. Once again, function is more important than genesis.

It's true, I did not happen to see the triumph of justice.
The lips of the innocent make no claims.
And who knows whether a fool in a crown,
a winecup in his hand, roaring that God favors him
because he poisoned, slew, and blinded so many.
would not move the onlookers to tears: he was so gentle.[195]

(Czesław Miłosz, "Counsels")

Yet clownish autocracy is different in certain respects from traditional autocracy – above all, because to some social groups it can appear to be an impossible phenomenon. Paradoxically, this can appear to be the case even when it actually exists, constituting a palpable reality. It seems impossible because it clashes with what we regard as the laws of common sense or as the prevailing order of the world.[196] It is impossible not only because it threatens to institute a harsh regime to which it is difficult for people to accustom themselves, but also because it alters the style of exercising power, introducing genetically populist elements and revising the rituals previously associated with kingly power. Marcolf on the throne has no capacity or desire to fossilize into a dignified form. He does not wish to be "stiff." He wishes to sow fear and to command absolute obedience, though he still retains some of his former customs, expressions, and tricks, even when – like Sancho Panza in Słonimski's poem – he wishes to forget about his lowly past and demands the same of his underlings. Accordingly, he changes the external trappings of power, transforming the facade. However, when he comes to power in a state previously ruled by a tyrant, he does not introduce any fundamental innovations to the actual design of the structure. Marcolf on the throne no longer holds the fool's license, though – as we may observe – he retains certain habits from the times when it gave him legitimacy. Ultimately, the fool's license can never belong to the ruler, even when he himself – like Caligula – is a confirmed lunatic. The fool's license can never belong to the ruler because once it becomes law, it ceases to be a sanctioned departure from the norm. During Marcolf's reign, this matter becomes somewhat complicated, since the fool's license can no longer function in its previous form. In a world ruled by a clown,

---

195 Czesław Miłosz, *New and Collected Poems: 1931–2001*, transl. Cz. Miłosz & R. Haas (New York: HarperCollins, 2003), p. 237.

196 The subject of these reflections is the evolution of a literary motif rather than historical events, even as analogies. Nevertheless, it is difficult not to permit myself to make a digression here. At the beginning of the 1930s, Hitler was, above all, a ranting clown in the liberal imagination. His rise to power seemed impossible. There is no need to recall that this imagination turned out to be precisely a lack of imagination.

the role of clown in its classical form is condemned to wither away. One might surmise in this situation that a person representing "academic gravity" or "academic dignity" could assume the role. Any examination of this rather theoretical possibility falls beyond the purview of this article.

Specifically, it falls beyond the purview of the article partly because Marcolf the king does not value this wisdom at all. Indeed, he probably fears it, preparing a whip for it like a hammer of witches:

Marcolf: Nobody forbids you, my vassals,
              from conviction or humility from imitating the wisdom – of
              counsellors!
Somebody: The wisdom of the world!
Marcolf: For such wisdom a whip today
              is what's needed – I have one somewhere,
              as all shall soon see.

                                                          (Kasprowicz)

This passage by no means concerns only the "wisdom of counsellors" – in other words, of the professional executors of the ruler's orders. Marcolf himself is no bureaucrat in the old style, but from the moment he seizes power he values the bureaucracy. He understands that it forms a reliable support for the throne. Yet this is not the most significant point here. After all, it is no secret that the blows of the whip against wisdom are not aimed primarily at the counsellors but rather in quite a different direction. As a clown, Marcolf had already expressed his deep distrust of theoretical reason. He opposed Solomon – who was not only the ruler but also the personification of such wisdom – with his own rough-hewn wisdom, which he had apparently acquired from life experience. In one version of the medieval tale, Marcolf convinces Solomon that nature is something higher than learning. Nobody taught the cat to hunt mice, and yet it performs this activity very effectively.[197] In the same way, a category as irrational and suspicious as instinct may take the place of knowledge in social phenomena (which are also at stake here). Marcolf does not abandon this attitude when he gains the throne. On the contrary, he intensifies it. There is no place for intellectuals in his state, just as there is no place for them in Guybal Wahazar's state in Stanisław Ignacy Witkiewicz's play (entitled

---

197 Here I am a drawing on the work of Julian Krzyżanowski, who analyzed this version
     of the tale, which emerged quite late in a nineteenth-century work by Józef Lompa.
     See: Julian Krzyżanowski, *Paralele* (Warszawa: Państwowy Instytut Wydawniczy,
     1961), pp. 471–473.

Guybal Wahazar). Intellectuals are immediately suspect. The clown turned king no longer has any desire to debate with them but wishes to treat them in a different and somewhat less courteous fashion. Now clownish wisdom – raised to the dignity of law – excludes the existence of any other type of wisdom. On the surface, it even resists closed and dogmatic wisdom, a wisdom that finds its only support in ritual books and is unable to develop or integrate social experiences in new ways.

Certainly, Marcolf is no dogmatist. He cannot be one, since he does not belong to the guild of commentators on sacred books. At the same time, he does not oppose this ossified thought to any new or adventurous thought since he is only prepared to acknowledge whatever has – or rather, appears to him to have – direct support in practical life. Accordingly, he is always anti-intellectual. Nevertheless, despite his constant references to practice, it would be difficult to call him a pragmatist. Above all, he cannot free himself from a certain set of established rules. He continues to define himself by them even when it seems to him that he has gone far beyond them or even overthrown them. The clown king is still dependent on the old overthrown king in whose court he once performed the duties of clown. He is still the shadow of this old king. He cannot (or does not wish to) overcome the tradition that invariably forms his only point of reference, for he simply does not know any other traditions. Even if he has heard of such traditions, they present themselves to him as alien, suspicious and sometimes even diabolical. Marcolf's pragmatism is not a principle of conscious long-term action. Instead, its essence lies in capitulation to immediate circumstances, and thus in complete dependence on the demands of the moment and previous experiences. This is a small-minded form of pragmatism, the pragmatism – as with Słonimski's Sancho Panza – of a lackey, who has intellectually remained a petty servant, even though he has seized the position of autocratic ruler. Such pragmatism negates both theoretical constructions and the products of the imagination, thus partly undermining its own existence – though this is quite another matter.

The burden of past experience not only manifests itself in this limited version of pragmatism, but also defines the clown king's style of being and mode of behaviour, which do not fit the usual images of how a king should carry himself. Marcolf retains certain habits and gestures from the time when his role was to play the fool. We have already referred to these as Marcolfian gestures. They are based on the introduction of clownish pranks into a social context that does not require them and perhaps even excludes them. An example of a Marcolfian gesture would be hurling a shoe at an opponent to shut him up. Here debate degenerates into mere barroom brawling. A shoe hurled by the man on the throne may testify to his human qualities, but it also constitutes a shocking disruption of accepted customs, violating the rules of the game. It is not "diplomatic." However, Marcolfian gestures are not limited to this type of action. Language forms a separate area of their operation. In this case, such gestures might include the introduction of an unexpected style that astonishes listeners with its bawdiness and boorishness, as it ignores the accepted rules. This means the use of the same arguments to which Marcolf appealed when he was His Majesty's clown, constantly converting the "high" into the "low." Yet such a conversion now takes on a different meaning, since the one-time holder of the fool's license has reached the top. Marcolfian gestures represent innovations only in the domain of external trappings. They do not change the system. They may not even make it less grim. They have ceased to reflect any ludic element. Now they possess the attributes to dominate as a model worthy of imitation. Nothing remains of their former clownish brilliance.

5 Labyrinth – the space of alienation

5.1 The labyrinth constructed in words

Unlike most other myths, in which the primary role is played by heroes, this one focuses on the place where characters operate. We tend to associate myths with specific figures: when recalling the story of Iphigenia, we usually speak first of its heroine, the ill-fated daughter of Agamemnon and Clytemnestra, and only later position her in particular places like Aulis or Tauris, where key moments of her biography took place. Similarly, with Prometheus – we know that he was chained to the mighty rocks of the Caucasus, but they do not acquire independent meanings and do not emancipate, as it were, in symbolic terms, remaining forever tied to the fate of the degraded titan, always secondary to him. Although these places have been individualized and named, they are still in the background. The same case is with the Olympus. Although it serves as the seat of gods, this place has never been crucial in mythology as it has no myth of its own.

In the myth of the labyrinth, this hierarchy of significance is reversed. Although it does feature certain stories and characters – otherwise it could only be the subject of a descriptive poem, a form not used for recording myths and one that has little in common with the mythological mode of thinking. Therefore, since it is impossible to have it any other way, characters operate in that specifically shaped space and enter into various relationships with it. However, these relationships differ from those established between Prometheus and the Caucasus, or between the Argonauts and Colchis, primarily because none of them – neither the place of punishment nor the place where the Golden Fleece was kept – have a specific character that would affect the fate of the mythological heroes, or determine the meaning, symbolism and further evolution of their storylines.

To avoid any doubts, it needs to be stressed that the myth of the labyrinth speaks of a space that has been specifically designed and organized – one of a very special character due to its peculiarity and original meanings. It is a space unlike any other, standing apart at least because it always affects the behaviour of those who have found themselves inside it, or even defines them. It cannot ever be neutral, indifferent or deprived of meanings. Thus, this myth speaks of a space that can never be "plain": merely empirical (even in the specific sense that this adjective can have in relation to myth), or merely physical, i.e., the kind that one simply finds oneself in and consequently perceives in an ordinary way.

This specially formed and developed space towers over the characters. Certainly, this does not go to such an extent that would completely overshadow such figures as Daedalus, Minos, Theseus, Ariadne, and the Minotaur. It is easy to reconstruct what has been said about them in the myth, to present not only their adventures but also their individual characteristics that clearly emerge from the mythological story. However, we shall not be recounting these stories here for they are well known and the present aim is not to paraphrase them for the sake of doing so. This decision has also other, more serious reasons. The myth of the labyrinth fused with a certain spatial construction rather than any series of narrative elements – this is the way in which its unique character manifests. Although that spatial image was endowed with various meanings throughout history, they have nevertheless always retained a more or less clear connection with their point of departure – the mythical labyrinth on the island of Crete, ruled by Minos. Or, in other words, one does not have to remember about Daedalus, Minotaur, Theseus, and Ariadne when getting to know the various versions of the labyrinth. Still, it is impossible to forget that this spatial image first emerged in early antiquity and was from the start infused with symbolical content.

This is also impossible because this symbolically organized space was at the same time real. Its first description was made by Herodotus, who did not hide his fascination with the Egyptian labyrinth.[198] Archaeological excavations carried out on Crete confirm that the labyrinth located there – the model and archetype of all later ones – is not just a figment of imagination but a particular and real place, although it had a symbolic dimension right from its beginnings. Labyrinths were also built later in various places and epochs, and with diverse aims in mind. However, it was always a demarcated and signifying space, one constituting something more than a spatial design isolated for some reason. It would carry a special message due to its links with beliefs or rituals, while its structure would correspond to some kind of a vision of the world, offering its more or less direct image. It is this kind of labyrinth – which has emerged in various cultures, often distant from each other in time and space, thus precluding communication – that is described in the excellent book by Paolo Santarcangeli.[199] I owe a lot to this publication, which constitutes an unrivalled compendium of knowledge on this subject. In this *summa*, the author reveals his multiple competences by shedding light on various aspects of the phenomenon,

---

198 Herodotus, *The Histories*, transl. R. Waterfield (Oxford: Oxford University Press, 1998), pp. 154–155.

199 Paolo Santarcangeli, *Księga labiryntu* [*Libra dei labirinti*], transl. I. Bukowski (Warszawa: Wiedza Powszechna, 1982). I have also used the French translation: *Le Livre des labyrinthes. Histoire d'un mythe et d'un symbole*, transl. M. Lacau (Paris: Gallimard, 1974).

revealing its religious, anthropological and aesthetic dimensions. Without taking them into account it would be entirely impossible to consider labyrinths (perhaps with the exception of those which, like garden ones, were built for the purposes of decoration or entertainment; however, they emerged relatively late and have a marginal meaning). This space *is* and *means* in equal measure. By "means" I wish to convey that this space refers to a certain set of images and texts that have codified it and become its vehicles, primarily myths.

However, this does not exhaust the subject. Labyrinths are spaces constructed anew, time and again, in words. This is not limited to cases when – as in the famous account of Herodotus – the object of interest consists of a real labyrinth, and the writer's task boils down to providing a description. In later periods this does not happen at all. Certainly, the knowledge of the Cretan labyrinth (and sometimes of other such places) lurks in the background; however, the point is not to present it, but to direct attention to the metaphorical meanings: the ones contained in the myth, and the ones that could be freely drawn from it, or even imposed on it. Literature ceaselessly produces its own labyrinths. Therefore, it would not be an exaggeration to say that today these places exist to a greater extent on the pages of novels and poems rather than in empirical space.

For the time being, we shall remain content with this general view. However, it might be added here – right at the very beginning – that the literary construction of labyrinths is made possible only by the fact that language offers countless spatial categories. Thanks to them and with their help (or mediation) we are able to speak of things that have no real connection to space. This question has been studied in depth by linguists, who have demonstrated that, for example, already at the level of grammar some basically spatial categories are formed in order to speak about time, among other things. Spatial metaphors constitute one of the fundamental elements of semantics.[200] This cannot be forgotten in any consideration of labyrinth as a literary theme, although this perspective naturally does not exhaust the topic. It has to be argued, however, that in literature, and even in everyday language, we do not just talk *about* labyrinths, but primarily *with* them.

This kind of space is deeply rooted in tradition and mythology. It rather "means" than just "is," and constitutes an unusually wide-ranging symbol. It recurs throughout the ages and has been employed to express diverse attitudes, ideas and beliefs. It seems as if it were destined to become – despite some fluctuations or deviations – the symbol of human existence, and of the individual's position in the world. As Mircea Eliade claimed in an autobiographical remark, "the trial of

---

200 For more information see: Georges Matoré, *L'espace humane* (Paris: La Columbe, 1962).

the labyrinth" defines the human condition.[201] It is a metaphor of the relationship between the human being, the world, and other people, as well as of the relation to oneself and one's internal life. This metaphor has been variously shaped, but almost without exception it refers to an existence led in an alien and hostile space, one that resists taming and grasping in psychological terms. It is a space in which we are cornered and continuously face the worst threat. Labyrinth proved to be such a space to everyone who entered it in order to tame the Minotaur, including Theseus. It has remained such for those who have never ventured into the maze-like space, full of crossroads and alleys leading nowhere, but nevertheless seem to have been sentenced to inhabit it forever, making it not the space of an adventure, even one ending with death, but one of everyday existence.

Labyrinth could be – alternatively – a welcoming space for the Minotaur (at least because he would not remember any other place), but this might not be certain as well because he did not find himself there out of his own will. Still, it remains doubtless that whenever we hear stories about being lost in a labyrinth (Cretan or any other), we do not identify with the weird monster or any of its counterparts, but rather with those brave ones who enter the labyrinth to combat the monster, or who have found themselves inside it for other reasons. A defence or praise of the Minotaur is contained in only one work I know – an ironic prose poem by Zbigniew Herbert, which reverses, if not the classical version of the myth, then at least its hierarchy of values.[202] However, this exception does not undermine the rule. We are incapable of identifying with the Minotaur, at the same time precluding the possibility of domesticating the labyrinthine space and settling in it. Anyway, a domesticated and tamed labyrinth is no longer a labyrinth, even if it were to be comprised of particularly crooked and winding passageways. One simply cannot feel at home in a labyrinth. It cannot be made one's own as this would contradict its very nature. If the Minotaur really considered it to be his private, cosy space – one corresponding to his aspirations and lifestyle, not hiding any secrets and mastered both materially and intellectually – it would then cease to be a labyrinth in some sense. It is, after all, a space of alienation.

We feel trapped in it and wish to find the exit. We lose our way. As Georg Simmel notes in the essay "The Stranger":

---

201 Mircea Eliade, *L'epreuve du labyrinthe. Entretients avec Claude-Henri Rocquet* (Paris: Belfond, 1978), p. 39.

202 Zbigniew Herbert, "Historia Minotaura," in: *Pan Cogito* (Warszawa: Czytelnik 1974). A similar theme appears in an essay that Herbert published earlier, titled "Labirynt nad morzem" ["Labyrinth at the Sea"], in: *Twórczość* 2 (1973), p. 31.

If wandering is the liberation from every given point in space, and thus the conceptional opposite to fixation at such a point, the sociological form of the "stranger" presents the unity, as it were, of these two characteristics. This phenomenon too, however, reveals that spatial relations are only the condition, on the one hand, and the symbol, on the other, of human relations.[203]

It is in the labyrinth that wandering entails being stuck, if not in a particular and strictly defined place, then in a much larger area; in both cases, however, space is always clearly demarcated and isolated. Such wandering radically differs from what we usually understand by this term, at least because one just cannot go for a walk in the labyrinth – it is not a space of touristic explorations or of casual strollers who wish to admire views. It has been rightly noted that the character thrown in the labyrinth has to be in constant motion, which defines his or her present condition.[204] Any stops or pauses would be like Stations of the Cross (with one notable exception we shall deal with separately). However, such manner of movement is not simply necessitated by the story's development, especially in 20th-century prose. Importantly, it simultaneously provokes the movement of thoughts, stimulating a cognitive process that is supposed not only to help protagonists become better acquainted with further, usually mysterious portions of that space, but also to aid them in orienting themselves and finding their way.

In an article titled "What Daedalus Told Ariadne, or How to Escape the Labyrinth," Paul G. Kuntz calls the myth of the labyrinth philosophical – "a myth of discovery" – because it shows a character overcoming fear and the feeling of being lost in order to solve the mystery and simultaneously ascertain that the world is in fact constructed on the basis of certain knowable and construable patterns.[205] Kuntz's interpretation seems to be overly intellectual and rational. Moreover, it disregards how the myth has functioned throughout the ages and how it functions today. Nevertheless, the fact that he emphasizes the cognitive dimension is certainly laudable. The labyrinth-exploring character not only

---

203 Georg Simmel, *The Sociology of Georg Simmel*, transl. K. Wolff (New York: Free Press, 1950), p. 402.

204 Colette Guillemard, *Le Labyrinthe romanesque de Lawrence Durrell* (Lille: Atelier Reproduction des thèses, Université de Lille III, 1980), p. 127.

205 I was unable to obtain this article, published in the October issue of *Monist* in 1966, but I am basing here on a detailed summary, backed with quotations, contained in the book by Enrico Garzilli, *Circles without Center: Paths to the Discovery and Creation of Self in Modern Literature* (Cambridge, Mass.: Harvard University Press, 1972), pp. 91–92.

keeps wandering, more or less chaotically, trying to find the right way among a tangle of paths, at the same time experiencing a feeling of entrapment in a closed space without any apparent exit but also attempts to learn about it and understand it. This goal is often pursued even if the protagonist does not believe – as Kuntz would like to believe – in the power of rational analysis or common sense to penetrate spatial complications and master them. This cognitive factor is a fixed component of the protagonists' existential situation – their attitude is not passive and they do not succumb to fatalism, surrendering to factors that shape their fate. Learning and understanding demand taking action and putting up resistance, even when such endeavours are doomed to fail.

The myth of the labyrinth has been considered here so far as if it had always been the same, displaying the same symbolic meanings. Naturally, as with all things in this world, it has been subject to evolution and its significance has changed with time. In some periods, it completely fell into oblivion and lost its symbolic vitality. French authors of one book on social space have drawn attention to the fact that in epochs characterized by classicist or positivist tendencies images of labyrinth disappear.[206] Santarcangeli speaks of "labyrinthine epochs."[207] This term is often used in reference to the baroque (mainly due to the suggestive book by Hocke[208]), Romanticism (which inherited a fascination with this type of space from the Gothic romance[209]), and primarily the 20th century, when various artistic currents (except for the classic avant-gardists[210]) turned to the labyrinth on numerous occasions and for various purposes. This essay focuses on the more contemporary obsession with the labyrinth, but I shall retain the fully understandable right to refer to the classic version of the myth and some of its versions developed later.

---

206 Abraham Moles & Élisabeth Rohmer, *Psychologie de l'espace* (Paris: Casterman, 1978), pp. 141–142. Such images tend to appear in the context of exiting the labyrinth. A great example of this is provided in a poem by Adam Asnyk from the cycle *Przeminął czas* [*Time Has Passed*]: "At that time, the song shall rise again, / Replenishing the wondrous energies / And lead from the labyrinth of dark dreams / Into the light of the day." In: Adam Asnyk, *Poezje* (Warszawa: Państwowy Instytut Wydawniczy, 1974), p. 339.

207 Paolo Santarcangeli, *Księga labiryntu*, pp. 40–41.

208 Gustav René Hocke, *Die Welt als Labyrinth* (Hamburg: Rowohlt, 1957). I am using the French translation by C. Heim: *Labyrinthe de l'art fantastique. Le maniérisme dans l'art européen* (Paris: Denoël, 1977).

209 Marianne Thalmann, "Labirynt," transl. A. Sąpoliński, *Pamiętnik Literacki* 3 (1978).

210 For more information see: Ernest Kuźma, "Przestrzeń awangardy," in: *Tekst i fabuła*, eds. Cz. Niedzielski & J. Sławiński (Wrocław: Zakład Narodowy im. Ossolińskich, 1979), pp. 168–170.

5.2 Various closings and openings

In the "Essay on Man" Alexander Pope wrote:

> Let us (since life can little more supply
> Than just to look about us and to die)
> Expatiate free o'er all this scene of man;
> A mighty maze! but not without a plan[211]

The perspective of the English rationalist is definitely an isolated case. In other epochs, such an account of the human condition ("A mighty maze! but not without a plan") would be considered contradictory or even totally impossible. Either the image of the labyrinth would not be recalled at all, or the idea of a pre-existing, rational plan would be outright rejected. However, we cannot neglect the fact that sometimes – even in contemporary times – there do emerge images of the labyrinth as a space that may not be exactly favourable but is at least not hostile. Unexpectedly, one such image can be found in Czesław Miłosz's *Visions from San Francisco Bay* (this may be surprising because his works also feature other kinds of labyrinths). The labyrinth emerges here as a metaphor of everything that humankind has created in the course of its history:

> For the threads spun by our ancestors do not perish, they are preserved; we alone among living creatures have a history, we move in a gigantic labyrinth where the present and the past are interwoven. That labyrinth protects and consoles us, for it is anti-nature.

Elsewhere he writes:

> For me the human labyrinth is splendid, spellbinding. Besides, it matters little what I think of it; what I am in relation to it is important.[212]

---

211 Alexander Pope, *An Essay on Man*, in: *Selected Poetry and Prose*, ed. R. Sowerby (London: Routledge, 2003), p. 151.

212 Czesław Miłosz, *Visions from San Francisco Bay*, transl. R. Lourie (Manchester: Carcanet New Press, 1982), p. 176 & 195. A different understanding of the labyrinth can be glimpsed in a short prose passage from the cycle *Unexpressed* [*Niewyrażone*] contained in the volume *Unattainable Earth* [*Nieobjęta ziemia*]: "Labyrinth. Constructed on a daily basis in words, sounds of music, lines and colours on paintings, shapes of sculptures, and architecture. Lasting since ages, it is so exciting to visit that anyone who becomes immersed in it no longer needs the world. It is fortified because it has been established in opposition to the world. However, the most surprising thing is that when one savours it for itself, it dissolves into thin air like palaces made of mist. What supports it is only the desire to exit somewhere onto the other side." In: Czesław Miłosz, *Nieobjęta ziemia* (Paris: Instytut Literacki, 1984), p. 31.

The vision of labyrinth as an experience that is dangerous, inviting tribulation and danger, but simultaneously leads to positive solutions, crystallizes usually when it is considered as a myth of initiation. The experience of initiation may be frightening, but the "fear of the world" it invokes is already brought under some control.[213]

Such accounts – let us emphasize once more – are rare, especially in the 20th century. It seems that Gustaw Herling-Grudziński expressed the zeitgeist when he claimed that labyrinths "perfectly convey purposelessness."[214] In most cases, the labyrinth is understood as an unwelcoming space, one that hides dangerous secrets, trapping and alienating its visitors. In this sense, it becomes, as it were, the quintessence of enclosed space, its most complete and condensed form, a special kind of "spatial negativity,"[215] or "negative space."[216] Deprived of a "plan" – not only a divine one, but also frequently a human-scale one too – it is opposed to open space, empirically and, even more so, symbolically. When considered in the most general terms, this opposition ought to be regarded as the most fundamental one: enclosed space would be negative, while the open one – positive (although, after all details are taken into account, it is certain that there will emerge facts and images softening this contrast, because there are many ways to open and enclose space[217]).

This juxtaposition is revealed most clearly when chthonic space is considered as the opposite of heavens: as a prison or simply the opposite of everything that remains outside it. The meaning of such contrasts does not typically depend on the gulf between opposing elements but is related to their axiological character. This allows for various revaluations of these spatial images and – primarily – for all kinds of intermediate states. Sometimes in a single work, or in a single author, both spaces can be valued equally negatively.[218] In other cases, however, the

---

213 Term coined by Aleksandra Olędzka-Frybesowa in: *W głąb labiryntu. Wędrówki po Europie* (Warszawa: Wydawnictwo Literackie, 1979), p. 279.

214 Gustaw Herling-Grudziński, *Dziennik pisany nocą (1973–1979)* (Paris: Instytut Literacki, 1980), p. 153.

215 Term coined by Jean-Pierre Richard in the essay "Figures du vide," in: *Microlectures* (Paris: Seuil, 1979), p. 43. This topic recurs in many of his other works. For example, he discusses Celine's enclosed spaces in the book *Nausée de Céline* (Paris: Fata Morgana, 1973).

216 Term coined by Algirdas Julien Greimas in "Pour une sémiotique topologique," in: *Pour une sémiotique topologique* (Paris: Seuil, 1976), p. 132.

217 A classic analysis of various spatial images can be found in Gaston Bachelard's *La poétique de l'espace* (Paris: Les Presses universitaires de France, 1957).

218 This case is discussed in the context of Alexander Blok's works of Zara Minc in: "Struktura 'przestrzeni artystycznej' w liryce A. Błoka," in: *Semiotyka kultury*, eds. E. Janus & M. R. Mayenowa (Warszawa: Państwowy Instytut Wydawniczy, 1975), p. 324.

clear boundary between open and closed space begins to be blurred, producing zones lying in-between, which seem to be symbolically ambiguous almost by definition, thus being prone to acquiring different, sometimes even accidental meanings.[219]

Let us repeat: there are different ways of closing and opening. In this way, emptiness – the kind of space that is clearly and unquestionably open – was generally valued negatively by representatives of the early modernist movement called "Young Poland."[220] Considered in abstract categories, emptiness could be seen, in a sense, as the reverse of labyrinth, but it nevertheless leads to the labyrinth in some cases and is symbolically akin to it. On the other hand, home is certainly an enclosed kind of space, but it seems to be the exact opposite of the labyrinth.[221] It is always a private, tamed and friendly space. Its enclosed character is not only harmless but also constitutes the condition of safety and simultaneously its component. It has not been imposed from the outside and is absolutely under control. The keys to the house are not an ordinary object – they are the sign of my mastery over the places I have developed the way I saw fit, and which no alien is allowed to enter. Such closing off isolates and separates, but does not entirely cut off my contacts with the world. It cannot do so, because I am in control of the situation. When I am at home, I am *at my own*, even if this home is not a literal home. It could be any space that is friendly and desirable,

---

219 The gradable character of the opposition "open-closed" is emphasized by Yuri Lotman in the context of works of Gogol ("Zagadnienia przestrzeni artystycznej," transl. J. Faryno, in: *Semiotyka kultury*, p. 258).

220 For more information see: Maria Podraza-Kwiatkowska, "Pustka – otchłań – pełnia. Ze studiów nad młodopolską symboliką inercji i odrodzenia," in: *Młodopolski świat wyobraźni*, ed. M. Podraza-Kwiatkowska (Kraków: Wydawnictwo Literackie, 1977). Let us add that, among these poets, labyrinth-related themes occur most often in works of Tadeusz Miciński. See: Edward Balcerzan, "Przestrzenie Tadeusza Micińskiego," in: *Oprócz głosu* (Warszawa: Państwowy Instytut Wydawniczy, 1971); Erazm Kuźma, "Oksymoron jako gest semantyczny," in: *Studia o Tadeuszu Micińskim*, ed. M. Podraza-Kwiatkowska (Kraków: Wydawnictwo Literackie, 1979), pp. 211–213; Maria Podraza-Kwiatkowska, *Symbolizm i symbolika w poezji Młodej Polski* (Kraków: Wydawnictwo Literackie, 1979), p. 230.

221 For a broader discussion of the symbolism of home see for example: Olivier Marc, *Psychanalyse de la maison* (Paris: Seuil, 1972); Alina Witkowska, "Białe ściany polskiego domu," in: *Słowianie, my lubim sielanki...* (Warszawa: Państwowy Instytut Wydawniczy, 1972); Stanisław Barańczak, *Język poetycki Mirona Białoszewskiego* (Wrocław: Zakład Narodowy im. Ossolińskich, 1974), p. 80ff.

regardless of its other characteristics. Krasiński expressed this perfectly in one of his love letters:

> [...] from what I gather, neither planets nor the sun have their homes – they are located not where these celestial bodies are at a given moment, but where they are headed. Similarly, the human heart is not at home where it is beating, but in its journey to that which it is beating towards, making you my home. Likewise, I am your home! We are at home only when we are together! Consequently, the universe will be *at home* when it meets God during its stellar journey. There is no other goal for the millions of millions of stars that venture into infinity![222]

Naturally, today nobody seems to be as eager as the Romantic poet to consider the entire universe as a space prone to domestication, but home is nevertheless always close (in the metaphorical sense) and valued positively. However, when it becomes a labyrinth, or even begins to resemble one, it ceases to be home. This happens for example in Andrey Bely's autobiographical novel *Kotik Letaev*, where the vision of home departs from other images prevailing in this kind of literature.[223] "Passages, rooms, corridors," he writes, "remind us of our body, give us the image of our body."[224] Both elements of this juxtaposition seem to the little hero to be incomprehensible and dangerous. Both the internal and the external world assume labyrinthine shapes. The "labyrinth of rooms" (sometimes referred to as "black" and sometimes as "ours") seems, as it were, to be the novel's leit-motif, which recurs on all sorts of occasions. Therefore, in this particular case, a house that approximates a labyrinth basically ceases to be a home.

Similar phenomena can be observed in prose works of Bruno Schulz, where the boundary between the friendly enclosed space and the hostile one (i.e., between home and labyrinth) is often blurred. "The structure of labyrinth can be identified in those images of home which [...] symbolize human beings or their psyches, and further in images of the city and night sky."[225]

---

222 Zygmunt Krasiński, *Listy do Delfiny Potockiej*, ed. Z. Sudolski, vol. 2 (Warszawa: Państwowy Instytut Wydawniczy, 1975), p. 546.

223 They are analyzed by Małgorzata Czermińska in the essay "Dom w autobiografii powieści o dzieciństwie," in: *Przestrzeń i literatura*, eds. M. Głowiński & A. Okopień-Sławińska (Wrocław: Zakład Narodowy im. Ossolińskich, 1978).

224 Andrei Bely, *Kotik Letaev*, transl. G. J. Janecek (Evanston: Northwestern University Press, 1999), p. 21.

225 Jerzy Jarzębski, "Czasoprzestrzeń mitu i marzenia w prozie Brunona Schulza," in: *Powieść jako autokreacja* (Kraków: Wydawnictwo Literackie, 1984), p. 193. A systematic and deepened account of this labyrinth can be found in Jarzębski's introduction to the "Biblioteka Narodowa" edition of Schulz's prose. Spatial images, highly

However, despite the above as well as other diversions, home is the embodiment of friendly space – one that is approved not only when it is considered from the perspective of individual experience, but also when viewed as an imaginative element typical for entire epochs in the history of literature. Thanks to studies by Teresa Michałowska and Adam Karpiński[226] we know how spatial images were formed in early Polish poetry (mainly in the Renaissance) and what they meant. Certainly, this period also had its own *loci horridi*, but the dominant pattern involved images of places considered to be homely, ones that would constitute both a favourable and natural environment. "For the landowner," Karpiński argues, "house and village are synonymous with the values they represent."[227] Real relationships between them would recede into the background. Regardless of the shape it would assume, in the kind of space whose centre is occupied by a home that is strongly marked in axiological terms there is no place for a labyrinth.

A labyrinth "without a plan" is opposed both to the friendly enclosed space, and to the great wide open, except for certain subtypes of the latter that would be valued negatively, like Young Poland's above-mentioned emptiness. It remains doubtless that what we are dealing with here is primarily the contrasting of symbols that are saturated with values rather than neutral spatial images. It could not be any other way because space is supposed to be not only a kind of place, even if endowed with unusual features, but also an expression of the existential situation. However, such contrasting can take many forms. In epochs that could not be said to favour labyrinths, or in works of authors fascinated mainly with open spaces, such enclosed worlds are simply rejected. Although they might be mentioned or even meticulously presented, this is done in a way that leaves little doubt about such space being neither one of the artist nor one of the characters – it is "alien space," although the sense of that adjective is different from what we

---

characteristic for this writer, are also analyzed by Wojciech Wyskiel in *Inna twarz Hioba. Problematyka alienacyjna w dziele Brunona Schulza* (Kraków: Wydawnictwo Literackie, 1980). In Schulz's prose the labyrinth encompasses all dimensions of the presented reality, while his visions are distinguished by immense poetic power. I do not discuss them in detail here only because so much has been already written on the subject.

226 Teresa Michałowska, "Wizje przestrzeni w liryce staropolskiej. Rekonesans," in: *Przestrzeń i literatura* (Wrocław: Zakład Narodowy im. Ossolińskich, 1978); "Kochanowskiego poetyka przestrzeni," in: *Poetyka i poezja* (Warszawa: Państwowe Wydawnictwo Naukowe, 1982); Adam Karpiński, *Staropolska poezja ideałów ziemiańskich: próba przekroju* (Wrocław: Zakład Narodowy im. Ossolińskich, 1983).

227 Adam Karpiński, *Staropolska poezja ideałów ziemiańskich*, p. 97.

usually associate with it. This is the case not only among landowner poets of the Renaissance but also among certain modern writers. In Polish literature, the main representative of this phenomenon is Julian Przyboś. In the conflict between enclosed and open space, victory is achieved in his poems by the latter, even when the theme of the labyrinth does occur, as in the poem "Bread and Roses" ["Chleb i róże"]. Openness is something more than an approved and desirable feature here: it constitutes, as it were, the fundamental characteristic of a world worth living in and praising. Sometimes this attitude is expressed directly:

> Walls – in walls – from walls I break away. I carry
> a sudden narcissus from the late spring,
> a flower so fragrant that feels unfamiliar; so gold
> and so snow-white,
> that I feel
> such joy, as if I embraced
> the whole world in the aroma's many hues[228]

Open space can be conquered and embraced in one way or another, but an enclosed one does not yield to any such operations, itself gaining dominance over humanity. This fundamental difference determines the literary representations of both kinds of space, and consequently – their symbolic capacity. A writer of open spaces notices – like Przyboś – the enclosed one but somewhat particularizes it, not expanding it to cover either the entire world or even its especially important and significant parts. Such authors treat this kind of space as one that can be always exited with a certain amount of effort. A writer of enclosed spaces, on the other hand, is naturally aware of the open one, but sees it as unattainable and does not link it to situations considered to be real and essential. Such authors' souls are – to recall Shakespeare's *Hamlet* – too narrow, feeling "the narrowness of the given reality"[229] regardless of the kind of space that is being represented, be it a prison cell, the maze of a great urban sewage system, or places that do not seem like a trap: a room in a tenement house, a modern metropolis, or any other. Although modern literature does not usually mention this explicitly, it is the human world that is too cramped, despite the fact that one can be "bounded in a nutshell" and consider oneself "a

---

228 Julian Przyboś, "Projekt wiosenny 1958," in: *Poezje zebrane* (Warszawa: Państwowy Instytut Wydawniczy, 1959), p. 475.

229 Karl Jasper's term developed in "Boundary situations" ["Sytuacje graniczne"], translated by A. Staniewska and included in: Roman Rudziński, *Jaspers* (Warszawa: Wiedza Powszechna, 1978), p. 197.

king of infinite space" (to recall *Hamlet* once more). However, in a "labyrinthine epoch" like ours there seems to be no escape from this nutshell, and no way to crack it, also in an act of mental liberation.

The role of the Shakespearian nutshell can be played – let us repeat – by almost any space. Sometimes it may be far from the classical labyrinth in terms of shape. Nevertheless, some of its properties are typically preserved. Labyrinths are usually placed low, on a horizontal plane, although it is possible to encounter vertical ones, too. Still, even if they climb upwards, they are positioned low, because the vertical dimension is principally subjected to the horizontal one. The clearest example of a vertical labyrinth is the set of visions found in Piranesi's *Carceri*. Even there, however, the multi-level symbolic constructions are not related to any "top," all the more so because the artist employed in them visions of hell found in the Italian tradition, albeit not limiting himself to Dante.[230]

Similarly, stairs are often a component of labyrinthine spaces in literature. Just like in Piranesi, they play a significant role in an excellent short story by Hermann Broch, titled "A Slight Disappointment."[231] Its protagonist wanders through the various levels of the city. A weird large building in which he has found himself appears to be one of its elements. The story does not introduce any juxtaposition of "top" and "down,"[232] the attic and the cellar. All we find is unclear and dangerous space, one that corners the protagonist and cuts off all escape routes.[233] The hero cannot gain control over such places regardless of the level he finds himself on. Such "tops" only have a relative character, strictly subordinated to the "down." Naturally, this affects the symbolic dimension of this space.

---

230 Hell-related analogies are emphasized in Marguerite Yourcenar's discussion of Piranesi. See: "Les Prisons imaginaires de Piranèse," in: *La Nouvelle Revue Française* 94 (1961). See also Wojciech Karpiński's essays on Piranesi in: *Pamięć Włoch* (Kraków: Wydawnictwo Literackie, 1982).

231 Hermann Broch, "Lekkie rozczarowanie," in: *Powrót Wergilego*, transl. A. M. Linke (Warszawa: Czytelnik, 1981).

232 The relativity of such juxtapositions is confirmed in one passage from Thomas Mann's *The Magic Mountain*. When Settembrini compares the stay in Davos to a descent into the abyss, making allusions to Hades, Hans Castorp reacts in the following way: "Into the depths, Herr Settembrini? But I beg your pardon – I climbed a good five thousand feet to join you up here." In: Thomas Mann, *The Magic Mountain*, transl. J. E. Woods (New York: A.A. Knopf, 2005), p. 222 (e-book edition).

233 For a discussion of the labyrinth's vertical dimension see: Yves Stourdzé, "Ville soustraite, cité calcinée, pouvoir ahuri," *Revue d'Esthétique* 3–4 (1977).

Labyrinth has been also introduced into the sphere of Christian symbolism, where it is always associated with that which is positioned low. If it appears at the top in sacred architecture – which is very rare – it loses its symbolic meanings and plays a solely ornamental role. In such cases, spatial images are not meant to be complex, even when the actual construction employs labyrinth-like patterns. It is a different case when they appear on the floor, e.g. in mediaeval cathedrals.[234] However, this was no longer done for decorative purposes, but to construct a highly meaningful space. Its sense and function have not been fully decoded to this day. One thing remains clear, though: it was supposed to be a long road (to be covered on one's knees), both symbolizing the pilgrimage to Jerusalem and marking a penitential trail. Either way, the labyrinth-based itinerary equalled – at least to a certain extent – a symbolic journey through life.

Although mediaeval floor labyrinths had no direct continuation and have fallen into oblivion, they are in a sense a model realization of the labyrinth's idea. Literature knows many different symbolic labyrinths because it possesses the unique ability to treat almost every space in such a way that it becomes a labyrinth. The limitations that emerge in this context stem from the general symbolism of spatial notions, specifically such oppositions as: top-down, open-closed, and between two types of closure (the positive one, subordinated to human will, and the one indifferent to our desires). Nevertheless, these limitations do not have to be absolute if the concept of the labyrinth is easily generalized, becoming a universal notion that corresponds to the world.

There are also other factors at play. Labyrinths constructed in literature do not have to be equipped with exactly those features that characterize the mythological labyrinth and are to this day associated with popular images deeply rooted in culture. A specific space may be presented as a labyrinth, not due to its mimetic conditions, but primarily or solely because this is how a specific character perceives it. This is not the property of literature only. Psychologists claim that perception and valuation of space is dependent, for example, on one's disposition or mood at the time of contact with that space.[235] The image of space – and consequently its symbolism – can be prone to various fluctuations, especially in

---

234 Some great analyses of the cathedral labyrinth are provided by Aleksandra Olędzka-Frybesowa in *W głąb labiryntu*, pp. 244–265. See also the corresponding passages from Paolo Santarcangeli's *Księga labiryntu*.

235 See for example: Antoni Kępiński, *Melancholia* (Warszawa: Państwowy Zakład Wyd. Lekarskich, 1974).

literature, which is privileged to present the setting in a highly subjective way, without care for intersubjective verification.

The greater the role of individual perception in literature, and the greater the consistency in presenting space from the perspective of the individual, the bigger its potential to resemble a labyrinth. This potential also depends on the force with which symbolic values are imposed on space, sometimes without any consideration for empirical matters. This happens particularly often in newer literature, where spatial visions are determined not only by the properties that could be objectively assigned to them but also – or even primarily so – by subjective interpretations, in which almost everything can become a labyrinth.

Obviously, in many instances, classical labyrinths are preserved, including such constructions as dungeons, backstreets, obstructed passages, corridors, caves, windowless rooms, houses with blocked exits, etc. These are – so to speak – specific letters in the alphabet of labyrinths, elements from which larger wholes are made. Such building blocks, however, are already filled with meanings and know no neutrality in terms of signification. Let us take a closer look at corridors for instance. Theseus was lost in them when he found himself in the Cretan labyrinth. A single corridor is not usually considered to be a labyrinthine space as one does not feel trapped or lost in it, although it could be a dangerous place. It is not by accident that Norwid used the following comparison: "a corridor long as nothingness."[236] Only a system of corridors can become a labyrinth – a vast and impenetrable network. The more difficult it is to retain control over a tangle of corridors, the clearer their symbolism is:

> I walk those corridors by torchlight
> Hearing water trickle down onto broken slabs.
> Deep into the mountain. In niches, busts of my friends,
> Their eyes are of marble. Only the light and shadow
> Throw over their faces a brief sour grimace of life.
> So, farther into the labyrinth leading to the dark interior,
> Where there are no kobolds, only the echo of my steps,
> Until the torch gutters out, and on the unknown bend
> Where it is fated, I will turn to stone. [237]

---

236 In the poem "Do Bronisława Z." All works of Cyprian Kamil Norwid are quoted here from the eleven-volume *Pisma wszystkie*, edited by J. W. Gomulicki (Warszawa: Państwowy Instytut Wydawniczy, 1971–1976).

237 Czesław Miłosz, "Those Corridors," in: *New and Collected Poems 1931–2001*, transl. Cz. Miłosz & R. Haas (New York: HarperCollins, 2003), p. 202.

It is "these corridors" – leading nowhere, dark and confusing – that are among the typical elements of negative space. In novels where the setting is urban, or the city is itself a protagonist, streets become their counterpart. Sometimes – as in the case of Durrell's prose, for example[238] – they acquire the rank of an obsessively recurring major theme. For characters wandering in the city (not to mention those who do so on its outskirts, as in Ernesto Sábato's novel *On Heroes and Tombs*), the usually narrow and winding streets (or sometimes even ones not having such features) create a functional counterpart to corridors. Naturally, they belong to chthonic space, which in itself is symbolic:

> We have long freed ourselves from the reign of ancient telluric gods
> we have been long immersing into the realm of chthonic deities.
> Trudging in a disorganized herd, a million puffing spectres,
> Escaped from torture cells and gas chambers, from graves, pits and horrors.[239]

Such space is always complicated and threatening, but it does not necessarily have to shatter our image of the relationships between particular elements. This allows ascertaining what is nearer or further away, what is higher or lower, etc. In this respect, this space does not have to diverge from any other. Consequently, its chthonic and closed character – i.e., fully labyrinthine – does not question traditional spatial relations, although respecting them is not a rule in narrative prose of the 20th century. In such cases, the effect of the labyrinth is created not through some, even very indirect mythological references, but primarily by way of questioning traditional, commonsensical spatial relations. The first one to obliterate them was Franz Kafka.

There can be no doubt that space in his works – which might be called non-Euclidean – has a highly symbolic character, as can be gleaned from casual reading.[240] It is particularly striking to observe the closed character of such space, rendered with incredible consistency, and its chthonic character, probably best visible in the short story "The Burrow" ["Der Bau"], an account of an animal burrowing an underground complex that never really becomes a safe zone,

---

238 This is discussed in detail by Colette Guillemard in *Le Labyrinthe romanesque de Lawrence Durrell*.

239 Alesander Wat, "Dawnośmy wyszli…," in: *Ciemne świecidło* (Paris: Libella, 1968), p. 106.

240 The symbolic role of space in Kafka is particularly emphasized by Hermann Pongs in *Franz Kafka: Dichter des Labyrinths* (Heidelberg: Rothe, 1960), as related by Mihály Sükösd in *Wariacje na temat powieści*, transl. A. Sieroszewski (Warszawa: Państwowy Instytut Wydawniczy, 1975).

despite the fact that this was its purpose.[241] The importance of such space for the author is also confirmed by the following confession:

> I have often thought that the best mode of life for me would be to sit in the innermost room of a spacious locked cellar with my writing things and a lamp. Food would be brought and always put down far away from my room, outside the cellar's outermost door. The walk to my food, in my dressing gown, through the vaulted cellars, would be my only exercise. I would then return to my table, eat slowly and with deliberation, then start writing again at once. And how I would write! From what depths I would drag it up! Without effort! For extreme concentration knows no effort. The trouble is that I might not be able to keep it up for long, and at the first failure – which perhaps even in these circumstances could not be avoided – would be bound to end in a grandiose fit of madness.[242]

Of course, Kafka never realized his "basement project," but he did not take it at face value – after all, his underground would always have a metaphorical character. And although the labyrinths in his works do not carry a single reference to the myths about Minos, Theseus, and the Minotaur, they are ubiquitous, not only due to their closed nature and unceasing sense of entrapment. It is omnipresent primarily because Kafka's space is organized in a way that precludes any brightness or transparency, as is fitting for non-Euclidean space. It is Kafka who demolished – with greater consistency than anyone else – the classical relations between the elements that form space. These constituent parts overlap and remain at an unpredictable distance to each other. There can be no certainty what is close or far, what is low or high. It is impossible to judge the distance between K., the geometrician, and the castle which he stubbornly approaches. The effect of this is all the more pervasive since Kafka treats this space as something obvious and apparently natural, not attempting to justify its character in any way, e.g. by utilizing dream visions or allegorical perspectives that would cancel the empirical dimension. What we observe here is precisely the labyrinthine effect.

Therefore, if we were to sketch a map of the regions where the labyrinth extends in literature, one end of the spectrum would be occupied by somewhat ordinary spaces corresponding to our commonsensical intuitions, while the other – by spaces similar to those developed in Kafka's works, which radically challenge

---

241 See the great interpretation of this short story in Heinrich Henel's essay "Kafka's 'Der Bau,' or How to Escape from a Maze," in: *The Discontinuous Tradition*, ed. P. F. Ganz (Oxford: Oxford University Press, 1971).

242 Franz Kafka, *Letters to Felice*, transl. J. Stern & E. Duckworth (New York: Schocken, 1973), pp. 602–603 (e-book edition).

our normal perception. These regions are immense since – let us emphasize this again – almost everything can acquire labyrinthine shapes and become an alien, tangled space that refuses to be fathomed and grasped. This is because labyrinthine spaces are derived from categories we encounter in this world. All places, including those that are well known, can become labyrinths, even ones that are not typically associated with maze-like qualities.[243]

5.3 Works stretched on myth

In the history of literature, the 20th century is "the era of the labyrinth." The same is not true for architecture, even after the demise of rigorous functionalism. Probably the only great 20th-century architect whose works contain clear references to labyrinth was Antonio Gaudí.[244] The image of the labyrinth is usually associated with alienation, anxiety, a sense of loss and entrapment, as well as lack of control over one's fate, and dependence on powers whose identification and understanding goes beyond human capabilities. Nevertheless, it refers – either directly or indirectly – to the literary mazes developed in previous epochs, mainly in Romanticism. It would be difficult to indicate a continuous line of this theme's evolution. Still, it would be equally risky to try demonstrating that in the 20th century references have been made to ancient myths without any historical mediation, and consequently that the labyrinth-related elements introduced by the Romantics have not played a significant role. As is typical in such cases, the history of images characterized by such symbolic capacity, and thus susceptible to meaning-related adaptations, constitutes a specific synthesis of continuity and discontinuity, links and breaks. One thing remains certain though: never

---

243 This is the way in which, for example, Alfred de Musset presents Versailles as a labyrinth in the short story "Les Mouches." For its interpretation see the text by Georges Poulet "Piranesi i romantyczni poeci francuscy," transl. W. Błońska, in: *Metamorfozy czasu* (Warszawa: Państwowy Instytut Wydawniczy, 1977)("Piranèse et les poètes romantiques français," *Nouvelle Revue Française* April-May 1966). A similar reading is offered by José Cabanis in *Saint-Simon l'admirable* (*Ten wspaniały Saint-Simon*, transl. A. Kijowski [Warszawa: Czytelnik, 1978]). This comparison has its own tradition. As Michel Butor observes in *Répertoire V* (Paris, Éditions de Minuit, 1982), already Charles Perrault wrote towards the end of the 17th century a work titled *Labyrinthe de Versailles* (pp. 103–147). In the Polish context, Wawel is described as a labyrinth by Wyspiański in *Wyzwolenie* [*Liberation*] (Act II, scene with Mask 7). Moreover, Rome's Castel Sant'Angelo has been frequently presented as a labyrinth (see: Gustav René Hocke, *Die Welt als Labyrinth*, p. 99).

244 See for example: Aleksandra Olędzka-Frybesowa, *W głąb labiryntu*, p. 265.

before has the myth of the labyrinth resonated so widely as in the 20th century. Nowhere in the past has it taken so many different forms.

It is not my purpose here to trace all the incarnations of this theme as this essay is not intended to constitute an erudite study belonging to the domain called *Stoffgeschichte*. However, it needs to be argued that the motif is encountered in abundance in all regions of literary and cinematographic creativity. It is heavily present in poetry[245] – also in Polish works of authors like Wat, Ważyk, Miłosz, and Jastrun.[246] It appears in drama, where it becomes a stage space without exit. In Sartre's *No Exit* hell is closely related to labyrinthine space. The character of such enclosed spaces to which the protagonists are confined is typically announced in the first stage directions. This is what happens in Sławomir Mrożek's *The Émigrés* [*Emigranci*]: a filthy den in which two unfortunates have found themselves is not the kind of space that would be treated in the same way as in a naturalistic play.[247] The work is dominated by meanings that carry at least indirect associations with the symbolism of labyrinths.

In film, spaces shaped like labyrinths are often the backdrop for great adventures.[248] However, this remains outside the scope of this discussion. The fact that the phenomenon is broader and more serious finds confirmation in such films as Buñuel's *The Exterminating Angel*, Resnais's *Last Year at Marienbad* or Robbe-Grillet's *L'immortelle*. The author of *Les Gommes* (who was also the screenwriter for the film by Resnais) set his story in labyrinthine places that are well known from literature: palace and city. The pull of contemporary novel is certainly detectable here, but it does not constitute, it seems, merely the consequence of the personal union of writer and film-maker. This is proven for example by Stanley Kubrick's famous film *The Shining* (1980). The garden labyrinth from the film's opening comprises a specific harbinger of the real labyrinth, in which terrible events will unfold later. The huge, abandoned hotel serves as the setting and appears as a counterpart to castles found in

---

245 Hocke mentions Juan Ramón Jimenez, Federico Garcia-Lorca, Jorge Luis Borges, Paul Eluard, Henri Michaux, and Jean Cocteau (p. 137). This list is naturally grossly incomplete, not only because it is limited to authors writing in French and Spanish.

246 It appears – more or less accidentally – in works of poets such as Kazimierz Wierzyński, Jarosław Iwaszkiewicz, Krzysztof Kamil Baczyński, Urszula Kozioł, Tadeusz Różewicz, Edward Stachura, and – among more recent lyricists – Krzysztof Boczkowski.

247 See: Stanisław Mrożek, *Emigranci*, in: *Utwory sceniczne nowe* (Kraków: Wydawnictwo Literackie, 1975), pp. 80–81.

248 It also appears in macabre works aimed to shock, as in the case of David Lynch's *Eraserhead* (1977).

Gothic novels. The film's labyrinthine story is certainly a reflection of novelistic visions of enclosed spaces.

It is a very broad phenomenon, both in historical and strictly contemporary terms. Labyrinth first emerged in narrative prose relatively early – it can be found in 18th-century adventure romance. Still, at that stage, it did not carry all of its later meanings and simply acted as the setting for the adventures experienced by the protagonist. The main character would be always capable of overcoming the labyrinth and other obstacles standing in his or her way.

Gothic novels are different in that respect, although they are also somewhat related to the adventure romance. One dissimilarity would consist in the fact that the Gothic as a genre found for itself a special kind of space that is highly characteristic. The affinity between an old castle and a labyrinth is something that is announced on the very first pages of Horace Walpole's *The Castle of Otranto*, a model work within this genre and its key forerunner.[249] Both adventure tales (often created only for entertainment) and Gothic novels influenced the way the theme of the labyrinth was developed in Romantic literature.[250] It acquired – at least among German Romantics who used it most extensively – meanings that are quite close to the ones prevailing in the 20th century. It ceased to be a space of adventure and was transformed into an existential one.[251]

Undoubtedly, realism does not belong with the "labyrinthine epochs," despite the fact that many of its representatives have taken city as their subject – a space that has grown similar to labyrinth in the 20th century. In most cases, however, when we glimpse enclosed spaces, they form the backdrop to adventures, not really imposing special meanings on them. Alexandre Dumas's *The Count of Monte Christo* is a good example of this. Enclosed spaces that are treated in metaphorical terms, thus approximating the symbolism of labyrinths, often occur in fantastic literature, which is akin to the Romantic

---

249 Among more recent works on the history of the Gothic romance see: Elizabeth MacAndrew, *The Gothic Tradition in Fiction* (New York: Columbia University Press, 1979).

250 Thalmann demonstrates this compellingly in his above-mentioned study, on which I base my own remarks. The role of enclosed space and various kinds of underground spaces in Romantic literature is discussed on many occasions in works of Maria Janion.

251 However, what must be mentioned is the Romantic fascination with the underground, which – as is confirmed by Novalis's *Heinrich von Ofterdingen* – did not have to be related to visions of labyrinth. The underground would not always evoke such associations in writers representing realism and naturalism. See: Kurt Ringger & Christof Weiand, "Aspects littéraires de la mine," *Revue de Littérature Comparée* 4.232 (1984), pp. 417–441.

tradition. It has been often pointed out, for example, that such themes obsessively recur in Jules Verne's novels.[252] Among the realists, however, they play an episodic role – Flaubert used them in one episode of his last novel, no longer a realist one but grotesque.[253]

Such relative poverty stands in contrast to the great abundance of labyrinth-like themes in 20th-century prose – an abundance that seems impossible to grasp. These themes rose to prominence already in the century's first decades, and have retained this status unshakeably and unquestionably. It would be difficult to indicate another symbol that has become so distinguished in modern prose, proving to be both far-reaching and lasting. The symbol's heightened activity, which has continued for so long, proves that this is not a matter of a passing fashion, or of some kind of a special coincidence that made things work in its favour. What we are dealing with here is a truly "unstoppable" symbol. It has not been relegated to the archive or simply forgotten for very long, at the same time not ossifying into a stereotype, a pure convention that cannot be used to express anything new or important (although it naturally appears in purely stereotypical or conventional forms – it could not have been otherwise).

Thus, by assuming various guises, references to the labyrinth appear among writers creating in many languages and representing different currents and styles, including the greatest: Mann, Joyce, and Borges. Still, there are two literary currents in which labyrinth-related themes perform an unusually profound role, becoming their trademark: Latin American prose, and the *nouveau roman*.

The former term is rather imprecise and general. Those who contribute to Latin American literature or have remained close to it could probably discern various currents and tendencies inside it, distinguishing individual stages in its historical evolution. However, this is impossible from the Polish perspective. Therefore, we need be satisfied with a general category. The only solace is that if someone were to look at Polish literature from the perspective of Argentinian La Plata, without being a specialist in the matter, they would certainly have to resort to equally unsubtle generalizations.

---

252 For more information see: Michel Serres, "Loxodromies des Voyages Extraordinaires," in: *La communication (Hermes I)* (Paris: Minuit, 1968); Marcel Brion, *L'Allemagne romantique. Le voyage initiatique* (Paris: Albin Michel, 1977), pp. 35–36; Roland Barthes, "Nautilus et bateau ivre," in: *Mythologies* (Paris: Seuil, 1957); Maria Janion, "Kuźnia natury," in: *Gorączka romantyczna* (Warszawa: Państwowy Instytut Wydawniczy, 1975), pp. 275–277.

253 Gustave Flaubert, *Bouvard and Pécuchet*, transl. M. Polizzotti, (London: Dalkey, 2005), pp. 44–55.

Latin American literature is labyrinthine to a degree unmatched by any other. This theme recurs constantly in works of Borges, acquiring the status of a leading symbol. Moreover, it plays a huge role in novels by Ernesto Sábato, appears in works of Julio Cortázar and José Donoso, and makes episodic entrances here and there, e.g. in *Paradiso* by Lezam Lima. I cannot explain such intense activity of this symbol in that particular region. Perhaps it stems from some special cultural conditions. It seems hard to imagine that this could simply boil down to the influence of one great writer – Borges – who personally discovered the labyrinth, revealed its many meanings, and finally imposed it on other artists. His impact seems undeniable, but it could explain the theme's success only if other writers who fell under his spell were mere imitators. This, however, is not the case – all the more so since they have pushed the theme of labyrinth in original directions, while Sábato made it the very foundation of his narrative constructions. In this case, labyrinth does not constitute a space of adventure, even if the narrated events could be called thus. It is rather a highly meaningful space in which a specifically understood life can unfold. What is more, it forms an unceasing problem faced by the cognizant subject, especially in Borges, for whom the labyrinth is an image of the cosmos and the model of a story that does not develop by following a straight line.[254]

In the French "new novel" the labyrinth appears very ofteln. Pierre Astier even claims that alongside with similar structures it constitutes in this current the common denominator of imagination.[255] In this respect, the most characteristic works would be *Passing Time* by Michel Butor, and *Dans le labyrinthe* by Robbe-Grillet. Naturally, however, these are not the only examples – labyrinths appear in other works of these writers, as well as in various books by other representatives of this current. Labyrinth can assume many shapes. For example, in Robert Pinget's *L'Inquisitoire* it assumes the shape of a huge building that seems to be somehow related to the ominous castles from Gothic novels. Its construction is as unclear and complex as the events that unfold inside it. As Astier pointed out, in Samuel Beckett's *Molloy* and Nathalie Sarraute's *Martereau* it is the forest that assumes a labyrinthine shape.

Still, the peculiarity and importance of this phenomenon cannot be reduced to the multiplicity of its forms since – to reiterate once again – almost any space could be treated as a labyrinth. As is known, the *nouveau roman* was accompanied

---

254 See: Enrico Garzilli, *Circles without Center*, p. 89.

255 Pierre A. G. Astier, *La Crise du roman français et le nouveau réalisme* (Paris: Nouvelles Éditions Debresse, 1968); for his discussion of the labyrinth see pp. 288–293.

by ample theoretical considerations. The role of space was particularly emphasized in them, with stress put on the aspiration to present only that which can be perceived from a given perspective. As befits a current that attempted to realize certain objectivist ideals (the concept of "objective literature" was particularly important to Robbe-Grillet[256]), such space was supposed to be primarily "empirical." Its goal was "to be" and not "to mean," or in cases when it is impossible to avoid, "to mean" only slightly, or bashfully.

This literary utopia of a space relieved from symbolism was not realized even to a small degree. Space became a "forest of symbols," even more so than in realist prose, in reference to which the creators and theoreticians of the new novel defined themselves. This happened at least because almost all places presented from the subjective perspective of the protagonist – the cognizant subject – are typically enclosed. This characteristic makes such spaces symbolic, all the more so since – as is the case in the above-mentioned works – they are augmented by references to myth, first and foremost the myth of the labyrinth.

In the "new novel" the enclosed space is – so to say – the space of cognition, and then – one of life in general. By its very nature, the world is unclear and resists any efforts to explicate it. It is a world in which the sense of loss is experienced not only by the wandering characters but also by narrators themselves. The paths they choose become a labyrinth. It is all the more distinctive and simultaneously meaningful because the aim of the narration is not to illuminate the labyrinth and impose order on it. On the contrary, it is the narrative itself that has a labyrinthine character – it is itself a call made from deep inside the labyrinth.

Let us repeat: the fascination with the myth of the labyrinth and the shaping of novelistic space in its image are not limited to Latin American literature or the *nouveau roman*. These tendencies have a much wider range, surfacing in all kinds of literary phenomena that are diverse in thematic, stylistic and philosophical terms. In 20th-century prose fiction, the labyrinth is not related to any particular school or trend, transcending all boundaries and extending from Joyce to Malewska, from Gide to Konwicki, from Bely to prose writers debuting in the 1980s: Włodzimierz Paźniewski and Jerzy Grundkowski.[257]

How does the labyrinth exist in the 20th-century novel? Or, to put differently: What evidence do readers find in the setting, accessible directly through reports

---

256 See the famous 1954 essay by Roland Barthes "Littérature objective," in: *Essais critiques* (Paris: Seuil, 1981).

257 In his parable-like prose the labyrinth is definitely a dystopian space. See: Jerzy Grundkowski, *Annopolis, miasto moich snów* (Kraków: Wydawnictwo Literackie, 1983).

and descriptions, that enable them to find the labyrinth's patterns, and then to identify and name them? In order to answer these questions, it becomes necessary to generally consider the forms and ways in which myth functions in 20th-century novel.[258] After all, despite its peculiarities related to being a spatial myth, the theme of the labyrinth is basically subordinated to certain general principles (perhaps with the exception of works where – as in Kafka – the mythological analogy emerges from the very shaping of non-Euclidean space that departs from classical notions).

Let us note right away that there are very few works that directly adapt the myth of the labyrinth, even if it is somewhat transformed or brought up to date (one example of such work would be the fascinating and original novel by Hanna Malewska, titled *Labyrinth*). Moreover, it is not an isolated phenomenon – it actually confirms the rule discussed in detail by J.J. White: insofar as drama usually preserves mythical stories, even when they are given an ironic or parodistic treatment, in novels myth occupies a rather more secretive dimension: one of subtext, allusion and indirect reference, becoming a kind of *basso continuo* that creates a harmonic basis on which various contemporary stories are told. What we are dealing with here are not novels that repeat or even transform myth, but ones that are somewhat based or "stretched" on it. The prime model of such a novel is, of course, James Joyce's *Ulysses*. Its case is all the more important here because this work's mythological counterpoint is constituted not only by Homer's epic poem, but also the myth of the labyrinth, one of the most important ones in Joyce's entire oeuvre.[259] Let us add that one novel based on myth appeared early in Polish literature, i.e., at a time when such an approach was almost without precedence – I am referring here to *Snowy Crop* [*Ozimina*] published in 1911 by Wacław Berent.[260]

It seems that the phrase "novel stretched on myth" is descriptively more accurate than the term "mythological novel" (sometimes used by White for example) insofar as in most cases it does not refer to works that paraphrase

258 I am basing here on two books: John J. White, *Mythology in the Modern Novel: A Study of Prefigurative Techniques* (Princeton: Princeton University Press, 1971); Eric Gould, *Mythical Intentions in Modern Literature* (Princeton: Princeton University Press, 1981). I owe a particularly substantial debt to White's study.

259 The scope and significance of the labyrinth motif in Joyce's work is well demonstrated in Egon Naganowski's monograph *Telemach w labiryncie świata* (Warszawa: Czytelnik, 1962).

260 I discuss this in greater detail in the introduction to the "Biblioteka Narodowa" edition of this book (Kraków: Zakład Narodowy im. Ossolińskich, 1974).

myths. Moreover, the term does not contradict the differentiations introduced by the critic but perfectly supplements them. Apart from novels that repeat myths (like Mann's *Joseph and his Brothers*, or Pavese's *Dialogues with Leucò*), White distinguishes: (i) novels in which the mythological story episodically overlaps with the modern one that constitutes the basis of the plot; (ii) novels set in contemporary times but reactivating the entirety of the mythological original; (iii) novels in which the mythological theme prefigures some element of the plot (e.g. a character or event) but does not encompass its entirety.[261]

There seems to be no reason against combining cases (i) and (iii) since they have more similarities than differences. As a result, we obtain two basic types of novels stretched on myth: in the first case the entire plot structure refers to the mythological model, and in the second – only some of its elements do so. The question of the extent to which a given work recalls a myth is important but does not exhaust the problem because this extent does not predetermine either the way in which the mythological counterpoint is introduced, or the meanings it is given.

It is beyond doubt that – as Eric Gould has indicated – *Odyssey* is not a simple paradigm repeated with some alterations.[262] This remark does not only refer to the work by Joyce – it is applicable in most cases of novels stretched on myth. Typically, the goal of adapting myths does not lie in mere repetition or the utilization of their accessible model for the purposes of composition. The fundamental matter always consists in the myth's visibility as a vehicle of meanings – a visibility that is either open and direct or formed like a gap (sometimes one that is difficult to notice), demanding from the readers a lot experience in reading texts that do not open up their meanings easily.

Obviously, this visibility is equally important in the case of the literary assimilation of the myth of labyrinth. In this case, however, it differs – or can differ – in that it does not have to involve references to the story as a factor that directly affects the plot's events. How are then references to labyrinth introduced into novelistic space? How is novelistic space positioned in relation to that other space which certainly belongs to archaic myth? One could answer that there are many ways. However, such a general and vague response could be not deemed satisfactory. Let us add then that some of them are quite simple.

Indeed, sometimes it suffices to merely use the word "labyrinth" to link some space to the mythical model, thus interpreting that space (and accordingly

---

261 John J. White, *Mythology in the Modern Novel*, pp. 52–54.
262 Eric Gould, *Mythical Intentions in Modern Literature*, p. 141.

directing the readers' attention). It is understandable that the word itself cannot always play that function, all the more so because it became widely used in most European languages, primarily as a metaphor, also in everyday use. In literature, it also appears in countless contexts and accidental phrases. This fact is certainly characteristic because it confirms how widespread the metaphor of labyrinth has become, making it firmly anchored in natural usage. However, this fact is not the subject of analysis here because this would lead nowhere. We shall only conclude that since such a role can be played a single word, references to the myth of the labyrinth stand apart from other references to mythological stories. It is not enough to say "Prometheus" to immediately recall the myth of a titan stealing fire for the benefit of humankind, or to say "Demeter" in order to momentarily activate the myth of changeable rhythms of nature. Still, the modest word "labyrinth" suffices to evoke appropriate associations.

Naturally, the matter is usually not limited to particular words. It is often the case that labyrinth-like spaces emerge as a result of open interpretation of places where the story is set, an interpretation offered either by the narrator, or – more often – by the characters. This is what happens in the above-mentioned episode from Mann's *The Magic Mountain*, titled "Satana," in which words uttered by Settembrini make Davos appear to be like hell, Hades, or precisely a labyrinth. This method of introducing references to labyrinth does not usually boil down to incidental analogies or explanations – evidence suggests that it is capable of imparting a general meaning on all spaces encountered in the work. In such cases, the protagonist views the world as a dark place (in all shades of this adjective): dangerous, enclosed and alienating, i.e., not allowing anyone to feel at home in it. In such cases, the world appears like a labyrinth, a territory where one is forced to go around in circles. In other cases, the novelistic space is presented as if it were a labyrinth from the very start, regardless whether characters become aware of this or not. Moreover, in each case, the fact of being "stretched on myth" can have a varying intensity and reveal itself to different degrees.

Nevertheless, there is one particularly "strong" method of introducing references to labyrinth that needs to be mentioned here. This method is referred to in theoretical accounts of novels using the French term *mise en abyme*, which has etymological roots in heraldry (one of its counterparts is work-within-a-work).[263] The myth of the labyrinth is introduced into some works through works

---

263 There are many theoretical works on this subject. "*Mise en abyme*" is discussed for example by Lucien Dàllenbach in *Le récit spéculaire (Essai sur la mise en abyme)* (Paris: Seuil, 1977).

of art that are discussed in it. Probably the most exceptional novel that employs such a technique is Butor's *Passing Time*. Its protagonist admires a cycle of eighteen tapestries depicting the story of Theseus in a museum located in Bleston where Butor's character arrives to spend one year. He also visits the cinema, where he watches a nature documentary about Crete. These works, especially the tapestries, become a specific leitmotif in the novel, affecting the way the protagonist thinks about himself and his position, as well about the place he has found himself in. As a result, they introduce a mythological dimension to this literary piece, making its case slightly different from other works "stretched on myth" discussed above. Parallels between mythological and contemporary history, between mythical space and the modern city, take shape in the consciousness of the character-narrator who describes his experiences, and before the eyes of the readers.

5.4 City

The main labyrinth found in contemporary literature – primarily in the novel – is the city. Such works leave no place for nature, and even if it does appear, this happens as a coincidence. Even in cases when this does not need special justification, nature is treated as a sort of peculiarity (sometimes critics speak of the "countryside novel," but nobody speaks of the "urban novel" because it is novel *tout court*). However, the city is never a neutral space, at least because it can be considered – as Lewis Mumford put it – to be "man's greatest work of art."[264] It is not a neutral space because it is saturated with meanings and constitutes a highly symbolic construction.[265] Clearly, writers who set their works in the urban environment cannot be indifferent to this.

Butor addresses the city as text.[266] In his perspective, this is viable because the city is always linked to inscriptions without which it could not exist. Those who are unable to read this writing find themselves – like a European in Tokyo, who does not know Japanese – in the situation of an illiterate person. Moreover, our understanding of the city depends, to a large degree, on various kinds of

---

264 After: Barclay Jones, "Prolegomena to a Study of the Aesthetic Effect of Cities," *The Journal of Aesthetics and Art Criticism* 4.18 (1960), p. 419.

265 This is underscored in the sociology of the city. See, for example, Raymond Ledrut in: *L'espace social de la ville* (Paris: Éditions Anthropos, 1968) and *Les Images de la ville* (Paris: Éditions Anthropos, 1973).

266 Cf. his essay "La ville comme texte" in *Répertoire V*. See also Lino Gabellone's essay under the same title, in: *Lingua e Stile* 2 (1976).

descriptions and accounts, which determine our understanding of the urban environment. A similar perspective is adopted by semioticians of the city, as in the case of Greimas's work quoted earlier.[267] Thus, the city is text, or discourse, and has its own poetics[268] because it is a signifying totality whose individual components are meaningful too. Thus, as Henri Mitterand argues, images of urban space found in narrative prose are not part of "geographical mimesis." Even when they are faithful, as he claims while discussing visions of Paris in a short story by Balzac, they depend on what is being said about the city in actual social practice. In this sense, "the novel is a topological meta-language of the second order" (second because it refers not only to the symbolic "language of the city" but also to the "discourse on the city").[269]

By making the city the space of their works, writers already operate in a domain that is deeply meaningful. One could even say that it is already ambiguous since the senses acquired by the city are not just varied but differentiated through contrasts, and full of irreconcilable contradictions. A city can be an "ecological niche" that protects humans from various dangers.[270] At the same time, however, it can concentrate in itself all kinds of dangers: being negative, alienating, and excluding any liberation. In short, it can be both a refuge and a hell-like labyrinth.

This ambiguity has accompanied literature ever since it became "urban." It surfaces already in Romantic poetry. Young Norwid – a poet for whom urban themes will play a significant role later[271] – gave vent to anti-urban passions with full force:

> I hate the city, I hate the shouting,
> The grand festivities and the brilliant lights
> [...]
> City – a gilded edge of the precipice!
> Stand there and look – a cold shiver
> Will shake your body from head to toe.
> City – a foretaste of hellish abandon.[272]

---

267 Algirdas Julien Greimas, "Pour une sémiotique topologique," p. 141.

268 Pierre Sansot, *Poétique de la ville* (Paris: Payot, 1971).

269 Henri Mitterand, *Discours du roman* (Paris: Presses Universitaires de France, 1980), p. 197.

270 See for example: Jean Duvignaud, *Le don du rien: essai d'anthropogie de la fête* (Paris: Stock, 1977), pp. 123–124.

271 See: Zofia Stefanowska, "Pisarz wieku kupieckiego i przemysłowego," in: *Literatura, komparatystyka, folklor* (Warszawa: Państwowy Instytut Wydawniczy, 1968).

272 Cyprian Kamil Norwid, "Wspomnienie wioski," in: *Pisma wszystkie*, vol. 1, p. 11.

Such aversion is not typically expressed as clearly and decidedly as in this case, usually assuming other shapes, following the "love-hate" model in which fascination can be very close to repulsion. Both emotions can have multiple causes, both philosophical and psychological.[273] Already at that point, however, i.e. in the middle of the 19th century, the city became a kind of a mythical space, both among writers representing the Romantic style and those leaning towards realism (it is not accidental that historians of literature speak of the myth of Paris, which appears in works of Victor Hugo and Honoré de Balzac). Thus, it was already at this point that city became a labyrinth, if not fully then through comparison. Indeed, labyrinth as a metaphor of a huge metropolis appears sporadically here and there. In the case of Paris, it emerged for the first time towards the end of the 18th century in a work by Sebastian Mercier.[274] One reservation needs to be made, however: comparisons to labyrinth do not always have to carry symbolic intentions as sometimes they might only be a way of accounting for certain properties of a given city in which visitors might get lost in the maze of streets. This happens for example in one of Kleist's letters, which contains an excellent, highly suggestive image of Würzburg.[275]

When the labyrinth appeared in 19th-century novels, it did not usually encompass the entirety of the city's space but functioned – as it were – as an episodic term (e.g. in a description of Coketown, a fictional city modelled on Manchester, featured in Charles Dickens's *Hard Times*[276]). A different situation presents itself in 20th-century prose, where the metaphor of the labyrinth almost always has a total character, not applying to this or that segment of the novel's space, but to

---

273 Mickiewicz's aversion to big cities stems – according to Zofia Stefanowska – from the fact that he was "a badly adapting provincial, for whom the very idea of city life was the opposite of nature" (Zofia Stefanowska, *Próba zdrowego rozumu: studia o Mickiewiczu* [Warszawa: Państwowy Instytut Wydawniczy, 1976], p. 169).

274 As reported in the overwhelmingly erudite book by Pierre Citron: *La poésie de Paris dans la littérature française de Rousseau à Baudelaire*, vol. 1 (Paris: Éditions de minuit, 1961), pp. 120–121.

275 Heinrich von Kleist, *Listy*, transl. W. Markowska (Warszawa: Czytelnik, 1983), pp. 113–115. This issue is also important in relation to paintings that present labyrinthine places as if in themselves. What I have in mind are old paintings from Siena, primarily by Ambrogio Lorenzetti. Seen today, their labyrinthine effects are explicit, although this seems to be justified in mimetic terms rather than symbolic ones.

276 For a discussion of Dickens's images of the city see: Raymond Williams, *The Country and the City* (New York, Oxford University Press, 1973), Chapter 15. The theme of the labyrinth, which recurs in Dickens's prose, is discussed by many critics.

the work as a whole. This is not only the case with books by Robbe-Grillet and Butor, where cities have fictitious names or have no names at all, but also with works of artists who have set their stories in places that are easily locatable on the map, sometimes even making them painstakingly and obsessively realistic. The global character of the metaphor of the labyrinth becomes clear once we become aware of the distinguishing features of Joyce's Dublin, Bely's Petersburg, Mann's Venice, Döblin's Berlin, Dos Passos's New York, Camus's Amsterdam, Durell's Alexandria, and Konwicki's Warsaw.[277]

The global character of the metaphor of city-labyrinth is not principally related in any direct way to what happens in that space, or at least this is not a crucial factor. Various terrible things happen in cities described by the naturalists, but these places have not typically become similar to labyrinth for that reason. For example, Zola's cities remain open against all odds.[278] The aforementioned global character manifests in the metaphor's structural character, i.e. not referring to that which can be only accidental, or to this or that part of space which would be treated as particularly tangled, unpleasant or dangerous. It is the city as a whole that constitutes the sphere of reference in this case, or – to put it differently – its design, understood as the basic and fundamental organization of space, which can seem entirely "devoid of any plan" from some perspective. It is no longer a question of "narrow courts upon courts, and close streets upon streets, which had come into existence piecemeal,"[279] and which themselves evoke labyrinth-related associations. They have not disappeared from our field of vision. On the contrary, newer prose addresses them more frequently and exhaustively than ever before. However, they have lost their particular character, ceasing to be enclaves that exist surrounded by rationally conceived zones one can grasp. What was a mere accident, and what was typical only of particular places or an individual district, has become radically generalized.

---

277 Tadeusz Konwicki is certainly the greatest writer of Warsaw in the 20th century, besides Miron Białoszewski. Labyrinth-related themes can be found in all of his novels set in Warsaw: from *Wniebowstąpienie* [*Ascension*] (1967) to *Rzeka podziemna* [*Underground River*] (1984). However, they have found fullest and most direct expression in the former work, one of the best Polish contemporary novels, which is still not as appreciated as it should be.

278 Michel Zéraffa claims that it was Baudelaire and the naturalists who began to portray the city in the way we now find discernible in contemporary literature. See his essay "Villes demoniaques," *Revue d'Esthetique* 3–4 (1977). The entire issue is devoted to urban aesthetics, and is characteristically titled "La ville n'est pas un lieu."

279 Charles Dickens, *Hard Times*, ed. G. Law (Peterborough: Broadview, 2000), p. 99.

Labyrinth became the blueprint of reality and its symbolic basis (let us also add – a plan without a plan). Through this fact alone it became the carrier and determinant of novel's crucial meanings. If the city acquires symbolic meanings thanks to its urban planning, then, of course, this process must be even more intense in literature. It is no accident that in all kinds of utopias cities are composed clearly and harmoniously. They are meant to match the new order in all aspects, expressing an undisturbed optimism and belief in a stellar future. A great example of this is provided by the urban projects from the period of the French Revolution.[280] Ideal cities know no closed spaces.

However, 20th-century fiction moved from utopia to dystopia. Novels have come to feature cities that have no clear-cut or rationally ordered spaces. These cities are governed by a different symbolic order, and this distinctness is highly significant, all the more so because it became generalized. Coming back to the main theme, the global reach of the discussed metaphor rests primarily in the fact that the labyrinth-like city is basically something more than just a city. Numerous studies on Joyce make claims that *Ulysses* and his other works present Dublin as a specific city-world. Fully embracing this argument, it should be added that although Joyce was a pioneer in this, implementing this equation with full, masterly consistency and achieving this goal on a massive scale, he was not alone in having done so. It seems that the literary construction of the city as the world has become something relatively common, despite being realized in many ways and with different consequences. The latter, however, remain outside the scope of this essay.

The city as the world was an unknown theme in the 19th century. It is for this reason alone that the symbol of the labyrinth could not become as widespread as it did in the 20th century. If the city, along with all that belongs to it – not only dark corners and winding thoroughfares but also broad alleys and clearly organized spaces (that seemingly have nothing to do with any maze whatsoever) – has become the world, the symbol of the labyrinth acquires universal features

---

280 They are the subject of an immensely interesting analysis done by Bronisław Baczko in " 'Od placu Rewolucji do placu Szczęścia…' Paryż wyobrażony czasów Rewolucji Francuskiej," in: *Archiwum Historii Filozofii i Myśli Społecznej* 23 (1977). See also the chapter "La cité géométrique" in Jean Starobinski's *Les emblèmes de la Raison* (Paris: Flammarion, 1973). Robert Klein even claims that city projects are always symbolic; see his "L'urbanisme utopique de Filarète à Valentin Andreae," in: *Le Forme et l'intelligible: Ecrits sur la Renaissance et l' art moderne*, ed. A. Chastel (Paris: Gallimard, 1970). Chastel argues that the utopian vision of the city first emerged before Thomas More's *Utopia* – namely in Antonio Avelino's (Filarete) *Trattato di architettura* (1460–1464). See: André Chastel, "La ville et l'utopie," *Le Monde* 8768 (23 March 1973).

too. This happens because it is no longer any particular place in the world (even a metropolis inhabited by millions) that becomes a labyrinth. It is the entire world that is seen as a labyrinth, which happens without Dublin ceasing to be Dublin (the same being valid for Venice and Berlin).

Thus, a city that is not considered to be like an ecological niche became the world in which life unfolds. It is not only the particular life of Leopold Bloom, Franz Biberkopf, or the figurines moving around Warsaw in Konwicki's *Ascension*, but life in general. The labyrinthine space of the city has something to do with allegory, although it differs from those allegorical spaces that appeared in mediaeval stories. One such departure would consist in that it is usually presented in a way suggesting the space's strictly empirical character, sketched in accordance with the principles of novelistic mimesis. However, this is not the most significant difference. It seems that another one is far more crucial. In historical allegorical stories, it was not only the space as a whole that had its second meaning but primarily its individual elements, which were endowed with distinctive senses and clear indications of value. In the labyrinthine space of the city-as-world things appear differently: its individual components may be entirely deprived of any additional meaning, not referring directly to anything outside it; nevertheless, such space would have a symbolic meaning as a whole. Even if one were to accept that we could speak of allegory in this context, it would be much more discrete and delicate than what we encounter in full-blown allegorical works.

These reservations pertain, to an even greater degree, to the characters who wander in such labyrinthine worlds. They are defined by the very fact of acting in an enclosed and internally twisted space. They cannot be indifferent to it as this space affects all their endeavours. This is where we see the emergence of the difference between the city presented in classic realism, and the labyrinthine city of modern fiction.

In realist prose, the city usually opens up all kinds of possibilities. This is what happens ("canonically," one might be tempted to add) in Stendhal and Balzac, or – with some divergences – in Dickens and Dostoevsky.[281] What emerges in those cases is a certain characteristic theme that recurs in various forms, namely through a young person arriving in a big city. The protagonist usually wants to

---

281 For a discussion of Dostoevsky's visions of the city see: Vladimir Toporov, "O strukture romana Dostoevskogo v sviazi s archaichnymi skhemami mifologicheskogo myshlenia" ["Concerning the structure of Dostoevsky's novel relative to archaic schemes of mythological thinking"], in: *Structure of Texts and Semiotics of Culture*, eds. J. Van Der Eng & M. Grygar (The Hague and Paris: Mouton & Co., 1972), pp. 225–302.

make a career and settle in the metropolis, but also – in some sense – bring it under control. This space, after all, is always one to be conquered, as if by its very nature; also, in cases when conquest fails, it remains the territory of basically unlimited mobility in psychological and social terms. This does not change even if the character's efforts do not lead to an aristocratic marriage, obtaining of wealth or political position, or even when they conclude with an outright defeat, as in the case of Stendhal's Julian Sorel or many characters in works of Balzac.

Heroes of novels in which the city becomes a world-labyrinth are not typically like Argonauts setting out to find the Golden Fleece – they do not earn anything, not even considering such goals but merely dealing with a welter of ordinary and usually banal things. At the same time, the theme of arrival at the city simply loses its former significance: even if it does not disappear, it degrades. Heroes are always already in the city, and even if they arrived there at some point in the past, it was so long ago that the novel does not offer any retrospection of these events, even when they reach back deep into their histories. They are in the city just like they are in the world. The city constitutes a space in which their lives unfold, and there is no escaping from it. This space is given once and for all, although one cannot conquer it and claim any mastery over it, not even in symbolic terms.

The city-world-labyrinth can have various hallmarks of the labyrinth. Sometimes they are very strongly marked, as in novels by Sábato, filled with tunnels and "underground sewers that form an immense, labyrinthine network stretching for thousands and thousands of kilometres"[282]; such a setting constantly reveals the "fetid labyrinth of incest and crime, slowly sinking once more."[283] The signs are not always as graphic as the above-mentioned ones. Sometimes they take the form of signals communicating that the novel describes places far removed from typical forms of urban space. For example, in one of Konwicki's works, it turns out that the square where the characters find themselves is actually "a labyrinth of squares assembled by the chaos of post-war life."[284] Elsewhere, the said signals may be even weaker, limited merely to allusions or brief mentions.

The urban space that becomes a labyrinthine world in the eyes of the characters is dominated by curved, twisted and variously tangled lines. This seems obvious as such space simply could not have any other properties. Moreover, its symbolic meanings appear clear too. However, what demands to be emphasized – and does

---

282 Ernesto Sábato, *On Heroes and Tombs*, transl. H. R. Lane (Boston: Godine, 1981), p. 354.

283 Ernesto Sábato, *The Angel of Darkness*, transl. A. Hurley (London: Jonathan Cape, 1992), p. 28.

284 Tadeusz Konwicki, *Wniebowstąpienie* (Warszawa: Iskry, 1982), p. 51.

not suggest itself easily – is its overcrowding. It is packed but not because of a flood of people. It is filled to the brim with things, usually scattered in disarray, regardless whether it is an interior space or an area generally accepted as open. This, however, does not stem from fear of emptiness but rather from an anxiety about accumulation and overload. This space – overflowing with random heaps of objects – is usually threatening. Its descriptions can contain significant catalogues:

> The traffic got snarled up, impeded and constricted by construction sites, cable laying, canalization pipes, concrete mixers, asphalt boilers. The snarl-up, the labyrinth, the knotty tangle, emblematic of losing one's way, of wandering and erring, the insoluble, inextricable knot, the ancients already had known the curse, had experienced the deception, found themselves ensnared, had lived it and thought about it and described it.[285]

This passage is important for the present discussion also because the writer introduces direct commentary, revealing the symbolism of this space, which is so rich in its chaos. It is in this kind of space, stuffed like an antique shop, that the character is forced to operate, although the supposed treasures turn out to be only oppressive pieces of junk. This is how the areas of such literary itineraries present themselves.

These peregrinations are peculiar to an extent that they cannot be reduced either to a journey that entails covering distant and basically unknown territories, or – for other reasons – to a wander. Wandering usually takes place in an approved space that appears friendly to the wanderers. They can be unhappy and at variance with the world, but their lack of adaptation is not projected on that space, even when characters employ spatial metaphors to express such a shortcoming.[286] Thus, even when they experience internal dramas, they do not necessarily have to be lost while wandering. The wandering figure also differs from the kind of person that Walter Benjamin refers to using the French term *flâneur*, notoriously difficult to render in translation.[287] *Flâneur* is not a plain

---

285 Wolfgang Koeppen, *The Hothouse*, transl. M. Hofmann (New York: W. W. Norton & Company, 2001), pp. 102–103 (e-book edition). As Georges Poulet aptly put it in "Piranesi i romantyczni poeci francuscy," "the theme of the labyrinth becomes the theme of people squeezing through crevices in thick matter" (p. 520).

286 For further discussion of the theme of wandering see for example: Bohdan Pociej, "Wędrówka," in: *Idea, dźwięk, forma. Szkice o muzyce* (Kraków: Polskie Wydawnictwo Muzyczne, 1972); Hanna Filipkowska, "Tułacze i wędrowcy," in: *Młodopolski świat wyobraźni*.

287 Walter Benjamin, "On Some Motifs on Baudelaire," in: *Illuminations* (New York: Harcourt, Brace & World, 1968); Walter Benjamin, "Paris, Capital of the Nineteenth Century," in: *Reflections* (New York: Harcourt, 1978).

stroller: navigating the crowd, he keeps looking for his own path and desires to remain himself. The hero of a labyrinth-based novel also does so – or at least has such potential – although accents may be distributed differently. Emphasis is placed here not on a search for some *itinerarium*, which would unquestionably belong to the character and guarantee that he retains his personality in the crowd. The most important aspect is that he has found himself in an alien space that cannot be tamed. It remains incomprehensible even when one becomes better acquainted with it.

Such wanderers could be arriving from an unknown city, which happens for example in Butor's *Passing Time*. This not a rule, however, as one can just as well wander in a home city or one that is already quite familiar. In Joyce's masterpiece, which has become the main model of such novels, it is Dubliners who wander through the streets of Dublin. Therefore, one's own space could also become untamed and unhomely. This is clearly on display in *Ulysses'* tenth episode – "Wandering Rocks" – which is often treated by critics as the culmination or a specifically condensed synthesis of the entire work.[288] Regardless of any circumstances, a hero of this type is an alien or a stranger, just like in a poem by Borges:

> The letters and the telegrams once sent,
> he wanders through the indeterminate streets,
> noticing oddities of no importance,
> thinking perhaps of Aberdeen or Leyden,
> more real to him than this labyrinthine grid
> of crossing streets, with no complexities,
> wherever it leads him, loose time of a man
> whose real life lies elsewhere, and far away.[289]

Wandering in the city becomes the main labyrinth-based theme, while the city itself – the embodiment of alienating space. The hero can feel this alienation and grows aware of it even when he faces only a "labyrinth of straight lines." Most often, however, the city constitutes a tangle of streets that are not lined in accordance with any ordering idea: maze-like streets do not really lead anywhere. In one of his essays Roland Barthes claims that the structure of Western cities, which feature a distinguishable centre, originates directly from Western metaphysics, which always assumes "the middle as the place of truth."[290] The concentric structure of cities is, therefore, a question of certain order, not only a strictly spatial

---

288 See for example: Egon Naganowski, *Telemach w labiryncie świata*, pp. 94–95.
289 Jorge Luis Borges, "The Stranger," in: *Selected Poems*, ed. A. Coleman (New York: Penguin, 2000), p. 219.
290 Roland Barthes, *L'empire des signes* (Genève: Skira, 1970), p. 44.

one but also philosophical. It is precisely in the labyrinth-based novel that this order is questioned. This also happens when novels are concerned with real cities that implement this idea of order. Still, questions of mimesis do not play a major role here, or are even bereft of all significance. What used to be called the "city's physiology" in the 19th century is no longer of interest here – it rather becomes important how the characters perceive urban space, not limited by a purely encyclopaedic knowledge of it. Moreover, attention is shifted to symbolic meanings carried by the object in question. In such cases, the centre, which was supposed to guarantee some kind of order, does not really differ from the fringes, peripheries or outskirts. A striving towards the centre does not equal aspiring to order and clarity as the centre is not different from any other spatial components – there is simply no centre in the city, just like there is no centre of the universe. It is not distinguished in any sense insofar as it belongs to the great space of wandering. Geometry – which, as Jean Starobinski argues, is the "language of reason in a world of signs"[291] – has no bearing in here. Those who wander in the labyrinth of streets and squares do not notice any sign of geometry – on the contrary, the space of wandering contradicts rationalized geometrical orders, even when it does not sink in chaos.

Any kind of space can become the space of wandering. It suffices to treat it as unclear, chaotically filled with various elements, or enclosed in some sense. Characters in labyrinthine novels could argue that to a certain extent they themselves create the space in which they move, providing it with specific qualities that vary depending on how one sees it, feels it, and behaves in it. All in all, spatial visions are not – let us emphasize again – subject to mimetic rules, not even when there is mention of particular places that have their firm place on the map and are filled with details rendered with meticulous precision. Such visions depend on a more or less open or mediated interpretation, and cannot be separated from it. The hero is not just in a certain situation and therefore in a certain space, but also reflects on it. In this sense, coming back to the article by Kuntz, the myth of the labyrinth is a philosophical myth. At stake here, however, is not the finding of solutions but the becoming aware of one's position and interpreting it – learning about one's situation and all that contributes to it. This also involves the city itself, which is both a labyrinth and the entire world.

In such novels wandering or roaming becomes the human condition. Among such works, we find Joyce's *Ulysses*, the model and masterpiece of this kind of prose, Marek Nowakowski's *Worms* [*Robaki*], Patrick Modiano's *Missing Person*, Sábato's

---

291 Jean Starobinski, *Les emblèmes de la Raison*, p. 59.

On Heroes and Tombs, and numerous works representing the *nouveau roman*. If these works contain overt references to the myth of the labyrinth, it is usually emphasized that the novel's protagonist differs from Theseus in that he or she lacks the Ariadne's thread.[292] There is no escaping from the labyrinthine city-world, and nothing could facilitate such a flight. Those who wander aimlessly, who are – as it were – doomed to wander, cannot leave the place where fate placed them.

The labyrinth-like city is leading one into a corner. Considered as a chthonic space, it constitutes – to employ a metaphor coined by Italo Calvino – a "city of the rat" that is never the "city of the swallow."[293] It imprisons, limiting the freedom of movement. It is this aspect that makes the 20th-century labyrinthine novel different from realist fiction, where the city could be strange or even hellish, but never really weighs down on the characters so much, branding them so profoundly. The walls do not just limit one's possibilities but are aggressive, regardless whether they belong to splendid buildings or meagre ruins that bear only a distant memory of former glory. In this alienating space where one can only wander around, characters are not just incapable of finding a guide, but fail to establish any communication as all interpersonal contacts become impossible in the deepest sense. This question, a broad and hugely significant one, shall be touched upon further.

Lastly, the status of the alienating city-labyrinth can vary. Sometimes it is ascribed unquestionable reality (often regardless of the subjective perspective from which we see it), and sometimes it is not clearly defined, occupying an uncertain space between reality and vision. At other times, it creates a specific oneiric reality, as in the following passage from Robbe-Grillet:

> Before I fall asleep the city once more rears before my pallid face, my features marked
> by age and fatigue, rears high before me, far behind me, all around as far as the eye
> can see, blackened walls, mutilated statues, twisted iron work, ruined colonnades
> whose giant shafts lie smashed amidst the debris. I am alone. Walking at random.

---

292 This is a popular motif. See for example Eugène Ionesco's remarks about Kafka's world
     as a labyrinth in which Ariadne's thread does not help anyone (*Notes et contre-notes*
     [Paris: Gallimard, 1962], p. 231). Emily Zants argues that the "new novel" offers an expe-
     rience of the labyrinth without any saving thread (*The Aesthetics of the New Novel in France*
     [Boulder: University of Colorado Press, 1968], p. 57). The idea is in fact older. In his notes
     to the poem "Source" ["Źródło"], Norwid writes: "—In this labyrinth of insolent crime / in
     the labyrinth of political crimes one's mind is lost: there is no thread here to follow / —All
     stands musty with halted progress—" (*Pisma wszystkie*, vol. 11, p. 384).
293 Italo Calvino, *Invisible Cities*, transl. W. Weaver (New York: Harcourt Brace Jovanovich,
     1978), p. 154.

Wandering, as if at random, among the unrecognizable fragments of what were pala-
tial homes, public buildings, private residences, gaming houses and houses of prosti-
tution, theatres, temples, and fountains. I am looking for something. It is beginning
to get dark. I cannot quite remember what it was. Can it really have been a prison? It
seems unlikely.[294]

5.5 Prison

We might follow Robbe-Grillet by asking the same question: "Can it really have
been a prison?" City – out of its nature closed, alienating and paralyzing – certainly
becomes much like a prison, or – like Denmark in Hamlet's nervous vision – actually becomes it. This is the case for example in William Blake's poem "London":

> I wander thro' each charter'd street,
> Near where the charter'd Thames does flow.
> And mark in every face I meet
> Marks of weakness, marks of woe.
>
> In every cry of every Man,
> In every Infants cry of fear,
> In every voice: in every ban,
> The mind-forg'd manacles I hear[295]

The city is described here with the help of prison-related metaphors. Blake is not
the only author to have done this. At least since Romanticism, this metaphor
is distinguished by great dynamism and broad range.[296] The genius behind this
invention, however, was not a writer but a visual artist – Piranesi – whose influence on literature has been huge.[297] City could become a prison[298] but it could

---

294 Alain Robbe-Grillet, *Topology of a Phantom City*, transl. J.A. Underwood
(New York: Grove Press, 1977), p. 10.

295 William Blake, *The Complete Poetry and Prose of William Blake*, ed. D. V. Erdman
(Berkeley: University of California Press, 2008) pp. 26–27.

296 This topic is taken up extensively and interestingly by Victor Brombert in *La prison
romantique. Essai sur l'imaginaire* (Paris: José Corti, 1975), where he discusses French
Romanticism. This part of my essay owes a lot to Brombert's book.

297 Piranesi's influence on literature is discussed by Luzius Keller in *Piranèse et les poètes
romantiques* (Paris: José Corti, 1966), and by Georges Poulet in "Piranesi i romantyczni
poeci francuscy."

298 This is also true for realist prose. The transformation of an industrial city into a
prison in Władysław Reymont's *Ziemia obiecana* [*The Promised Land*] is analyzed
by Magdalena Popiel in the essay "Od topografii do przestrzeni mitycznej: analiza
przestrzeni w 'Ziemi obiecanej' Reymonta," *Pamiętnik Literacki* 4 (1979).

equally be the whole world. Prison itself is a labyrinth, or a part of it.[299] It has its own architecture, comprised of dark corridors, dungeons and cellars, windowless cells, etc. Its function is obvious and does not require any explaining. It outright determined the character of this symbol and its literary uses. Prison is an archetype and – as it were – a synthesis of all enclosed space.[300] One reservation needs to be made here. Since times immemorial, prisons have played an important role in social life, history, and – in its own way – culture[301] where it has always been the subject of narration and description. However, in stories about the fate of imprisoned authors it is never a symbol and never acquires generalized meanings – it simply constitutes one of the parameters characterizing the terrible experience. This happens basically independently of the period in which such accounts were produced: from Silvio Pellico's *My Prisons*, which relates his experience of Austrian casamates, through Kazimierz Moczarski's *Conversations with an Executioner* [*Rozmowy z katem*] and Aleksander Wat's *My Century* [*Mój wiek*], as well as other, numerous prison-related accounts. The experience of being confined is in itself so terrible that it does not need any further symbolic additions. In non-fiction prose, which communicates personal experience, prison is only a prison – this is sufficient.

Things are different in the case of fiction, where prisons acquire – as if on their own – certain symbolic meanings. This is encountered in all literature, regardless of style and period, perhaps with the exception of the least ambitious adventure stories meant only to provide easy entertainment. It seems that the horribleness which decided about prisons being nothing more than prisons in non-fiction determined the symbolic character of poetry and narrative pieces. This is also true of realist prose, which (at least seemingly) avoided direct symbolism, as in the case of Dickens. However, it is precisely in works of this author – as Northrop Frye observed[302] – that the prison is transformed into a labyrinth, which in turn becomes a symbol of the society that limits individual freedom. Furthermore, the same can be said about novels by authors who have developed prison-related

---

299 It was already Plutarch who compared the labyrinth to a prison (quoting people of Crete). See: Paolo Santarcangeli, *Księga labyrintu*, p. 118.

300 Erving Goffman, "On the Characteristics of Total Institutions," in: *Asylums: Essays on the Social Situation of Mental Patients and Other Inmates* (New York: Anchor Books, 1961).

301 See Michel Foucault's *Discipline and Punish: The Birth of the Prison*, transl. A. Sheridan (New York: Pantheon Books, 1977).

302 Northrop Frye, "Dickens and the Comedy of Humors," in: *The Victorian Novel: Modern Essays in Criticism*, ed. I. Watt (Oxford: Oxford University Press, 1971).

themes through references to their own experiences. A good example of this is Jean Genet's *Notre-Dame-des-Fleurs*, a work in which the metaphor of labyrinth appears as well ("The labyrinth is more tortuous than the summing-up of judges"[303]). This case proves – it seems – that the demands of literary fiction, which raises the empirical to the rank of a symbol, are greater than the pull of personal experience. Thus, symbolization has become an unavoidable point in the rulebook of literature.

The theme of the labyrinth-like city foregrounds aimless wandering in an enclosed space – one that is limiting and restrictive. The quality of being enclosed, however, can have varying degrees: the prison is a kind of space whose isolated character precludes wandering (which demands at least a minimum of freedom) or makes it epiphenomenal. In the theme of the prison – treated either as an independent labyrinth or its part – it is the absolute closing off that acquires a dominant position because in this case the walls are literally entrapping. This "literalness" becomes, in turn, the subject of a symbolic generalization. As Sartre claims,

> [...] man is closed inside and does not cease to be related to all these walls that surround him, and never forgets that he is bricked up there. All these walls create one prison – this prison is life [...].[304]

Brombert adds:

> Sartre, the teacher of freedom, is obsessively attracted, it seems, to the metaphor of imprisonment.[305]

The author of *No Exit* is not isolated in this. It appears to be almost a rule that the more a writer is concerned with freedom, the more often he or she employs the metaphor of prison.

Before proceeding to discuss this paradox (or perhaps only an apparent paradox), one more issue needs to be addressed. We have approvingly embraced the claim made by Colette Guillemard that all labyrinthine stories involve characters moving along mistaken paths – they cannot ever see the labyrinth from one perspective only. Naturally, prison precludes any shifting of the point of view but does not seem to question what is crucial for the labyrinth, confirming to be its subtype.

---

303 Jean Genet, *Our Lady of the Flowers*, transl. B. Frechtman (New York: Grove Press, 1987), p. 131.
304 From *Critique de la raison dialectique* (1960); after: Victor Brombert, *La prison romantique*, p. 189.
305 Ibid.

However, what emerges in this context is a theme most clearly connected to the entire complex of labyrinth-related ideas, one that somehow links imprisonment to movement. It is the theme of being trapped on a ship, or of the prison ship as a floating jail. Its history extends pretty far back into the past, perhaps even to ancient adventure romance. It may also be related in some way to the mediaeval theme of the ship of fools, which also recurs in various forms (suffice to mention Milos Forman's *One Flew Over the Cuckoo's Nest*). Its modern history begins, however, with Edgar Allan Poe's *The Narrative of Arthur Gordon Pym* (1838). Stories by the American Romantic writer abound in labyrinthine spaces in many forms.[306] This particular tale about a ship that turns into a clink for the eponymous hero occupies a particularly prominent position. A similar theme of a prison ship appears in novels by Jules Verne, as well as in contemporary works, e.g. in Julio Cortazar's *The Winners*, which combines elements of psychological insight, the novel of manners, and the poetics of allegory. First and foremost, however, this theme is encountered in Teodor Parnicki's historical novels. His monographist – Małgorzata Czerwińska – titled one of her book's chapters "Imprisonment and journey":

> Despite the seeming contradiction between the two terms, both spatial images were combined by Parnicki into a single theme. We can easily recall how often his heroes are put in prison: Łukasz, Mr de Puertocarrero, Atanazy and Typotius in *A New Fairytale* [*Nowa baśń*], as well as Leptynes in *Circles in the Sand* [*Koła na piasku*]. However, there is such a diversity of kinds of imprisonment: arrest in a ship cabin aboard the "Concord of Nations"; a guarded palace of the hostage Chozroes, and the hideout of the hunted Markia (in *Word and Body* [*Słowo i ciało*]); Papal palace chambers in Avignon, where Stanisław is locked in *Only Beatrice* [*Tylko Beatrycze*]; castle ruins surrounded by military forces in the desolate mountains of the Caucasus (in the third volume of *The Face of the Moon* [*Twarz księżyca*]); a chamber bricked-up from outside (in *Aetius's Death* [*Śmierć Aecjusza*] and *Kill Cleopatra* [*Zabij Kleopatrę*]). The perfect place of imprisonment is always the inside of the ship: in such context, characters in novels by Parnicki have a particularly clear feeling of seclusion and isolation, in which they are cut off from the outside world and the broader society. If being trapped on a ship that is lost in the vast seas provides a better sense of isolation than any other kind of imprisonment on land, then how much clearer it has to be in the case of a ship hidden *under* the water's surface! Thus, "Nautilius" – where the protagonists of *Identity* [*Tożsamość*] find themselves – would be the perfect model of enclosed, isolated and finite space.[307]

---

306 This is particularly emphasized by Bernard Marcade in "Pour une psychogeographie de l'espace fantastique: Les architectures arabesques et grotesques chez E. A. Poe," *La Revsue d'Esthetiqsue* 27 (1974), pp. 41–56.

307 Małgorzata Czermińska, *Teodor Parnicki* (Warszawa: Państwowy Instytut Wydawniczy, 1974), p. 187.

Such floating labyrinths are nevertheless a highly specific and isolated phenom-enon. The most typical symbol of complete and absolute imprisonment is still a landlocked jail, surrounded by thick walls, containing windowless cells locked from outside, and extending deep underground, where dungeons and sometimes torture chambers are located. Such prisons may take various forms: constructions drilled on rocky islands that are inaccessible due to high security; strongholds, citadel or old castles, in comparison to which the castles of Otranto from Walpole's Gothic novel appear gentle and welcoming; and finally, buildings erected in accordance with the period's latest architectural rules of functionality and rationality. Such details do not tend to affect the theme's symbolic develop-ment. Prisons acquire secondary meanings simply through being enclosed: not because of their spatial development but solely by virtue of their function.

At this point we can return to the main theme – that of freedom and impris-onment. However, there is more to it than a simple juxtaposition of a space that allows for freedom of movement and a space that prevents it. Such contrasts have a fundamental function in non-fiction, but in fiction they become generalized. This is also because prisons are often treated in the latter case not as a place of temporary isolation, but a symbol of the human condition. As Krasiński wrote in one of his letters:

> Life is a plaiting of compulsions. Human freedom is only internal and ideal – not external and real! While in prison, I can still retreat from slavery in spirit, but not with my body. That is why one's dignity is not hurt when surrounded by prison walls – it would suffer only if the spirit accepted these walls and respected them. More or less all of life's situations are such prisons. Power and happiness can be found only when the internal, ideal freedom perfectly matches the outside one – when the latter embodies the former so that both are equal. However, it is not usually a question of will but God, prov-idence, fate, or coincidence! Within my power, there is only my spirit, but not my body or the world! I have to keep making spiritual efforts to guide my body, and successfully struggle with the world.[308]

The opposition of freedom and imprisonment finds a model form in Krasiński. The walls that surround people do not have to be the walls of any particular prison. Life and world are the prison here, while freedom can be found primarily by not succumbing in spirit to all that limits the individual – by resisting the "plaiting of compulsions." Krasiński lends a universal, almost heroic dimension to the disagreement with imprisonment, acknowledging the moral significance of rebelling and fighting. Byron does the same in the first stanza of the "Sonnet on Chillon" that precedes the long poem *Prisoner of Chillon*:

---

308 Zygmunt Krasiński, *Listy do Delfiny Potockiej*, vol. 1, p. 279.

> Eternal Spirit of the chainless Mind!
> Brightest in dungeons, Liberty! thou art:
> For there thy habitation is the heart—
> The heart which love of thee alone can bind;[309]

Here, freedom is primarily an internal value. Those who end up in prison are the ones who cherish this value to the greatest degree. One peculiar feature of Byron's long poem – a great monologue on the horrors of life in the casamates – is that it develops no clear opposition between enclosed and open space, the world inside the walls and one outside them. They both resemble a prison, so the prison located at the Geneva Lake is only one particular manifestation. After so many years there is no point in escaping as it would lead only to another prison. One can only miss the sight of the Alps. Thus, the space of imprisonment is somewhat basically domesticated:

> These heavy walls to me had grown
> A hermitage – and all my own!
> And half I felt as they were come
> To tear me from a second home:
> With spiders I had friendship made,
> And watched them in their sullen trade
> Had seen the mice by moonlight play,
> And why should I feel less than they?[310]

The poem's intellectual premise seems paradoxical: the Byronic monologist – rebel and victim of persecution – has psychologically domesticated the space of the prison, claiming it as his own, because he had come to the conclusion that the entire universe is, in fact, a prison. This space – approved only because "the whole earth would henceforth be / A wider prison unto me" – is not, however, "his own" space in the ordinary meaning of the phrase. It constitutes, as it were, solely a point that he had grown accustomed to, one located in the vast expanse of strangeness.

Byron's paradoxical perspective does not diminish in any way the functioning of the "space of dead emptiness" as an existential metaphor, or even magnifies its prominence. Prison – a station in the world's labyrinthine structure, where no one alights out of their own will – not only positioned itself as the opposite to freedom but also became an occasion to express the attitude of pursuing freedom. This is also true when it turns out the prison is not just one particular

---

309 George Gordon Byron, *The Prisoner of Chillon, 1816* (Oxford: Woodstock, 1993), p. 1.
310 Ibid., p. 21.

space, surrounded by thick walls and covered by buildings whose main function is to prevent movement, but simply the universe itself.

The architecture of prisons can be sometimes fantastic, unusual and Piranesian, but they nevertheless always have to serve their primary function. A good example of this is contained in Borges's story "The God's Script," where the labyrinth acquires a whole range of forms:

> The prison is deep and of stone; its form, that of a nearly perfect hemisphere, though the floor (also of stone) is somewhat less than a great circle, a fact which in some way aggravates the feelings of oppression and of vastness. A dividing wall cuts it at the centre; this wall, although very high, does not reach the upper part of the vault [...]. A long window with bars, flush with the floor, cuts the central wall.

However, this is not an ordinary sphere of isolation and suffering, unique among others of this kind that are more welcoming to people. The architecture of the prison, as fantastic as it may seem, is the architecture of the world:

> A man becomes confused, gradually, with the form of his destiny; a man is, by and large, his circumstances. More than a decipherer or an avenger, more than a priest of the god, I was one imprisoned. From the tireless labyrinth of dreams I returned as if to my home to the harsh prison.[311]

A prison that is both labyrinth and world does not leave any place for rebellion. It weighs down on man and destroys him, doing so in the most ruthless way of all the labyrinths constructed in literature since Romanticism, even though it never had its own Piranesi.

5.6 The labyrinth of Babel

Regardless whether labyrinths take the form of cities or prisons, they neither support communication nor facilitate favourable conditions for establishing contacts, thus precluding dialogue. Such spaces do not only limit but paralyze movement, restricting exchanges and consequently all relations with other people. "I am alone," every inhabitant of the labyrinth could say, repeating after the protagonist of the novel by Robbe-Grillet. This remains true not only when there is literally no one around, but also in situations when one is in a crowd or among the few others who are also wandering or remain locked up. One could say – borrowing a phrase from E.T. Hall – that the labyrinth is always a "sociofugal

---

311 Jorge Luis Borges, "The God's Script," transl. L. A. Murillo, in: *Labyrinths. Selected Stories & Other Writings*, eds. D. A. Yates & J. E. Irby (New York: New Directions, 2007), p. 166 & 168.

space."[312] It is such, however, not as a result of individual choice – it simply could not be otherwise. Walls separate the protagonist from other characters even when they enter a seemingly free conversation; there is no ground for it to become a deepened exchange of opinions or experiences, one that would lead to the development of a shared mental universe. This space is sociofugal not because one avoids conscious contacts in it, but because they are impossible to establish. It is sociofugal to a very high degree, effectively being the space of misunderstanding.

In this, it is like the Tower of Babel[313] – the kind in which languages are mixed not only among tribes but also in individuals. Here, two images blend: that of a tower containing people from whom God has taken their common language, and that of a labyrinth. This mixture is not recent but old. Charles Baudelaire touches upon the Tower of Babel in one stanza of "The Parisian Dream," equipping it with features typical for labyrinths:

> Babel of endless stairs, arcades,
> It was a palace multifold,
> Replete with pools and bright cascades
> Falling in dull or burnished gold.[314]

Certainly, he is not the first author to do so. Although it may be difficult to ascertain whether he had forerunners in literature, it seems to be beyond doubt that he could base on a strong tradition in painting. I have not come across any works discussing iconographic themes and representations related to this building that symbolizes the mixing of languages (I do not know whether such studies exist). However, even when applying a casual and amateur perspective basing an incomplete and fragmentary material, one can argue that such iconography does exist. There is the famous painting by Pieter Bruegel, although a single work – even an unquestioned masterpiece – cannot be the basis for claims about iconographic conventions. Still, it appears that many Flemish and Dutch paintings do present the Tower of Babel in a way similar to that adopted by Bruegel.[315]

In painterly visions, the Tower of Babel takes the form of a truncated cone, in some sense deformed, irregular, departing from those architectural images

---

312 Edward T. Hall, *The Hidden Dimension* (New York: Anchor Books, 1990), p. 108.

313 For more information on the labyrinth and the Tower of Babel see: Paolo Santarcangeli, *Księga labyrintu*, p. 212.

314 Charles Baudelaire, "Parisian Dream," in: *The Flowers of Evil*, transl. J. McGowan (Oxford: Oxford University Press, 1998), p. 207.

315 See the paintings: Maerten van Valckenbroch, *Tower of Babel* (1595, Old Masters Picture Gallery, Dresden State Art Museums) and Hendrick van Cleve, *The Building of the Tower of Babel* (Rijksmuseum Kröller-Müller, Otterlo).

in which order and harmony come to the fore. The very choice of a cone is significant because it had special symbolic meaning in the Middle Ages and subsequent epochs. "The perfect world," Keller writes, "is represented by a sphere, while an imperfect one – by a cone."[316] This naturally does not exhaust the matter. The cone that represents the Tower of Babel as belonging to an imperfect world is not any ordinary cone. It was not evenly truncated – instead of a roof or top there are many asymmetrically arranged levels, cragged and yet without towers that would signify a symbolic path to heaven. Moreover, the whole structure is perhaps slightly yet clearly slanted, possibly contradicting the rules of architecture. Still, could it have been any different if its task is to symbolize human fate after the Fall, made so problematic by the expulsion from Eden?

There is more. The Tower of Babel, or at least its image preserved in European imagination by Bruegel, consists of countless windows, or rather holes. These "openings" have different shapes and sizes. Positioned in diverse ways, they do not seem to follow any rules of symmetry, and certainly do not constitute "windows onto the world" that would facilitate learning about what lies outside the building. They are rather "channels of communication" in a world where all human communication has been rendered impossible. Each of those openings speaks in a different language, making this space again one of misunderstanding. In this case, the discussed effect is perhaps achieved more clearly than anywhere else.

Analogies to the labyrinth suggest themselves almost automatically. Would it not be possible to imagine a syncretic entity named "the Labyrinth of Babel"? Both spatial images share certain features although the labyrinth is rather horizontal, while the Tower – out of its nature – clearly vertical. Both question the ordered structure of the world, lending asymmetry a symbolic meaning. In a space that is difficult to master, because the marked-out paths or corridors do not lead to a clearly defined point, one cannot establish any communication. In turn, in a space where no communication is possible because everyone speaks in a different language, one cannot help but wander. In both, it is not only the case that there is no one who could provide the information as to which path to choose, but it is also impossible to pose that very question. The Labyrinth of Babel could be a secluded place, an isolated negative space, but may also be generalized – like the labyrinthine city or prison – and become the world itself. This can be observed on a woodcut by an excellent Dutch graphic artist M.C. Escher, titled *Tower of Babel*. In works of this artist, the theme of the labyrinth recurs obsessively, while the labyrinth-like Tower

---

316 Luzius Keller, "Piranesi i mit spiralnych schodów," transl. M. Dramińska-Joczowa, *Pamiętnik Literacki* 1 (1976), p. 259.

becomes the symbol of a world drowning in chaos. According to Redekop's study devoted to the representations of labyrinth in Borges and Escher, this woodcut is a sort of a counterpart to Borges's "The Library of Babel"[317]:

> The universe (which others call the Library) is composed of an indefinite and perhaps infinite number of hexagonal galleries, with vast air shafts between, surrounded by very low railings. From any of the hexagons one can see, interminably, the upper and lower floors. The distribution of the galleries is invariable. Twenty shelves, five long shelves per side, cover all the sides except two; their height, which is the distance from floor to ceiling, scarcely exceeds that of a normal bookcase. One of the free sides leads to a narrow hallway which opens onto another gallery, identical to the first and to all the rest. To the left and right of the hallway there are two very small closets. In the first, one may sleep standing up; in the other, satisfy one's fecal necessities. Also through here passes a spiral stairway, which sinks abysmally and soars upwards to remote distances. In the hallway there is a mirror which faithfully duplicates all appearances.[318]

If Piranesi were not preoccupied with fantastic prisons but rather took to imaginary libraries, he could envision one of them in this way. However, this is not of primary importance here. In Borges's story, the library did not only become cosmos. When equalled with the Tower of Babel, it turned into a special space of misunderstanding. This is made all the more characteristic and telling because the library constitutes – out of its very nature – a space of communication, even when it equals the universe. Its transformation into the stony reality of the labyrinth is not, however, an idea that originated with Borges.

This concept appears in a Polish novel, published exactly thirty years before "The Library of Babel" was written: *Snowy Crop [Ozimina]* by Wacław Berent. The idea was later developed too, for example by Umberto Eco in *The Name of the Rose* (1980).[319] Finally, it made episodic appearances, among other places in José Lezama Lima's *Paradiso*. In *Snowy Crop*, it is a private library that metamorphoses into a labyrinth in which a professor from Kraków finds himself towards the end of a party:

> The electric lamp blinked, as if it were connected to the wiring responsible for turning off lights in other rooms. Lost in a labyrinth of shelves and startled from reverie by the impulse, he hears the regular beating of hooves indicating that the last carriage just took off from the gate. Everyone left. He was completely alone, forgotten by all in this labyrinth of books.[320]

---

317 Ernest H. Redekop, "Labyrinths in Time and Space," *Mosaic* 13 (1980), pp. 97–113.

318 Jorge Luis Borges, "The Library of Babel," transl. J. E. Irby, in: *Labyrinths*, p. 62.

319 See the article by Wojciech Skalmowski titled "Biblioteka," in: *Tygodnik Powszechny* 13 (1983), p. 8.

320 Wacław Berent, *Ozimina* (Kraków: Zakład Narodowy im. Ossolińskich, 1974), pp. 160–161.

These are not just irreverently used metaphors – the library-labyrinth plays an important role in the creation of the space developed in this novel. The metaphor finds its continuation:

> He recovered and – having banished shadows from before his eyes, and bleak thoughts from his head – began to search for a way out from the maze of shelves. Finally, when he left the labyrinth's tangled paths, the pearly dawn revived his sight […].

Later, the narrator speaks of a "maze of library shelves." Admittedly, the labyrinthine space of the library we encounter in Berent is not particularly threatening or generalized. It defines the situation in which the protagonist of this episode finds himself, indirectly referencing certain complexities of Polish culture. However, it is beyond doubt that it too constitutes a specific domain of misunderstanding. The Kraków professor wanders in the maze-like library on his own, and is aware of his loneliness, not only because the sounds of the party have faded, but primarily because he has spent all his evening submerged in those noises.

In a world that becomes a lot like the Tower of Babel or a labyrinthine library, it is language itself – as a means of communication – that develops into a labyrinth too. One could suspect that this is an accidental metaphor that does not deserve special attention. However, it seems that the situation is actually quite the opposite, which is confirmed by the fact that "labyrinthine" can refer not just to the complex structure of the linguistic system, but rather to language as the fundamental and basic component of the human condition in total. Therefore, in such an account language would constitute a labyrinth not just because it is so difficult to embrace its structure, but because it marks out labyrinthine paths through its own particular functioning. As Wittgenstein remarks:

> Language is a labyrinth of paths. You approach from *one* side and know your way about; you approach the same place from another side and no longer know your way about.[321]

Thus, language creates various paths that may lead – equally probably – right to the target or astray. In this sense, I lose orientation when I look at a specific place from a different perspective, when I frame it using different categories, or – in a nutshell – call it differently. All space is dependent on how we address it, as a result of which all space can be labyrinthine.

Language's labyrinthine character was also discussed by a thinker representing an entirely different philosophical tradition than Wittgenstein – Georges Bataille.[322]

---

321 Ludwig Wittgenstein, *Philosophical Investigations*, transl. G.E.M. Anscombe, P.M.S. Hacker & J. Schulte (Oxford: Blackwell, 2009), p. 88e (emphasis preserved).

322 Georges Bataille, "Le labyrinthe," in: *Oeuvres complètes*, vol. 1 (Paris: Gallimard, 1971).

In the essay "Le labyrinthe," he argues that because being is mediated through language, humans use it to learn about everything, including themselves. Consequently, human world has the structure of a labyrinth. Even if the linguistic labyrinth[323] does not determine the world-labyrinth, it certainly co-creates it.

It could be assumed that the linguistic labyrinth, or language as one of the major components contributing to the labyrinthine structure of the world, is discussed primarily by those who remain distrustful and suspicious of language, those who do not believe it could be an adequate means of cognition, securing what we could call easy communication. This idea – even if it is not consciously acknowledged – simply has to have a special relation to literature, which has turned the vision of labyrinth into one of its major themes. In a labyrinth it makes no use to even pretend that language is transparent or that words correspond to things – it is impossible to fantasize about speaking directly and clearly. All belief in easy communication is ruled out. If we accept that the labyrinth has developed its own rhetoric, then it would be characteristically one of darkness, one that questions even itself. This clearly reveals a similarity between the labyrinth and the Tower of Babel.

Naturally, in a labyrinth one does not question the social character of language. This is impossible even in a space developed so peculiarly. Language functions in it in such a way that particular idiolects cannot enter into full contact with others, as if they became separated to a high degree – as if each speaker leaned his or her head out of one hole in the Tower of Babel, articulating something incomprehensible to those popping their heads out from neighbouring openings. The space of misunderstanding strongly manifests here its properties.

Sometimes ordinary misunderstandings occur in this space. In a stunning essay, David Daiches demonstrates that in older literature misunderstandings (including verbal ones) were treated as the point of departure in comical scenes, not only in comedies. However, already at the very beginning, he makes the reservation that today things are different:

> One of the most frequently discussed themes in modern literature throughout the whole western world is alienation. Not only does the artist often feel himself alienated in our society: every individual, in virtue of his individuality, is seen as locked in his private consciousness and so unable to communicate adequately with his fellows. This is felt as a dilemma, often a tragic dilemma.[324]

---

323 This metaphor was employed by the famous philosopher of language Max Black, who used it in the title of his work *The Labyrinth of Language* (New York & London: Frederick A. Praeger, 1968).

324 David Daiches, "Misunderstanding as Humour: An Aspect of the English Comic Tradition," in: *More Literary Essays* (Edinburgh: Oliver & Boyd, 1968), p. 19.

A fundamental change has occurred. It seems as if one register were replaced with another, contradictory one. The inability to establish contact not only ceased to amuse anyone but has acquired a different meaning, becoming the expression of human existence. This is completely different from any transformation of the criteria of comedy or sense of humour. Former comical characters – who were not only the focus of a series of misunderstandings (often specially arranged) but would also become their victims – could be seen today as truly tragic figures.

Let us consider the eponymous character from Molière's comedy *Monsieur de Pourceaugnac*. This provincial from Limoges – not in his early youth anymore – arrives in Paris to marry a fair, young and dowered girl. He falls victim to an intrigue meant to prevent the marriage, as well as to many situational and verbal misunderstandings. The good-natured stranger does not know the rules of the capital and cannot communicate with anyone in Paris due to his small-town intellectual categories. He is abused by dishonest doctors, and even imprisoned (Erast, the fiancée's admirer, tells the physician: "I particularly recommend you not to let him slip out of your hands, for at times he tries to escape"[325]). This poor Pourceaugnac does not meet with any empathy or even a shade of understanding. Moreover, from beginning to end he is a comical figure embodying all features of the traditional character of an unfortunate suitor.

Let us imagine a contemporary writer adapting the story of *Monsieur de Pourceaugnac*. Despite the same, equally conventional ingredients, the meanings would be completely different. The big city would not be treated anymore either as a favourable or even neutral space, but would become threatening and alienating. The stranger from Limoges would no longer be a naïve provincial, who takes whatever happens around him at face value, but would rather acknowledge the situation he has found himself in, and feel his strangeness, problematizing it in some way or another. The whole story could be told only from his perspective – not from an objective one and certainly not through the eyes of the scheming tormentors. They would in turn become dangerous persecutors, or the embodiment of fate, while imprisonment would turn from a humorous episode into a special instance of alienation. In such an account of Pourceaugnac's story we would find key elements of the labyrinthine world: hostile metropolis, imprisonment, and the utter inability to communicate with others. The comic character of an unfortunate suitor would seem to stand before judgment. Thus,

325 Moliere, *Monsieur de Pourceaugnac*, transl. C. H. Wall (Project Gutenberg, 2004). Online: http://archive.org/stream/8prnc/8prnc10.txt (accessed 26 April 2017).

the world of comedy would slip, with baffling ease, into a reality straight from works of Kafka.

Let us return to the main theme: the mixing of languages. In Molière, Pourceaugnac's inability to communicate with anyone is – according to Daiches – the source of comedy. In Kafka, or anyone else who would want to develop a similar theme in a 20th-century work, such comical quality would completely evaporate. Nobody wants to laugh in the labyrinth, also because the actions, gestures, and thoughts of those who have found themselves in it cannot be presented from the outside. In the context of a labyrinth, language either ceases to be a means of exchange or allows for it only to a very slight degree. It serves to deliver monologues, rather than to enter any dialogues.

Among writers whose works develop settings that are modelled on, or resemble labyrinth, the themes of misunderstanding acquire various positions in the hierarchy of importance. As it turns out, among Latin American prose writers they play a smaller role, whereas in representatives of the *nouveau roman* they perform an important function, especially in Robbe-Grillet and Butor. It is difficult to discern what determined such a distribution of emphases though it may be quite meaningful that – as it seems – a major context for *nouveau roman* was created by existentialism. Although this philosophical current may have been indeed rejected by the "new novelists," literature often finds itself in a close relationship with those styles, currents, trends, and ideas that it programmatically and consciously undermines. The world becomes a Tower of Babel of idiolects.

This happens in Butor's *Passing Time* or – perhaps, to an even greater degree – in Robbe-Grillet's *Dans le labyrinthe*. The language of the protagonist (who is usually identical with the narrator) becomes distinct; in it, we may observe the surfacing of various categories that are not shared by others. In the labyrinth, a specific anti-rhetoric is being developed: words are – as it were – doomed not to reach their addressees. Whereas visions of labyrinth-like cities are dominated by the theme of wandering, and visions of prisons feature a sense of being trapped, in accounts of spaces of misunderstanding it is the theme of alienation that comes to the fore. All three combined form the image of the modern labyrinth, at the same time indicating two further aspects: the internal labyrinth and labyrinth as a form of speech.

5.7 Internal labyrinths

Borges writes:

A man sets out to draw the world. As the years go by, he peoples a space with images of provinces, kingdoms, mountains, bays, ships, islands, fishes, rooms, instruments, stars,

horses, and individuals. A short time before he dies, he discovers that the patient labyrinth of lines traces the lineaments of his own face.[326]

Labyrinth never creates an intimate space but can be treated as if it constituted an expression of the human internal world, as if there were no boundary
between where one is and what one carries inside. Thus, one is inside a labyrinth (*only* there in extreme cases, or just to a certain extent in less radical
accounts) because one's interior is labyrinth-like. One cannot liberate oneself from the labyrinth because there is no basis to lift oneself from the maze
(especially this kind of maze!). It is only possible to project it outside and
shape reality by taking oneself as a model. If one acknowledges the existence
of the internal labyrinth, one at least knows what world he or she lives in, and
what this life entails, which allows problematizing one's position. Failing to do
so, one falls victim to illusions, making mistakes that could have been avoided.
In one work by André Gide, Daedalus, the designer of the Cretan labyrinth,
comments on the terrible fate of his son Icarus by saying that he "could never
escape from the labyrinth, and did not understand that the labyrinth was
within himself." "He thought," Daedalus continues, "that he could only escape
by way of the heavens, all terrestrial routes being blocked." [327] Icarus, as we
learn from his father, had mystical inclinations ("The infinite calls me!") and
miscalculated his potential to soar high. By relating to Theseus the story of his
son, Daedalus expresses the main idea of Gide's work. Theseus's account does
not constitute only a report of his descent into the labyrinth, where he achieved
what he desired, and returned with the help of Ariadne's thread. It is a story
of a journey into the internal world. This internalization of the labyrinth[328] is
all the more discernible in this case because the narrative constitutes – at least
seemingly – only another version of the myth in its classical form. Such internalization can assume different shapes, and have varying degrees of intensity.

The weakest version – a liminal one, one could argue – is encountered whenever space is not introduced simply as a labyrinth but appears to acquire its
features, for some reason, in the eyes of characters.[329] For example, one may

---

326 Jorge Luis Borges, *Collected Fictions*, transl. A. Hurley (Harmondsworth: Penguin,
      1999), p. 327.
327 André Gide, *Oedipus and Theseus*, transl. J. Russell (London: Secker & Warburg, 1950),
      pp. 91–92.
328 This is discussed by interpreters of Gide's last work, for example by Enrico Garzilli in
      Circles without Center.
329 One could speak, in this context, of labyrinthine epiphany: at a sudden glance,
      the labyrinth is transformed into an ordinary and banal space, undistinguished

have deemed it alien or ungraspable, as a result of which it became obscure. This happens in one section of *Cosmos* by Witold Gombrowicz[330]:

> I even walked into the kitchen on some pretext to check up on Katasia's mouth one more time. But the trouble was that there was so much of everything, the labyrinth was expanding, lots of things, lots of places, lots of events, isn't it so that every pulsation of our life is composed of billions of trifles, what is one to do? That's it, I didn't know what to do.[331]

It would seem that this perspective is not original in any way, simply being part of the repertoire of techniques found in the modern novel, where space is presented in the way it appears in the protagonist's consciousness. This, however, is a slightly different case, at least for two reasons. Firstly, the labyrinth "was expanding" (not just "being" in a static way) in the novel's setting, which was never enclosed despite being limited. At the same time, it constitutes a domesticated space to those occupying it. Thus, in this case, the labyrinth is, as it were, a temporary space, directly dependent on the state of the character's consciousness. Secondly, this dependence became openly articulated and clearly problematized before the eyes of the reader. Drawing on Antoni Kępiński, one could say that the lived space comes to dominate over the real one.[332]

To repeat, in the above-quoted passage from *Cosmos* we observe the first stage of that process. A more advanced one comes to light when the narration develops variously shaped correspondences between labyrinth treated as an unquestionable or even objective spatial configuration, and labyrinth as one's intimate property, a structure that organizes the space of the internal world. In the face of this, two answers are possible: either one lives in the labyrinth and moves inside it because one carries it deep within, or one's internalized space is labyrinthine because one finds him- or herself surrounded by the labyrinth from all sides, doomed to wander in it, unable to escape regardless of any possible attempts. The two answers differ primarily in how they distribute accents.

---

in any way. One suggestive account of such an epiphany is found in the April 1938 section of Julien Green's *Diary 1928–1957* (New York: Harcourt, Brace & World, 1964).

330 The space of this novel is analyzed, among others, by Janusz Pawłowski in the essay "Przestrzeń w 'Kosmosie,'" published in the volume *Przestrzeń i literatura*.

331 Witold Gombrowicz, *Cosmos*, transl. D. Borchardt (New Haven: Yale University Press, 2005), pp. 91–92.

332 Antoni Kępiński, *Melancholia*, pp. 73–75.

The shaping of the relationships between the outer and inner labyrinths does not seem to be guided by rules indicating a causal relationship between the two, nor do they form a parallel. Such procedures would be too easy. What can be rather observed is the blurring of the boundary between the outer and inner labyrinths, between one's inside and his or her surroundings. Consequently, what emerges is a homogeneous world, a peculiar labyrinthine totality. One example of this would be Butor's *Passing Time*, where the protagonist-narrator moves freely from introspection to description and can thus present, without hindrance, the many sides of his labyrinth.

In such a homogeneous world, the ontological status of the labyrinth becomes principally uncertain. Where is it really located? Do the winding corridors and stairs exist in the novel's reality, or were they born in a delirium of the protagonist, who does not care about the truthfulness of his accounts in the world he inhabits? Readers of labyrinthine novels must often ask themselves such questions. Characters themselves do so, for example in the aforementioned novel by Bely:

> After twenty years my bit of strange dreams had become reality…—
>
> —(maybe the labyrinth of our rooms is reality; and – reality is a snake-legged monster: the *reptile Uncle Vasya*; maybe: the incidents with the old woman are arguments with Afrosinya the cook; the hurricanes of the red world are the stove in the kitchen; the whirling torches are sparks; I don't know: it could be…)
>
> The fellow student laughed.[333]

It is true that in Bely's work such questions have special justification insofar as it features a game between the consciousness of a child and that of the narrator – between the aspiration to present the world naively and the necessity to conceptualize it. The issue is not limited to such cases. The problematic character of the labyrinth was given the most elaborate expression in Robbe-Grillet's novel *Dans le labyrinthe*.[334] Gérard Genette claims that it is impossible to differentiate in this work between scenes set in contemporary reality, and

---

333 Andrey Bely, *Kotik Letaev*, pp. 31–32.

334 This has been the subject of numerous analyses, including Bruce Morrissette's "Le dédale de création romanesque: 'Dans le labyrinthe,'" in: *Les romans de Robbe-Grillet* (Paris: Éditions de Minuit, 1963); Stephen Heath, *The Nouveau Roman: A Study in the Practice of Writing* (London: Elek, 1972), pp. 137–152; Betty Rahv, "The Labyrinth as Archetypal Image of the New Novel," in: *From Sartre to the New Novel* (New York: Kennikat Press, 1974), pp. 99–148; Pierre A. G. Astier, *La Crise du roman français et le nouveau réalisme*, pp. 288–289.

ones that are remembered or imagined.[335] Moreover, it is impossible to establish the ontological properties of the labyrinth, which fills the novel's entire space. Therefore, one cannot ascertain where it is granted undoubted existence and where it could be considered to be a product of the characters' delirium. One thing, however, is certain: the labyrinth cannot be separated from the protagonist because he is the reason for its existence. It is in this sense that the maze is "internal."

However, this occurs on a different basis than in *Theseus*. In this work, published shortly before his death, Gide makes his excursion into the labyrinth refer to a journey deep inside oneself (akin to journeys made into the middle of the earth in literature from the turn of the 19th and 20th centuries). Even if it is not an allegorical journey, the kind that was eagerly practiced in mediaeval writings, it certainly welcomes such an interpretation. Still, such a reading cannot be applied in any way in the case of works like those by Robbe-Grillet. This is impossible because in these novels the external labyrinth is not a representation of the internal one, and does not symbolize it. Entirely different kinds of relations are established here. In Gide's prose, the existence of the labyrinth as something real and as a symbol is unquestionable. However, it can be doubted in the case of Robbe-Grillet because in his works the labyrinth is created as a projection of the protagonist's personality – it is his expression and a consequence of his cognitive acts or sometimes perhaps the outcome of basic, dispassionate observation. Therefore, labyrinth would function in a way suggesting that it rests on several ontological principles at the same time. Here, differently than in myth or in works that remain faithful to its fundamental narrative structure, no excursion is made into the labyrinth: in this case, one *is* the labyrinth and carries it inside him- or herself.

Moreover, the labyrinth is provided in this variant with yet another dimension: a temporal one. The labyrinth of time is not only a literary idea consisting in the translation of the concept of maze from one sphere to another. This subject is also tackled in works that analyse social images of space.[336] Existing and functioning in a different way than any ordinary labyrinth, its temporal subtype becomes – as it were – a second-order metaphor. Literary protagonists can always assume that the labyrinth which takes the form of the city, prison, or even the Tower of Babel is distinguished – even when it is born in a delirium – by

---

335 Gérard Genette, "Vertige fixé," [postface to:] *Dans le labyrinthe* (Paris, Collection 10/18, 1964), p. 282.

336 Abraham Moles & Élisabeth Rohmer, *Psychologie de l'espace*, pp. 234–235.

an unquestionable existence, as a result of which it can exist apart from the characters even when it is clearly the creation their minds. The temporal labyrinth is a different case because it is formed in a mental act whose facticity cannot be suppressed or regarded as having a minor significance. Thus, the temporal labyrinth cannot be ascribed the kind of existence that a spatial one has because it is born only due to one's specific way of thinking about time, the way of getting to know it, or the way in which one feels lost in it.

As a rule, the temporal labyrinth does not exist independently but is always linked to the labyrinth whose original model was Daedalus's construction. Butor's *Passing Time* is often mentioned above as an example of a great labyrinthine novel. However, if one is to give credence to the confessions of the author himself, its development was fundamentally shaped by Butor's experiences from Manchester – primarily his sense of being lost in time:

> This is why the theme of the labyrinth is so important in this book. It is not only a spatial labyrinth (the classic one, constructed by Daedalus to give shelter to the Minotaur, and later solved by Theseus thanks to the thread given to him by Ariadne) but also a temporal one; the entire book is a labyrinth inside time, with the thread of sentences performing the function of Ariadne's thread.[337]

This temporal dimension of the labyrinth naturally emerges not just in this novel. For example, it holds great prominence in Robbe-Grillet's *Dans le labyrinthe* or in works of Sábato. Butor's self-commentary presents the phenomenon in great detail and carries a further implication to which I shall return later. In the meantime, it needs to be emphasized that the "labyrinth inside time" can only be an internal labyrinth because it depends on a clearly subjective perspective.

The internalization of the labyrinth took the clearest and often purest form in poetry. One explanation of this could be that poetry is free from constraints that stem from the novel's very nature and cannot be rejected even in those works that programmatically depart from classic forms of fiction. Poetry simply does not have to introduce the labyrinth into broader conventions related to narration and storytelling. Labyrinth is, in this case, a purely internal space. In an untitled poem, Urszula Kozioł writes:

> By closing our eyes we open up darkness
> and formlessness envelops us
>
> up a thread
> attached to the wall of a breath

---

337 Georges Charbonnier, *Entretiens avec Michel Butor* (Paris: Gallimard, 1967), pp. 98–99.

we climb
toward the possibility
of a skein
not knowing if it's been given to us

fingers percuss
fingers hurt themselves on sounds
fingers retreat burnt by too close a signal

"the awesome figure
whose centre's everywhere and circumference nowhere"
lives also within us[338]

Poetry, especially that of the 20th century, has developed something like an original internal geometry, as well as a specific internal architecture. However, such geometry and architecture are not indifferent constructions, but ones that surround from all directions and – just like the tears in the poem "Wall" ["Mur"] by Tadeusz Różewicz, which develops the theme of being trapped – "lodge deep in our bodies."[339] Here, unlike in early modernist poetry of the Young Poland movement, there is no descent – the theme of introspective exploration, aiming to find something that would be reminiscent of a bleak chthonic space, has been abandoned. This happened as if it were not necessary to travel into the depths in order to discern the labyrinth within oneself, or at least some of its elements. Just like the wall in the poem by Różewicz, or the "awesome figure" from Kozioł's poem, the labyrinth is everywhere and encompasses all, not really demanding any special exploration.

In Polish poetry, the most consistent development of the theme of an internal labyrinth can be found in late poems by Mieczysław Jastrun, beginning – it seems – from the volume *Geneses* [*Genezy*] published in 1959.[340] This theme takes numerous forms in his works, determining the shape of the surrounding

---

338 Urszula Kozioł, *Poems*, transl. R. Grol-Prokopczyk (Austin: Host Publications, 1989), p. 67.

339 Tadeusz Różewicz, "Mur," in: *Poezje zebrane* (Kraków: Wydawnictwo Literackie, 1957), p. 374. Originally published in the volume *Poemat otwarty* [*Open Poem*].

340 I have written about it more extensively in a review titled "Metafora przestrzeni zamkniętej," *Twórczość* 6 (1959). My view was then questioned by Jacek Łukasiewicz, who claims that the space found in Jatrun's poetry is basically open; see: Jacek Łukasiewicz, *Mieczysława Jastruna spotkania w czasie* (Warszawa: Czytelnik, 1981), pp. 447–448. Nevertheless, I abide by my diagnosis because to my mind the entire body of Jastrun's work from the last 25 years of his career abounds in visions of enclosed spaces.

reality, and – primarily – creating a bleak space of the subject and becoming perhaps a fundamental existential metaphor[341]:

> Still the same landscape of the labyrinth.
> The inside of the ear with eardrum, anvil and malleus.
> The iris of an eye in which seeing is realized.
> There is no exit.
> There is no key.
> There is no key to the precipice.
> There is no star that opens the heavens.
> I am doomed to myself.
> There is no exit.
> […]
> Slaves to their own existence,
> Living on a daily rate,
> Walking the circle's circumference,
> Prisoners of the Great Circle.[342]

"There is no exit" – this theme appears particularly often in visions of internal
labyrinths. One just cannot wander around in it like in a city – it rather imposes
itself mainly because, like the strictest prison, it renders escape impossible. In the
poem "Light from Another World" ["Z innego świata światło"], which concludes
Jastrun's last volume of poetry, an exit appears but there is no doubt as to what
it means:

> A steep staircase opened beneath me
> leading to a tunnel underground
> where letters
> on the wall spelled
> the saving phrase: "Way Out."[343]

There is no doubt here because the poem imposes only one interpretation. The
saving exit is simply death. There is no point in dotting the i's here by adding
that such an "exit" is ironic, all the more so because death was never considered

---

341 Jastrun, who has developed the theme of the labyrinth so interestingly, is also the
author of an essay titled "Labyrinth" included in the volume *Mit śródziemnomorski*
(Warszawa: Państwowy Instytut Wydawniczy, 1962). Unfortunately, its conclusions
are lofty yet banal.

342 Mieczysław Jastrun, *Genezy* (Warszawa: Państwowy Instytut Wydawniczy, 1959),
pp. 87–88. Part of the cycle *Milczące monologi* [*Silent Monologues*].

343 Mieczysław Jastrun, "Light from Another World," in: *Polish Poetry of the Last Two
Decades of Communist Rule: Spoiling Cannibals' Fun*, eds. & transl. S. Barańczak &
C. Cavanagh (Evanston: Northwestern University Press, 1991), p. 17.

to be a good solution for exiting the labyrinth. Accordingly, the labyrinth itself would become the space of death. Examples of this are numerous – it suffices to recall the already quoted poem by Miłosz ("Those Corridors") or lyrical works of Aleksander Wat.

This also pertains – perhaps crucially – to the internal labyrinth. After all, this metaphor has not been used, almost as a rule, to convey psychological subtleties and complexities, but rather to foreground existential meanings. It speaks about the internal situation and, simultaneously, about one's position in the world – the fact of being closed off from many directions at the same time.

5.8 Labyrinthine storytelling

So far, my discussion of 20th-century literary labyrinths did not account for the ways in which they are introduced, as if it were an irrelevant issue unworthy of closer analysis. However, one cannot help but ask whether certain tendencies are not revealed in this area, and whether such narrations involve specific forms and situations that have crystallized along with the frequently recurring visions of labyrinths, which ceased to be spaces of adventure and became spaces of life, soaking up many, often profoundly important meanings. Have there developed independent forms of narration and description? Or: Is there a representing labyrinth distinct from the represented one? Have there emerged specific ways of labyrinthine discourse? Naturally, the labyrinth related to speech phenomena is only a metaphor and one that functions differently than the entire maze theme since it has been adapted to the sphere with which it has not come into contact before. Although this metaphor may seem risky here, we shall not abstain from answering the above questions.

Let us begin by recalling that the category of the labyrinth was used in relation to storytelling already by Krasiński. In a letter written shortly before the Spring of Nations, or "in the eve of revolution" as he put it himself, he was addressing the great Berlin political trial in which many death sentences were passed. He wrote:

> It would be worthwhile, I repeat, to quickly write and publish a few words in order to explain the matter at hand – just a few because they bring back to the public the forgotten horrors. This should also be done anonymously so as not to harm the reputation of the authors. The public craves for solid and systematic accounts of these crimes. Many have found it difficult so far to make sense of all the threads in this labyrinth.[344]

---

344 Zygmunt Krasiński, *Listy do Delfiny Potockiej*, vol. 3, p. 502.

Admittedly, the reference to labyrinth is made here in passing, but it is never-theless worth attending to. According to Krasiński, labyrinth could be likened to a story that is full of holes, inconsistently composed or simply incoherent – one in which readers cannot tie the threads together and find out about their interrelations. In a nutshell, the labyrinth indicates lack of clarity, one that has not been assumed in advance but stems from external circumstances, as the poet has made clear. Such cases cannot be passed over, although they are not the focus of the present discussion.

This is because in such a perspective labyrinth may refer to any complicated narrative that appears obscure and impenetrable, regardless of its subject matter. The questions that need to be posed are different. How are labyrinths narrated? How are they described? At first, it seems paramount to acknowledge that taking up this theme does not immediately entail selecting a particular narrative form – this is not about formal designation. Whatever happened in the laby-rinth can be narrated in different ways, even without disturbing the linearity of successive events or of narration, as is, for example, the case with the traditional picaresque novel. There can be no doubt, however, that 20th-century labyrin-thine novels are not as simple as a handshake. They reveal a strong tendency to narrate the complex labyrinthine structures (in which the unfolding events are usually not fully logical) in a way that corresponds to their complexity. Thus, it might be concluded that there exists something like "labyrinthine storytelling" or "representing labyrinth."

We would generally encounter it in narrative works, particularly in novels. Short lyrical pieces are different insofar as the labyrinth does not constitute a component of the story and rather becomes part of the general imagery, somehow functioning like its other elements. It could be the subject of descrip-tion, meditation or allegory. However, a specific distinction needs to be made in poetry, one that often imposes itself: speaking about the labyrinth, and speaking in the labyrinth (or from inside it). Of course, one does not automatically involve the other, but – as a rule – the "speaking in the labyrinth" has to be somehow thematized, even delicately or indirectly, in order to make it discernible to the readers. Otherwise, the properties of the labyrinth may appear to be not only unmotivated but also dysfunctional.

Narrative works basically follow the same principle. Thus, in order to discern the properties of labyrinthine writing they have to be linked with the theme of the labyrinth, although this mode of narration constitutes a broader phenom-enon that can appear in works that touch upon diverse matters. This issue shall be tackled later because in some cases the discreetly thematized labyrinthine quality of narration turns out to be a more influential factor in developing the vision of the labyrinth than the labyrinthine components of the world represented in the work. At this point, it might be only ascertained that narrative works, especially novels, feature broad and diverse possibilities for thematization, at least because of the very scope of the work's structure, whose volume can seem almost limitless in this matter.

It seems that such thematization should be considered in broad terms, including all, even extremely subtle and indirect references to labyrinths. In this perspective, the phenomenon referred to earlier as narration "stretched on myth" – crucial in contemporary fiction – functions (or at least can function) as a thematizing factor. Sometimes all it takes to emphasize the labyrinthine nature of fictional space and draw the readers' attention is to make a single reference – not even to the entire myth but to its single element, or even one characteristic detail. As much as it is of great import, the quality of being "stretched on myth" is not a specific indicator of labyrinthine prose because most 20th-century novels that refer to mythology share that attribute.

Here, the key factor is not speaking *about* myth but speaking *in* myth, or – to put it differently – with the help of the myth. In contemporary literature, the myth of the labyrinth cannot be narrated from outside just like one narrates a "good old" story. Nor can this be done in the moralizing mode that sets up an example or facilitates easy allegorization. In order to speak about the labyrinth one needs to be inside it. This principle remains in force in contemporary literature probably without exception. That is why the labyrinth has become something more than a theme – it turned into an existential situation, consequently one of speaking.

What does it mean, however, to "speak from the inside of the labyrinth"? At this stage of the discussion, it becomes permissible to state – without bothering about details, and refraining from additions and reservations – that it means speaking in and from a space that can be considered alien, and consequently dangerous and impenetrable. Moreover, this space is often compared to the Tower of Babel. In this situation, all traditional rhetoric becomes obsolete as it assumes not only establishing direct communication with the ones addressed but also retaining clarity of the form used to do so. However, in a space that itself becomes a stress-inducing factor, such directness and clarity cannot be relied upon. No speeches are made in the labyrinth, and no distance can be secured – the kind that is typical of traditional epic accounts. The rhythm cannot be stately and undisturbed, while the voice cannot be balanced and free from stammering as in the case of a singer performing a showpiece aria.

The above points relate in equal measure to the narrator and to the characters. In many instances, it is difficult to strictly demarcate the two, not only in the case of first-person narration. Still, one thing remains certain: although the labyrinth is not a factor that determines the characters in an absolute manner, it is bound to influence their behaviour and ways of speaking. It does not leave space for characters such as ones developed in classic realist novels – ones that have a continuous biography (even if only some episodes are reported in the story) and a consistently sketched psyche. There is no room for them because the labyrinth does not accommodate any classical features. Thus, in the 20th century references to this classical myth have helped shape a literature that is programmatically anti-classical, also in the terms of its modes of expression.

When we consider the "speaking in the labyrinth," the discussion is not limited to words uttered by individual characters, who have found themselves inside it for one reason or another, and are unable to leave it despite such attempts – words that have become "calls from the depth." Entire works also have to be considered because in one form or another, more or less directly, they speak about the individual inside the maze, and can be likened to the labyrinth. This is the case with James Joyce's *A Portrait of the Artist as a Young Man*[345] and *Ulysses*, Borges's short stories, as well as novels like Donoso's *The Obscene Bird of Night*, or Sábato's *On Heroes and Tombs*, and finally – numerous works representing the *nouveau roman*.[346] In Polish literature this is certainly encountered in Konwicki's *Ascension*. Thus, we are dealing here not only with works that are built on the myth of the labyrinth, but also with books that themselves become labyrinths of some kind.

If we were to scrutinize the basic properties of those novels where the labyrinthine quality is elevated to the rank of a formal principle – properties that do not have to appear *en bloc* in every work that could be classified as labyrinthine – it would be necessary to begin with the specific construction of time. In the discussion of labyrinth as internal space attention was drawn to its temporal dimension. It seems fitting to return to this subject now and consider it from another perspective.

In broadest terms, the labyrinth is not only a spatial category, but also a temporal one, as is pointed out in Butor's confession quoted above. The labyrinthine aspect of time means that it is so complex and multi-layered that both the protagonist and the narrator are unable to control and grasp it. However, it is

---

345 Egon Naganowski, *Telemach w labiryncie świata*, p. 71.

346 See the above-mentioned studies by Astier, Zants, and Rahv, as well as numerous reviews and articles that accompanied the publication of these novels.

not a question of time slipping away. If this were the case, it would be difficult to speak of labyrinthine consequences. Instead, analogies could be drawn with impressionistic moments that cannot be seized and prevail over any forms of lasting. The point is that those fleeting moments as well as longer stretches of time (i.e. "duration") overlap in a way that precludes any direct subordination of one to the other. Just like the labyrinth *sensu stricto* usually distorts any traditional configurations of space, in this case deformation affects those temporal relations that we deem to be obvious attributes of "normal" time. Continuity disappears and perspective is distorted, not allowing to order the stream of time, reveal its direction, and indicate the dimensions of its constituent parts. Finally, this kind of temporality – again, just like the spatial labyrinth – looms over the novel's entire world and weighs down on those who have been affected by it. Such temporality is making one feel trapped even though it is not the great time of history measured in epochs. In this respect, it does not differ from traditional temporality found in novels that do not know long duration.

One of the main factors that decide about the labyrinthine quality of time is that its ontological status remains uncertain. We witness the blurring of the boundary between "objective" and "subjective" time – the time in which characters live, and one they experience at a given moment. Shaped in this way, time cannot remain linear, just like the labyrinthine space is not patterned in any straightforward way. Clear analogies can be discerned here: time is fragmented into corridors that twist and turn, and whose relations question everything that would be linked to the images of the world organized in accordance with rules of geometry.

The fact that time lacks ontological clarity has profound significance and is directly linked to another property of labyrinthine storytelling, namely something that could be termed as the indeterminacy or mutability of modal frameworks in which the novel's events are presented. In classical narration, storytellers do not allow themselves (or readers) to have any doubts in this matter. It has to be clear whether a given event belongs to what we assume to be the reality represented in the work, or to the protagonist's imagination, constituting his or her hypothesis, supposition or speculation. Naturally, since the times of Cervantes classical novels relate dreams or whatever else that seems to appear before the character's eyes, but such situations are clearly marked. The labyrinthine novel, however, works differently. The modal framework supposed to indicate what region of the novel's reality the depicted element belongs to, or to inform directly about this, is not clear and in many cases becomes entirely blurred. Naturally, this process not only affects time but can also govern everything, including the labyrinth itself. In some cases, the boundary between the labyrinth that could be the subject of some "report," and the labyrinth born in the protagonist's dreams or hallucinations cannot be determined at all, entirely obliterating the modal frameworks that formerly served as the basis for orientation. As a consequence, readers are supposed to find themselves inside the multifarious ontological labyrinth along with the characters. This radical solution was implemented by Robbe-Grillet in the novel I often refer to here.[347] In this and similar cases it seems legitimate to speak not of the labyrinth as a theme or motif, but of work-as-labyrinth.[348]

In works that could be classified in this way, all linearity is questioned – in both story and plot. Certainly, the subject itself does not entail this – taking it up does not have to lead to such consequences. This is inevitable, however, when the labyrinth becomes a formal principle – one that goes beyond any technical solutions developed in the course of the novel's evolution. To quote T.S. Eliot,

> History has many cunning passages, contrived corridors
> And issues, deceives with whispering ambitions,
> Guides us by vanities.[349]

This happens not only when "history" is considered in broad, grand terms, but also when it refers to humbler events of smaller scale, as well as to stories in which they are reported. The "cunning passages, contrived corridors" no longer belong with the described objects but become elements of storytelling itself. Perhaps this is what Maurice Blanchot intended to convey in the enigmatic passage on "storytelling characterized by labyrinthine movement."[350]

Such "labyrinthine movement" manifests, firstly, in the breaking of those rules of continuity and coherence that were, as it seemed, inviolable within the art of narration. This disobedience is many-sided because it involves both the sequencing of the facts that form the subject of the account and the perspective or point of view from which these facts are presented. Secondly, it manifests

---

347 Genette discusses this in the essay quoted above.

348 This is what Borges does in "The Garden of Forking Paths" when he equates labyrinth, book and novel: "In all fictional works, each time a man is confronted with several alternatives, he chooses one and eliminates the others; in the fiction of Ts'ui Pên, he chooses – simultaneously – all of them. He creates, in this way, diverse futures, diverse times which themselves also proliferate and fork" (transl. D. A. Yates, in: *Labyrinths*, p. 40).

349 Thomas Stearns Eliot, *Collected Poems 1909–1962* (New York: Harcourt, Brace & World, 1963), p. 30.

350 Maurice Blanchot, "Le secret du Golem," in: *Le livre à venir* (Paris: Gallimard, 1959), p. 112.

without leading to any clearly formulated meanings and facilitates such modelling of signification that can either make senses unclear or eliminate any conclusive messages. Moreover, it does not impose anything on the readers. Anyway, after they are acquainted with the labyrinth's interior this could not even be possible. At this point, we approach a certain paradox, one that is crucial for labyrinthine literature: although it is mainly fascinated with enclosed spaces, which it takes as its main subject, by doing so it moves closer to the formula of an open work, in the sense given to the term by Umberto Eco.[351] "Labyrinthine movement" does so also because, by developing a vision of such space, it does not offer any guidance meant to aid the readers in orienting themselves in the tangle of twisting corridors, backstreets, or roads leading nowhere. Ultimately, the "openness" of the work allows emphasizing the enclosed character of the space depicted in it.

At the same time, this precludes any allegorization of the labyrinth. This is particularly worth underlining because narratives of journeys in alien and alienating spaces could easily be made allegorical. As is well known, journeys of all kinds have been the subject of stories since times immemorial. Their main meaning and reason for existence was that they could be read as allegories – vehicles of moral instruction. Any attempt at allegorizing contemporary labyrinthine works would immediately reveal not only its pointlessness but also the violence used against these works, which is entailed in this approach. The "labyrinthine movements of storytelling" ensure that allegorization is impossible, making contemporary stories about finding one's way in the labyrinth, or simply being inside it, into a complete opposite of an allegorical journey, which has its own beautiful tradition in older literature.

The labyrinthine movements of storytelling are particularly significant in those works where the theme of the labyrinth operates discreetly in the depicted worlds, nevertheless having a fundamental meaning for them as wholes. In Polish literature, one example of this is provided by Adam Ważyk's *Labyrinth* [*Labirynt*], a long poem that received little attention when it was published and has later fallen into nearly complete oblivion.[352] The poet's intentions are heralded already in the very title, which greatly affects the understanding of this work. Its story is set in the first quarter of the 20th century, and comprises a set of loosely connected narratives that are purposefully banal and whose

---

351 Umberto Eco, *The Open Work*, transl. A. Cancogni (Cambridge: Harvard University Press, 1989).

352 Adam Ważyk, *Labirynt* (Warszawa: Państwowy Instytut Wydawniczy, 1961).

nature seems more typical of novels of manners rather than poetry (those stories are similar to ones told in Ważyk's novels *Family Myths* [*Mity rodzinne*] and *Epilogue* [*Epilog*]).

These stories feature relatively few themes that would be directly related to the labyrinth. The image of a "long corridor" appears several times. The corridor is dark and at one point likened to a labyrinth tunnel. Here and there one can discern typical labyrinth-related elements like the "wall with false windows," but they are not many and certainly do not determine the long poem's character or justify the choice of its title. In this case, the labyrinth is primarily a component of a narration, introducing events that do not form clear causal chains but are chaotically reminisced by the narrator in fragmentary form and deprived of any stable meanings. The narrator cannot fully control them. The poem ends thus:

> [...]
> images in disarray
> loose stretches of time that cannot be united
> the pendulum swings of fading memory
> nobody's past

This constitutes a reference to one of the work's early parts:

> The day is just the same like anywhere else
> yellow like a half-smoked topaz
> Nobody could merge even if they wanted
> that which is or that which was
> torn links in chains of memories
> nothing connects, only dreamy
> visions marching
>   the past a labyrinth
> that leads no one knows where

Ważyk is interested here in the "temporal labyrinth" which he wrote about in connection with films by Robbe-Grillet, or the "labyrinth as a symbol of time stopped" which he mentions in an essay devoted to Borges.[353] When one attempts to describe and present the labyrinth of time, it approximates the labyrinth of narration. This is what happens in this long poem written in prose-like verse, which tells stories of uninteresting characters entangled in uncompelling events. What is more, the banality of reported stories and, even more so, the modesty of

---

353 Both essays in: Adam Ważyk, *Gra i doświadczenie* (Warszawa: Państwowy Instytut Wydawniczy, 1974); quotations from p. 135 & 150, respectively.

expression, strongly emphasize – maybe by way of contrast – the story's labyrinthine character. Ważyk's long poem certainly ranks among the boldest attempts at developing a labyrinthine mode of storytelling.

As we follow such narratives, we can discern how the labyrinth has kept growing, encroaching on further territories. Unsatisfied with what previously constituted its undisputed domain, it began to seize acts of speech and literary forms. Thus, it appears that Santarcangeli was right by claiming that

> labyrinth has no boundaries of form, while the guise it assumes in a given epoch and in a given social context will always be the *hallmark of a certain style*, of some concept of life, and of some lifestyle.[354]

5.9 Claustrophobic view of the world

The forms of literary labyrinths are limitless. They seem to outdo real (though also symbolic) labyrinths in the kinds of shapes they can assume, seizing upon various domains. Such lack of boundaries is even more overwhelming in this epoch of the labyrinth, when it has become a hugely popular symbol of great potential and significance. One of the heroines in the novel by Hanna Malewska issues the following warning:

> The labyrinth? No, I won't tell you anything about it. Even if it is no longer there, even if it is covered in rubble, and your Mycenae lords celebrate entirely different secrets in Knossos, it is better to remain silent about the labyrinth. This is what I've been taught and nothing that I've experienced can make me unlearn it.[355]

Nevertheless, she does not remain faithful to her own words, speaking about the labyrinth in a way that suggests it would be impossible to avoid. Speaking about it thus seems a real necessity. In this, she is not isolated, which is confirmed by a large portion of 20th-century literature. She also speaks about the labyrinth because she cannot, in fact, remain silent about it, although it remains uncertain if she really wants to speak about it. She speaks even when it makes her cringe. She speaks differently, but often in a way that could be easily called labyrinthine. Her speaking – regardless of the form it takes – always has to be something more than a description of a labyrinth or a guide to its winding corridors: it is meant to be an attempt at liberation, one that is made again and again, although it always

---

354 Paolo Santarcangeli, *Księga labiryntu*, p. 42.
355 Hanna Malewska, *Labirynt*, in: *Labirynt; LLW czyli Co się może wydarzyć jutro* (Kraków: Znak, 1970), p. 83.

feels uncertain and problematic since there is no guarantee it will succeed, all the more so because contemporary Theseuses have no Ariadne's thread.

Nevertheless, before we consider the issue in greater depth, it is necessary to attend to one thing that basically constitutes the main subject of these considerations. Once again I wish to pose the following question: What types and kinds of experiences does the metaphor of the labyrinth express in the 20th century? This entire essay constitutes an attempt at answering that question, but it seems that some issues still need to be added here. The visions of the labyrinth are a metaphor of human existence but have not been incorporated into the language used to speak about history, both ancient and contemporary. As a rule, they refer to certain metaphysical premises, or sometimes psychological ones, while everything that stems directly from current history recedes into the background. Of course, I am aware that the juxtaposition of existence and history may seem dubious and prone to break under serious criticism since it is difficult to imagine existence outside history. However, this juxtaposition is not considered here as a general one – it refers merely and only to the presently discussed subject. In this context, the existential and historical metaphors may not be complete opposites but certainly crystallize in different regions.

For the sake of completeness, one cannot fail to notice that the metaphor of the labyrinth sometimes refers to particular historical events. Krasiński, whose epistolary prose abounds in images of enclosed spaces, wrote in the summer of 1846 to Delfina Potocka:

> Please find enclosed the plenipotentiary's second letter, which announces that the peasant rebellion was pacified in Knyszyn. However, such actions only provide the impulse for future uprisings. We indeed live in terrible times: Muscovite soldiers are used to punishing and pacifying Polish peasants, who are incited to rebellion by Muscovite agents. Can you see what labyrinth this is? Verily, a terrible future has been fashioned for us living now. Poland will lift itself from it, but what about us? We won't! Still, one needs to fight as if we were to uplift ourselves and emerge victorious [...].[356]

Attempts at employing the metaphor of the labyrinth to history are also made contemporaneously, which is confirmed for example by Mieczysław Jastrun in the poem titled "Franz Kafka":

> Franz Kafka had an inkling of it all, by the black
> Angels stabbed, long before the death
> Of his three sisters. They ran quickly up the ladder

---

356 Zygmunt Krasiński, *Listy do Delfiny Potockiej*, vol. 3, p. 93.

Of Auschwitz smoke, assumed into heavens by their braids
Cut long before. He had in his hand a single thread
From the black ball of wool, a single thread that could
Lead out from the terrible Labyrinth
Or lead straight into the gas chamber.[357]

Beyond doubt, however, such attempts are isolated, which allows one to argue that the metaphor of the labyrinth did not really penetrate into the language used to speak of 20th-century history, and has not become one of the widespread and established images employed to present, problematize and assess it. It seems fitting to ask why, all the more so since the 20th century saw the consistent and ruthless construction of "total" institutions, to recall Goffman's study I already mentioned before.

It would seem that the labyrinth should be particularly lively in literature testifying to the horror of concentration camps, surrounded by barbed wire, or ghettoes enclosed within high walls – an archipelago of crime spread around the world from lands of perennial ice to the burnt sands of deserts. Still, it would be difficult to find even a slightest trace of the most horrible labyrinth in works that speak of gas chambers, institutional cruelty and crime – the worst experiences of the 20th century. Thus, this metaphor is missing from the "testified history" because it has never been used to think about "experienced history" (the two terms were coined by Jerzy Jedlicki).[358] They are missing, even though among its many meanings the labyrinth is also the space of death.[359]

This striking and significant absence is nevertheless not accidental. It seems to stem from a rule whose operation we might observe in contemporary times, but which has perhaps been at work also in the past. If one was the participant and (even more so) the victim of history, or its witness, one does not speak of the "experienced history" in order to reduce it a certain general pattern or idea, which could perhaps lead to generalization but at the same time would deprive that history of its particularity, stripping it of its individual and unique character that seems to be its most important characteristic. "Testified history," especially when witnessed at first hand or at small distance, thus precluding dissociation (and eliminating it from the process of reading), simply does not need any such metaphysical props, even when one finds at his or her disposal a symbol that could – as it seems – be particularly fitting.

---

357 Mieczysław Jastrun, *Genezy*, p. 47.
358 Jerzy Jedlicki, "Dzieje doświadczone i dzieje zaświadczone," in: *Dzieło literackie jako źródło historyczne*, eds. Z. Stefanowska & J. Sławiński (Warszawa: Czytelnik, 1978).
359 Paolo Santarcangeli, *Księga labyrintu*, pp. 172–173.

Labyrinth – a space that is always enclosed and alien – has not been incorporated into the language used to report direct historical experiences. It could become part of "history's language" only when that history already turns into a distant past and ceases to be a component of the direct experience of contemporary people, itself becoming a potential example, material that could be used in a fable, or an object for various generalizations.

The existential metaphor, which serves to present the human condition, seems to have been excluded from historical entanglement, also because it has a general and universal character that history could obscure. One could assume that historical particularization would be more expressive and significant than all that would be related to the human condition. This does not mean, however, that the visions of the labyrinth, so frequent in 20th-century literature and important for it, have been entirely separated from all historical experience. If the former penetrated into the latter – which nevertheless seems doubtful – then this would have been achieved in a very indirect manner, certainly not as an openly addressed subject.

Labyrinthine visions might have made their way into historical experience by way of that which comprises the main obsession of the literature in which the theme of the labyrinth functions, namely the obsession with being trapped. Of course, the fact that contemporary history ceaselessly produces total institutions – all kinds of camps, prisons and penal colonies – does not constitute the only or even the main reason for the above obsession, though it certainly played some role in its development. The chief category with which we might grasp the meanings of labyrinthine literature is the claustrophobic view of the world.[360] It is revealed almost independently of whichever particular space is in its direct focus: a windowless prison cell with the door bolted from outside; a city one cannot possibly leave because there are no roads allowing that; or finally, a universe that overwhelms one from all directions and does not leave any chance for liberation and escape. One is therefore trapped both in a miniature space, having at one's disposal only several square meters, and in a wilderness, wandering and being unable to opt out. One is trapped because this is also part of human fate. Thus, all human endeavours aimed at lifting oneself

---

360 The claustrophobic factor in the construction of the theme of the labyrinth is especially emphasized by Sami-Ali in the book *L'espace imaginaire* (Paris: Gallimard, 1974), where the author adopts a psychoanalytic perspective: "[…] the limited is identical to the unlimited, and the introduction of the symbolic theme of the labyrinth explains the reason for this: claustrophobia is the fear of being enclosed inside the mother's body after this body became hostile" (p. 18).

from entrapment are doomed to fail. Even when one encounters stairs, it may turn out that – as in the case of Piranesi's works – they lead nowhere, into the void. However, it is impossible to grow accustomed to confinement, much less to approve of it, at least because it continuously incites fear. In an enclosed space one can be only an eternal exile because the labyrinth is an invariably alien space.

One can attempt to tame the labyrinthine space by speaking about it. Consequently, describing a labyrinth would equal attempting not only to grasp it but also to escape from it. This is exactly what literature continues to consciously do. Speaking about the labyrinth would be a form of overcoming it. One character from Butor's fiction puts this problem in the following terms after being thrown inside a labyrinth of an alien city:

> The rope of words that uncoils down through the sheaf of papers and connects me directly with that moment on the first of May when I began to plait it, that rope of words is like Ariadne's thread, because I am in a labyrinth, because I am writing in order to find my way about in it, all these lines being the marks with which I blaze the trail: the labyrinth of my days in Bleston, incomparably more bewildering than that of the Cretan palace, since it grows and alters even while I explore it.[361]

A similar thesis is formulated in Malewska's novel[362] where one of the characters makes the following claim:

> I won't be able to explain this to you. The real song opens that which is closed and – as it were – forbidden. It is also the shortest way through the Labyrinth.[363]

However, is the shortest way really the one leading to an exit? We might have doubts about this. Can words crush the walls of the labyrinth? If this were the case, literature would not have been preoccupied with labyrinths for such a long time, arriving at some point at the conclusion that it is already a settled matter. However, labyrinths cannot be solved with words. As in the ending of the novel by Konwicki, characters might wonder: "Should we return there or there?"[364] Still, how does the former "there" differ from the latter? Is it really not going to be another labyrinth?

July-September 1985

---

361 Michel Butor, *Passing Time*, transl. J. Stewart (New York: Simon and Schuster, 1960), p. 169.

362 See Stanisław Grygiel's article about this novel: "Argument kłamcy, czyli pojednanie z labiryntem," *Znak* 11 (1971).

363 Hanna Malewska, *Labirynt*, p. 48.

364 Tadeusz Konwicki, *Wniebowstąpienie*, p. 249.

Appendix

Richard III and Prometheus – on *New Liberation* by Stanisław Ignacy Witkiewicz

No historian of literature who begins to write about Stanisław Ignacy Witkiewicz on the 100th anniversary of his birth can possibly shake off the conviction that everything has been already said with regard to Witkiewicz's oeuvre – that this body of work has been basically interpreted. It is difficult to think otherwise after the publication of books by Gerould, van Crugten, Sokół, Szpakowska, Michalski, as well as several edited collection and numerous articles by Błoński, Ziomek, Pomian, Puzyna, and Degler. These great scholars, and others whom I fail to mention, have not only established a rich canon of knowledge but primarily developed a certain mode of speaking about Witkiewicz. It is too early to subject this mode to revision. Although this would be very ambitious, it is not the aim of the present essay. I am fully aware of my dependence on my predecessors. The goal I have set before myself is much humbler: it boils down to rephrasing some of their claims and supplementing the interpretation of one particular work.

Indeed, this article could attempt nothing more, especially because it takes as its subject the drama *New Liberation* [*Nowe Wyzwolenie*] – one of the most frequently analysed and most thoroughly described dramas by Witkiewicz.[365] The traditional point of departure in interpretations of this highly original one-act play is to establish its relationship with Shakespeare's *Richard III* and Wyspiański's *Liberation* [*Wyzwolenie*] – two dramas that Witkiewicz drew on while composing his own work.

One of the basic features of Witkiewicz's plays is what Jan Błoński has termed their "parasitical character" – a concept he puts in quotation marks and deprives of its pejorative meaning.[366] Indeed, *New Liberation* constitutes an intriguing case as its author has never given any traditional dramatic form to his stage works; instead, he has drawn their components from diverse sources in an ostentatious manner, without showing any anxiety about constructing his artistic worlds

---

365   I am basing here on the version edited by Konstanty Puzyna: Stanisław Ignacy Witkiewicz, *Dramaty*, vol. 1 (Warszawa: Państwowy Instytut Wydawniczy, 1962), pp. 263–286.

366   Jan Błoński, "Teatr Witkiewicza," *Dialog* 12 (1967); he also discusses these issues in his other studies of Witkiewicz.

from prefabricated elements. Witkiewicz is aware that – as Błoński aptly put it – "in this cocktail, it is the mixture that is original and not the ingredients…"[367] To reveal that original character, however, one needs to consider the individual elements.

Traditionally, studies of Witkiewicz's dramas examine their relationship with certain models, attempting to establish whether we deal with parody, paraphrase, allusion or adaptation.[368] In this respect, his dramatic works are more complex than those by Gombrowicz, where parody prevails. I shall not engage in making such distinctions, although I cannot deny that they are justified. It seems to me that the most useful category would be a general one; however, I would prefer to employ the concept of "intertextuality" instead of "parasitical character." All dramatic works of Witkiewicz – certainly including *New Liberation* – have an intertextual character. They abound in references to more or less known works or their components (e.g. characters, situations, phrases), as well as to certain subtypes of dramatic works that have been developed in the genre and are now clearly part of a longer tradition, for example the psychological play from the turn of the 19th and 20th centuries.

Such references manifest in various ways. For example, sometimes the entire work somehow reproduces an earlier one, as in the case of *Country House* [*W małym dworku*], a drama that approximates parody. Sometimes, however, references have a more isolated character, surfacing only in particular places and not affecting the entirety of the drama. Witkiewicz's allusions can also figure differently: at times, they are conceived in such a way that in a single drama, or even in a single scene, we encounter overlapping references to works that are completely unrelated, occasionally even ones coming from different epochs and representing varied, often contrasting styles. This peculiar manner of Witkiewicz constitutes a classic example of the phenomenon that has come to called intertextuality. This is because his "parasitic" mode is not related to the genesis of a particular piece, but belongs to its very semantic structure. This is the only case in which we can speak of intertextuality. In other words, in order to properly read a given drama, it is necessary to become aware that its components have been drawn from tradition. The fact that a certain element originates in Shakespeare, Strindberg, Rittner, or Wyspiański

---

367 Jan Błoński, "Introduction" to: Stanisław Ignacy Witkiewicz, *Wybór dramatów* (Wrocław: Zakład Narodowy im. Ossolińskich, 1973), p. lxxxv.

368 Jerzy Ziomek, "Personalne dossier dramatów Wiktacego," in: *Studia o Stanisławie Ignacym Witkiewiczu*, eds. M. Głowiński & J. Sławiński (Wrocław: Zakład Narodowy im. Ossolińskich, 1972).

becomes meaningful in itself. For this reason, the fascinating analyses that trace the sources of the individual elements found in Witkiewicz's dramas are profoundly significant.

Needless to say, by making intertextuality the cornerstone of his literary practice, Witkiewicz did not write works with the aim to dazzle his readers with erudition and boast his firm anchoring in European culture. Such questions were entirely irrelevant to him, all the more so since he gave himself the right to freely employ borrowed elements because they would usually interest him only insofar as they contributed to achieving his own literary goals. One could even risk the claim that his attitude to tradition is quite instrumental. What is more, he granted himself the license to combine elements from the history of literature largely without any rules: virtually any two components can come into contact. This is facilitated by the fact that Witkiewicz ascribes a special role to intertextual practices, which have become a major factor – perhaps the crucial one – in developing the grotesque. Writers dismantle the world of literary history, breaking it down into individual components, just like they would resolve petrified social images into constituent parts so as to reassemble them into a new text and a new world: a grotesque text and a grotesque world.

Here we arrive at the matter that is central to the interpretation of *New Liberation* – "one of the most mysterious dramas by Witkiewicz," as Błoński wrote.[369] An immensely original and innovative work, it simultaneously approximates a centon. This has been thoroughly discussed and analysed by Błoński, Sokół and Gerould (to whom I am greatly indebted in this respect).[370] These researches have indicated which historical elements Witkiewicz utilizes, and what function they acquire in his work. Therefore, my own attempt at interpreting this drama does not aim to extend the repertoire of patterns woven into this peculiar centon, although I do hope to indicate one that has been passed over by my predecessors. The following analysis of *New Liberation* may allow perhaps demonstrating the specific character of Witkiewicz's intertextuality and its role in developing the grotesque.

Shakespeare's *Richard III*, Wyspiański's *Liberation*, as well as the psychological drama developed at the turn of the 19th and 20th centuries are the

369 Jan Błoński, "Introduction," p. lvii.
370 Lech Sokół, *Groteska w teatrze Stanisława Ignacego Witkiewicza* (Wrocław: Zakład Narodowy im. Ossolińskich, 1973), pp. 88–98; Daniel C. Gerould, *Stanisław Ignacy Witkiewicz jako pisarz*, transl. I. Sieradzki (Warszawa: Państwowy Instytut Wydawniczy, 1981), pp. 142–160.

main (and hugely diverse) ingredients that Witkiewicz used to construct his own work. References to the great historical play and the symbolist drama that broke the conventions of its period are revealed already in the short "Prologue," written in verse in 1906. This highly peculiar text in a sense performs the function of what French literary theorists call *mise en abyme*, i.e., it is a play-within-a-play, a miniaturized version of the drama incorporated into the larger work. This, however, is not the only remarkable thing about this short piece.

Basically, everything in this 24-line-long poem astounds. It remains an open question whether it was a standalone piece when it was first written – certainly it seems like an excerpt from a larger, unknown work. However, this is not crucial. More importantly, this prefatory part does not meet one requirement that seems obvious with regard to a dramatic prologue. The context – vital for every work, especially one written for the stage – is highly unclear here. It seems we deal not with one situation, but four. One sentence is spoken by the Chairman and one monologue is easily identifiable as uttered by the allegorical Soul. Moreover, it seems entirely possible that the last passage is a poetic account of a dream.

However, who is speaking in the first, longest part? The themes that recur there may suggest that it is Richard III, but upon closer examination it turns out that he is surely not the speaker but rather the subject. Another important argument against this hypothesis is that the said passage does not resemble a Shakespearian monologue, neither parodying nor caricaturing it. Actually, this excerpt resembles something else entirely, namely the choir parts from antique tragedies, or the monologues of their protagonists. What is more, it stylistically recalls Polish translations of Greek tragedies. Even if we assume that this connection was established with the mediation of Wyspiański, in whose works the antique tradition is very much alive, this does not change the whole situation. Furthermore, this hypothesis is confirmed by the fact that the first line contains an address to Typhon, a little-known figure from the Greek mythology. One popular encyclopaedia provides the following description:

> In Greek mythology, Typhon is a terrible monster, the youngest son of Gaia and Tartarus. He has the body of a giant, but snakes instead of legs. Higher than mountains, he could reach the stars. [...] Instead of fingers he had a hundred dragons' heads. His eyes spit fire and his mouth – tar.[371]

---

371 *Mała encyklopedia kultury antycznej*, ed. Z. Piszczek, vol. 2 (Warszawa: Państwowe Wydawnictwo Naukowe, 1962), p. 393.

This surely brings us closer to the main body of the drama. Would this mythological theme be the aforementioned component I wish to add to the repertoire of the drama's ingredients?

To verify this, it suffices to consult Aeschylus's tragedy about Prometheus. In one of his monologues, the protagonist speaks about the terrible rage of Typhon, who was a fire-spitting enemy of Zeus. What we deal with here is direct textual dependence. Witkiewicz could not read the drama in the Greek original (he did not know the language), but in 1906 he had three Polish translations to choose from, namely ones by Józef Szujski (1866), Zygmunt Węclewski (1873) and Kazimierz Kaszewski (1895). The best-known rendering by Jan Kasprowicz was published later and cannot be taken into account here (anyway, Typhon's theme was obscured in it).[372] This unexpected dependence indicates something more than just another ingredient of Witkacy's cocktail. It allows shedding a new light upon the entire drama, primarily the figure of Richard III. Commentators often make note that titans are frequently the heroes of Witkiewicz's plays.[373] The discussed reference to Aeschylus's tragedy confirms this observation.

The overlapping of the figures of Prometheus and Richard III is further proved not just by what the Shakespearian hero says in Witkiewicz's play but also by the position he finds himself in. We learn about this in the stage directions to the first scene:

> King Richard III stands on the left, resting his back against a pillar. From time to time he makes motions as if he wanted to move away from the pillar and leave. He is prevented from doing so by masked Murderers who are pointing daggers at him and hiss loudly by prolonging the sound of the letter "A" = "AAAAA."

Thus, for an extended period in the drama, the king is stuck at the pillar, which performs the function of a rock. He ceaselessly attempts to free himself from that spot but is stopped by two dangerous guardians. Richard III was never in such a situation either as a historical figure or as a character in a tragedy by Shakespeare. In Witkacy's play, he is a morally degraded Prometheus positioned in a space that combines elements of a Gothic hall and a middle-class salon. Dramas by Witkiewicz allow free mixing of such components. However, establishing this does not really exhaust the subject.

---

372 The translation by Kasprowicz was published first in the magazine *Sfinks* 1–2 (1909) (I owe this information to Mr. Roman Loth). The first book edition was published in 1912.

373 This problem is analyzed by Jerzy Ziomek in an article quoted above, where he also disusses earlier studies on this subject.

The myth of Prometheus is too important and too saturated with various meanings to allow limiting oneself to such a general treatment of the question. Assuming that the figure of Richard III was conceived as an allusion to Prometheus – and thus indirectly to his entire myth, which has taken so many shapes in history – one could explain certain structural properties of *New Liberation*. The allusion to the myth of Prometheus and the drama by Aeschylus fully explains the references made by Witkiewicz to antique tragedy, including the first passage of the Prologue, which features a mythological theme and is discussed above. Nevertheless, it is not just about Typhon because he is in fact of secondary importance. The antique component allows grasping the specific rhetorical structure of that introductory passage – a structure that cannot be explicated in any other way.

Furthermore, the assumption that Richard III alludes in this context to Prometheus allows making sense of some of his lines, beginning with the very first one:

> Let me rest for just a little while. Ah! Damn butchers!!! [...] My back is in pain! The bloody wall digs into it, and my hump hurts like a great ulcer. When will this torment end? When will I stop settling into these rough stones?

Moreover, it allows to better understand something else, namely Richard's peculiar behaviour, at least in some scenes. Up to a certain moment, he does not participate in any "salon action" and remains on the margin, although the attention of recipients and other figures is directed towards him. This specific manner consists in the fact that Richard plays the role of the commentator of the events that unfold in the salon. However, his utterances are not like traditional asides – his lines resist being reduced to a convention, even if we assume that they are delivered within the framework of parody. His short monologues at the pillar have a parodic character, but the object of parody is different as it targets the choir of ancient Greek tragedy. In these parts of the drama, Richard's lines remain, as it were, above those of other characters, and above the events presented on the stage. I primarily refer here to those delivered at the end of the first scene, and to two further ones in the second scene: one about the pragmatists, and one closing the scene. It is significant that these monologues delivered by Richard occur at the ends of scenes, i.e. in places where he is able to reveal and express the meaning of what has just happened in other areas of theatrical space.

Another element of the play's dramatic structure that is somehow related to ancient tragedy is the characteristic moment in the plot's development – *anagnorisis*. It is parodied in the entrance of Joanna, who recognizes that Florestan is her son, whom she has not seen in ten years, and that Richard III is her lover from a distant past.

Doubts could be raised with regard to this. Are these parodic references to Greek tragedy actually related in *New Liberation* to the myth of Prometheus, or do they exist independently of it? It seems that they are, at least because Prometheus is not only the hero of a myth but also the protagonist of one of antiquity's greatest tragedies. The highly indirect reactivation of the myth of Prometheus facilitates the introduction of an entire complex of elements related to Greek tragedy and simultaneously motivates their presence in the drama. This explains at least the parody of *anagnorisis*, despite the fact that this moment does not occur in the tragedy by Aeschylus. Broader issues become relevant in this context. When Witkiewicz alludes to the great works from the past, he does not aim to reproduce them faithfully but rather ensures that the reference is discernible to the audience. Sometimes the writer's attitude to the historical elements he utilizes is simply nonchalant.

However, let us return to Prometheus. His allusive presence in *New Liberation* not only allows to indicate the originality in the construction of the character, who turns out to be someone else than it seems at first but also facilitates displaying the relationship of this drama to Wyspiański's *Liberation* and locating it in historical and literary contexts that are crucial for interpretation.

The theme of Prometheus appears twice in the drama by Wyspiański: in the dialogue between Konrad and Mask No. 10 (Act II, lines 595–608), and in the speech of the Director (Act III, lines 651–655). It is, however, only one among many references to mythology. Witkiewicz does not reactivate particular mythological episodes in the discussed work. The issue is far broader. It could not be argued that the theme of Prometheus plays a larger role in Wyspiański's drama, but the problem of Promethean attitudes has a significant place both in this particular play and in his other works. It has the status of a "problem" because this matter is crucial for both the drama's main protagonist, Konrad, and the poet himself. It could not be otherwise because Wyspiański polemicizes in this way with Polish Romanticism, specifically foregrounding the question of Prometheanism. Despite its formal innovation and complexity, *Liberation* is a political work that refers to matters that were widely discussed in Poland at the beginning of the 20th century. However, it is not a Promethean drama; on the contrary, it questions the attitudes and gestures of the Romantics rather than repeats them, although without diminishing their significance and gravity.

Witkiewicz, who took up the Promethean theme in *New Liberation*, was not interested at all in its current political aspect, which Wyspiański found vital. However, it seems that he has surpassed Wyspiański in degrading the

myth of Prometheus. It is difficult to speak of an either direct or indirect literary polemic with Wyspiański – in this matter, it would be rather pointless. By
making the cruel and tyrannical Richard III, ruthless in his struggle for power,
the new incarnation or counterpart of Prometheus, he divested the myth of the
last remaining elements of the splendour it once had. Commentators of *New
Liberation* have indicated various ties linking this work with Wyspiański's drama.
The degradation of Prometheus and the related questioning of certain important
themes that have accompanied Polish culture for a long time since the times
of the Romantics seem to be the essential connection. In this way, Witkiewicz
gave expression to anti-Romantic tendencies, which were typical for European
literatures (including the Polish one) just after the First World War.

It is here that we encounter the problems of the historical and literary contexts
that seem to be so important for interpreting *New Liberation*. I would like to
primarily draw attention to two groups of phenomena. As I have already emphasized, both in this drama and in most other plays by Witkiewicz all kinds of
things could be combined: elements of Greek tragedy, Shakespearian drama, psychological drama à la Ibsen, etc. The range of ingredients in this mix – described
by Błoński – seems not to be limited in any way. However, is such juxtaposing
of all kind of components an unprecedented artistic initiative? This question is
particularly important when asked concerning to *New Liberation*, also because
of references to Wyspiański. In *Liberation* he introduces various themes from
antiquity, not limiting himself to mentions of Prometheus, but also referencing a
Muse and the Erinyes. However, this drama is not the most typical representative
of such tendencies, which manifest far more clearly in two other works: *Acropolis
[Akropolis]* (1904) and *November Night [Noc listopadowa]* (1904). Wyspiański
offers in them an astonishing synthesis of mythological, Christian and traditionally Polish historical themes. Similar syntheses were made by another favourite
writer of Witkiewicz – Tadeusz Miciński – and by Wacław Berent in *Snowy
Crop [Ozimina]* (1911), though the latter work represents a slightly different
approach. These syntheses have been saturated with various symbolic meanings.
Such cultural syncretism – as this phenomenon could be called – was treated
seriously by representatives of the generations before Witkiewicz, but for him
it became incorporated into grotesque playfulness. Not only was the repertoire of possibilities extended, but the general rules for the functioning of such
juxtapositions changed. Allusions, quotations, parodies, adaptation – all kinds
of manifestations of intertextuality – became one of the main factors, or perhaps
even the main component in the construction of the grotesque theatre and the
grotesque world. This strategy of Witkiewicz's, however original and off-handed,
is nevertheless strictly correlated with what has been achieved in this respect by

the writers representing the early 20th-century Young Poland movement. This is especially visible in the case of *New Liberation*.

Giving a grotesque character to cultural syncretism becomes particularly significant in the case of the modernization of the myth of Prometheus. This is so not only because it was a heroic myth reactivated by the Romantics, but primarily because this myth changed its status in the 20th century.[374] In its traditional, heroic version, it appears almost solely in derivative works. Furthermore, it also made its way into grotesque works, where its protagonist became not just an unheroic figure but even a comical one. A pioneering role was played in this by André Gide's *Prometheus Illbound* [*Prométhée mal enchaîné*] (1896), soon translated into Polish by Miriam and published twice. It seems that even if Witkiewicz did not know the original, he must have become acquainted with this work when it was printed in the magazine *Chimera*. It does not seem plausible to trace a direct relationship, but that is certainly not the point. What is crucial, however, is that Prometheus was subjected to de-heroization: brought down to the contemporary world and presented on its background. Bearing in mind the emergence of this grotesque version of Prometheus, one has to admit that Witkiewicz's drama, in which the degraded hero appears under the mask of the cruel King Richard III, is firmly rooted in its literary context.

I am focusing here chiefly on Richard III, weirdly associated with Prometheus, as if I had forgotten that he appears in *New Liberation* on the backdrop of a middle-class salon, and that he participates in events that parody other forms of drama. In this respect, however, one finds it challenging to add anything to what the authors of outstanding studies of this work have already stated; therefore, it suffices to refer to them, particularly to Błoński, Sokół, and Gerould. Still, I would like to consider one more issue, namely the question whether all that emerges in *New Liberation* could be treated as a parody of certain previous models – one conceived in advance. I have one particular case in mind. Gerould claims that the fact that one of the main characters has the name Florestan indicates a reference to Beethoven's opera *Fidelio*. This seems doubtful because no significant ties to the opera can be identified, while the name itself could have been chosen purely accidentally – an option that cannot be rejected if we consider Witkiewicz's way of handling proper names. If some genealogy were to be found for Florestan, it could be traced elsewhere, albeit still in the field of music. Robert Schumann – who was not only a great composer, but also an outstanding

---

374 A history of the myth of Prometheus in literature is presented by Raymond Trousson in *Le Thème de Prométhée dans la littérature européenne* (Genève: Librairie Droz, 1964).

author of texts on music – developed in his essays three figures that are his *porteparole*: Eusebius, Florestan, and Master Raro. The extravagant Florestan was supposed to be the embodiment of poetic inspiration (Schumann introduced this figure into his own compositions – the sixth movement of the cycle *Carnival*, op. 9, bears the title "Florestan").[375] Schumann was a particularly revered composer at the beginning of the 20th century, which makes it plausible that he might have been the source of the name used by Witkiewicz. However, I would not ascribe too much meaning to this because even if this guess were true, it would not affect the drama's interpretation in any significant way. Moreover, the name Florestan appears – as Alain van Crugten has kindly brought to my attention[376] – in many French popular plays from the end of the 19th century, which could also have influenced Witkiewicz's choice of the name for his character. As it seems, we need to assume that not all ingredients of the author's original cocktail have equal bearing. In other words, constructing from prefabricated elements (it is not an accident that some experts speak of Witkiewicz's "ready-mades"[377]) does entail establishing some kind of hierarchy. In *New Liberation*, the key element is Richard III, behind whose mask lurks Prometheus.

As is widely known, Witkiewicz considered *New Liberation* to be among those plays that come closest to the idea of Pure Form. Though this concept is not always clearly defined, it has been the subject of numerous interpretations. I would like to point out one specific moment, which has been already emphasized by Jerzy Ziomek. "The central problem for the explication of the Pure Form," he writes, "is the question of art's mimeticism."[378] An inversely proportional ratio is involved here: the further a work moves away from a mimesis-based aesthetic (as understood in the 19th century), the closer it would be to the ideal of Pure Form. Mimeticism is left behind when intertextuality – the foundation of grotesque – becomes so visible and exhibited that it focuses the attention of the recipients. In other words, they cannot treat the work as making a direct statement about the world, or as reproducing those models and schemas

---

375 Henryk Swolkień, *Robert Schumann* (Warszawa: Państwowy Instytut Wydawniczy, 1973), pp. 182–183.

376 In a discussion about this essay, which was first presented as a paper during a session devoted to Witkiewicz, held in the Department of Slavic Studies at the University of Amsterdam (21–22 March 1985).

377 Włodzimierz Bolecki, *Poetycki model prozy w dwudziestoleciu międzywojennym* (Wrocław: Zakład Narodowy im. Ossolińskich, 1982), p. 72; the author refers to earlier works of Kamila Rudzińska, Magdalena Nowotna-Szybistowa, and Ryszard Nycz.

378 Jerzy Ziomek, "Personalne dossier dramatów Wiktacego," p. 95.

of speaking about it that are considered to be its direct imitation. Intertextuality becomes here a matter of specific mediatisation. It can serve this function all the better because in Witkiewicz it is not connected with any care for faithfulness to any model; on the contrary, the writer gives himself the right to do whatever he pleases with a given model: primarily, to introduce it into contexts in which it had never appeared before, or even could not. Such intertextuality – let us emphasize it again – is not only directly related to the grotesque but also ceaselessly generates it. It would be difficult to find a better example of this mechanism than the drama *New Liberation*.

The grotesque intertextuality that realizes the ideal of Pure Form, or at least approaches it, is also a task meant to be realized by the recipients, not just the interpreters who are traditionally expected to reveal the ingredients that make up the work and indicate their meaning. When encountering *New Liberation*, every reader or member of the audience has to become aware of the fact that the drama contains something from Shakespeare and something from a psychological drama, something from Wyspiański and something from one of the greatest Greek myths (as well as from the tragedy inspired by it). The intertextuality of Witkiewicz, saturated with ludic elements, does not constitute a show prepared by an erudite wishing to prove his being deeply rooted in European culture. It has rather become one of the fundamental methods of constructing meanings.[379]

---

379 When I was writing this essay (and when I published it in 1985 in *Pamiętnik Literacki*), I was not aware of the book by Wojciech Sztaba *Gra ze sztuką. O twórczości Stanisława Ignacego Witkiewicza* (Kraków: Wydawnictwo Literackie, 1982), which simply escaped my attention. It is Sztaba who first discerned the theme of Prometheus in *New Liberation*: "Richard III, trapped at the pillar by threatening daggers, takes on the role of Prometheus whether he likes it or not. [...] However, the choice is rather surprising – Richard III is one of the darkest characters in Shakespeare's royal chronicles" (p. 138).

Bibliographical note

Essays contained in this volume were previously published in the following places:

"The Mask of Dionysus" – *Twórczość* 11 (1961), later reprinted with slight changes in the volume *Młodopolski świat wyobraźni*, ed. M. Podraza-Kwiatkowska (Kraków: Wydawnictwo Literackie, 1977);

"Narcissus and His Reflections" – *Twórczość* 10 (1980);

"That Ridiculous Prometheus" – *Pismo* 4 (1981);

"A Portrait of Marcolf" – *Twórczość* 8 (1974);

"Labyrinth. The Space of Alienation" – written in 1985, it was not published before;

"Richard III and Prometheus. On *New Liberation* by Stanisław Ignacy Witkiewicz" – *Pamiętnik Literacki* 4 (1985).

CROSS-ROADS.

POLISH STUDIES IN CULTURE, LITERARY THEORY, AND HISTORY

Edited by Ryszard Nycz

www.peterlang.com